I Hear Them Calling My Name

Books by Chet Fuller

Spend Sad Sundays Singing Songs to Sassy Sisters (poems)
I Hear Them Calling My Name:
A Journey Through the New South

CHET FULLER

I Hear Them Calling My Name

A JOURNEY THROUGH
THE NEW SOUTH

Houghton Mifflin Company Boston 1981

Library of Congress Cataloging in Publication Data
Fuller, Chet.
   I hear them calling my name.
   1. Afro-Americans — Southern States — Social conditions.
2. Poor — Southern States. 3. Southern States — Social
conditions. 4. Fuller, Chet. 5. Southern States —
Description and travel — 1951—   I. Title.
E185.92.F79   975'.00496073   80-27093
ISBN 0-395-30528-4

Printed in the United States of America

S 10 9 8 7 6 5 4 3 2 1

The author is grateful to Alfred A. Knopf, Inc., for
permission to reprint portions of "Prime" and "Georgia Dusk"
from *The Panther and the Lash: Poems of Our Times,*
by Langston Hughes, copyright © 1967 by Langston Hughes.

For my family, on both sides,
    and their endless acts of love.

I

Down Here
on the Ground

Only the children know what to ask
soon they will answer
their own questions
with lies
— C. F.

1

In Fear and Trembling

FOR ME, it began strangely. To this day, I do not know whose idea it was in the first place. I assume it was born somewhere between the sixth and ninth floors of the building where I work as a newspaper reporter — somewhere in the minds of the middlemen of management on the sixth floor and the inhabitants of the plush corporate offices on the top floor. My own entry into this project was sudden and traumatic. We had just gone through a changing of the guard at the paper: a new managing editor had been installed. Everything was up in the air. There would be a change in style, heads would roll, many would have to go. We all sat around the newsroom trying to determine who would be led to the firing squad first.

Jim Minter, the new managing editor, had the reputation of being a pipe-smoking ogre. He was once quoted in a local magazine as saying, "I've always wanted to be rich enough so that if I'm plowing a field and a mule doesn't do what I want him to do, I can just shoot him and buy another one." His reputation reached the sixth floor long before he showed up. He had previously served in the same position on the morning paper, which is housed two floors above the *Atlanta Journal* where I work. It is said that when he first took over there he really "kicked ass and took names," fired people left and right, and changed the paper around, got it moving again. The *Journal* newsroom was in an uproar, and our fears were compounded by the fact that we all spent time speculating about when and where Minter would strike. In our minds, there seemed to be no pleasant alternatives. Sooner or later we would all be called into Minter's office one by one, fitted for a blindfold, and scheduled for the firing squad; or else be banished to the backwoods of Douglas County or some other rural beat. And there I was, at twenty-eight, soon to be a hopeless case — a washed-up newspaper man looking for a place to stretch out and expire.

In this kind of atmosphere, between assignments — which seemed to come at wider and wider intervals — I would sit at my desk thinking of the time when I had been young and promising with no place to go but up. It was on such an afternoon that Bob Lott, one of the assistant managing editors, a tall rope of a man, soft-spoken, with thick brown hair and boyish eyes, sidled up to my desk and spoke these ominous words: "Minter wants to see you in his office." I swallowed. I followed Lott into the glass office, where Minter was sitting alongside Jim Rankin, the other assistant managing editor. Lott and Rankin were smiling. After I sat down, Minter spoke.

"Chet," Minter said, puffing on his ever-present pipe, a cloud of smoke circling his head like a sinister halo, "I want you to resign from the paper February first."

"Okay," I said coolly, though I was about to collapse in the chair. The faces of my wife and children flashed through my mind, and I saw them ragged and hungry. I didn't have another job lined up. But I was determined to be tough; I would go out like a champ. They would respect me. It had come to this. There was a terrible silence. My body shook, but I was determined to appear calm. I still had my self-respect. I checked their faces. There were no smiles now. Go ahead, give it all to me. Come on! Minter took his pipe out of his mouth slowly, coughed, and replaced the pipe. They all stared at me. It was like hanging out of the window of an airplane flying 30,000 feet above the ground.

Minter cleared his throat. "But we'll pay you anyway," he said.

"That's better," I blurted. We all laughed at the same time. "What the hell is this?" I wondered.

"Chet," Minter said, "there's a young woman who works for

us [at his home], and I don't think she has all that much education, but she works hard. She doesn't want all that much out of life, just a decent life. Can people do that anymore?"

"What do you mean?"

"I want you to find out what it's like for people trying to make it in the South now," he said. "People without much education, but hard-working. Can they make a decent life for themselves?"

"Not just an economic thing," Lott said. "Are there people in the South still getting their necks stepped on, being discriminated against?"

"In other words," Rankin added, "what has happened in the South in the last decade or so? How much was accomplished by the civil-rights movement? Are things any fairer than they used to be?"

"We want to get behind the government reports, the statistics," Minter said, "and find out how poor people are really living in the South. What do you think?"

I sat there puzzled. What kind of discussion was this? Where had it all come from? I was skeptical. Could it be some kind of setup? But for what reason?

"What if we get you a camera, some old clothes, and — I think you'd have to have a beat-up car," Minter said. "You could travel around trying to find work; see what it's really like out there. How you'd be treated."

"One of us could be your contact," Rankin said.

"Yeah," Minter said, "but very few other people here would know what you're really doing. I want you to tell everybody in the newsroom, and anybody else who asks, that you're quitting the paper to freelance, that you're going to finish up a book. How do you think it sounds so far?"

I was beginning to get a picture of what they were proposing. Still, I was shocked. First of all, I couldn't believe they were willing to try such a grand scheme. It was a noble idea, but it would be terribly expensive and possibly very dangerous.

"It sounds interesting," I finally said.

They seemed a little annoyed. They were expecting a more enthusiastic response. I was undecided as to whether such a project would prove much at this point in time. Ten years ago, perhaps, it would have been possible to find out all kinds of terrible things; but we'd been through the civil-rights movement, the war on poverty, affirmative action, and other programs designed to help those at the bottom in America.

"You understand we don't want anybody to know who you really are," Minter said, "because it could be dangerous. If some of these sheriffs in these rural counties found out what you were doing — I'm not saying this will happen, but I think we ought to cover all the bases — they could cause you a lot of trouble." We discussed the proposed assignment for a few more days and I finally agreed to try it.

"Whatever you need in the way of equipment or clothes, we'll get it," Minter said. "I think you ought to spend the next week or so figuring it all out — where you'll go, how you're going to work it, what name you'll use. You're going to have to become somebody else. You can't talk the way you do now," he said with a smile. "This project could take about six months. We can arrange for you to visit your family some weekends, though," he added with an impish grin as he walked away.

At the end of the week, I gave notice to Bob Johnson, then city editor, that I was leaving the paper to finish a novel. He was out sick at the time, so I called him at home. I hated to lie to him. Bob had helped me a lot during my development as a reporter. It seemed cruel to keep him on the outside, but I followed orders. (He was later told about the project, not long after I had left to begin it.) Over the next two weeks, I told my friends and colleagues the same story. It was difficult, for they had all come to mean a lot to me in the six years I had been at the *Journal*. We had been through all the fires, tornadoes, elections, murders, trials — the big, breaking stories. There were so many good memories, and for some unexplainable reason I felt as if I were really leaving and would never see them again. On the final Friday that I was to work, I cleaned the remaining items from my desk (I had been moving since I first gave notice of my departure) and quietly slipped away before quitting time. I felt as if a part of my life were ending. As I walked out into the crisp February air, I couldn't get my feet to move fast enough. I was afraid I wouldn't get to my car before one of my colleagues caught up and invited me to have a couple of beers. I knew I couldn't have survived a round of beers with my friends while concealing such a big lie inside. I broke into a trot.

After I "left" the paper, there were still two weeks of preparation before I would be free to leave on my ominous assignment. I had worn a goatee for many years, but the beard had to come off, because it gave me a kind of militant appearance that would ruin everything, I thought. Then the hair had to be cut short and combed back, which made my face look fatter and gave me the appearance of a hardluck jackleg preacher, the kind I remembered so well from my childhood. I bought a number of old shirts, khaki pants, and work pants from junk shops. The car — a faded green-gray 1969 Chevy Impala — was bought about forty miles south of Atlanta in a town called Griffin, where my parents had grown up and lived before they came to the big city. I wanted to buy the car in a small town, so that it would not have a Fulton County or DeKalb County license plate and the people I encountered on the road would think I was from a small town in Georgia. I established a residence in Griffin and had my driver's license changed to reflect the small-town address, so that it would be difficult for anybody to trace me back to my real address and occupation.

After the camera and small tape recorder were purchased, all that remained were lessons in farming — identifying various farm equipment and operating different kinds of tractors, so I could be convincing when I told people I had worked as a farm hand and at other odd jobs. The lessons were conducted by Minter one Saturday on his farm in Fayetteville, Georgia, south of Atlanta. I rose early that morning, put on old clothes, and negotiated the various highways and back roads, following a map Minter had prepared, until I came upon the 150-acre spread that is Minter's home.

It was a long session, rather like a one-day boot camp. We fed cattle, drove tractors about the yard, and held discussions on planting, cultivating, and weeding. I was taught the difference between a harrow and a plow, and how to tell a Massey-Ferguson tractor from a Ford or International by the color. As we sat in the cab of Minter's pickup, riding from one pasture to another to feed the cattle, he told me about his own parents and up- bringing; how he had been raised on the land, farming much of the very ground we were riding on. And, indeed, dressed in his faded jeans, work boots, and long-billed cap, he looked more like a man who made his living from the soil than a newspaper editor.

"If I could make a living at it," he told me sincerely, "I'd be farming right now. That's *real* work."

It was touching, the care he was taking to make sure I had a good chance of pulling this thing off; his love of the land and the way he spoke of his father; the way he seemed to know everybody in the little community surrounding his house. Once we stopped at a graveyard next to an old church where a thin, wiry black man was digging a grave, with sticks stretched out on the ground to guide him. Minter asked who was being buried. When the man called the name — even though it was that of an elderly black woman — Minter recognized it. He knew the family. This was a side of Minter we never got to see in the newsroom, a tender side, a side I will never forget. On that day we were not employer and employee, not managing editor and reporter, but men who shared an interest in people and trees and flowers and grass, men who understood each other, if only for that brief period of time. At that moment, sitting in the cab of that squeak- ing pickup rocking over rugged roads, it did not matter that I was black and he was white. I didn't even think of us in those terms. It was a rare moment; a time when I looked at him and saw the father of two boys. A husband. The boy in him. A man at home behind a plow. A man who remembered his friends. A man who beamed if you let him show you his tractors or the fence he and his sons had spent ten years of their lives putting up.

• • •

I could delay no longer; it was time for me to go. I had been dreading actually starting on this journey, for deep inside I felt that it would cost me a lot. Although I had no way of knowing until later just how much it would cost, I knew there would be a certain amount of pain and inconvenience, and some awkward, scary times. I don't know if I can adequately describe all the fears I had as I dressed that morning, February 22, 1978, to begin the trip to Charlotte, North Carolina, 250 miles away. I dressed slowly, sitting for a long time on the bench at the foot of the bed, thinking about what might happen. Thinking that I was going to miss my family — my youngest daughter was less than a year old, and doing all the cute things babies her age do. I didn't want to be taken away from her then, for she was about to crawl and was cutting teeth. What if I never saw them again, never got back here? What would happen to them? What if something went wrong? Suppose I got arrested in some tiny country town or remote county and was slapped away in jail. Would they ever find me? How long before anybody would know? Could I even do it? Could I pull it off? What if I fooled nobody? What if the whole damn thing failed, turned out to be just a colossal waste of money? Wouldn't a disaster like that follow me everywhere? Ruin my professional reputation? Could I fit in? Small towns are hard to penetrate. The people are suspicious of outsiders, and that's what I would be, an outsider — always outside, alone, under suspicion. How could I get people to talk to me?

I was going into another world, a land where I had little control. I was giving up my education. The official line on me was to be that I had only an eleventh-grade education, that I was basically unskilled, but a hard worker, having worked in restaurants, done farm labor, yard work, construction, and other menial jobs. The blanket protection of my press card was gone. My suit and tie, gone. People would no longer be able to tell immediately that I was somebody important. And what about this world I was entering? A world of poor people struggling to survive. I knew about poverty, having come out of the lower class myself. I knew about being desperate. I had seen the violence that exists in that world of human misery, where sometimes the quenching taste of vengeance is all a person has.

I was scared because it had been a long time since I belonged to that world, since I grew up poor in the Simpson Street and Summerhill sections of Atlanta, where you could sit on your porch on Friday nights and hear arguments, fights, and shootings going on in nearby houses and often in the streets. It was like living in a theater — a theater of the absurd in the round — for violent plays were always being acted out around you, with several performances a day on weekends. When we lived on Atlanta Avenue in Summerhill, in the shadows of Atlanta Stadium, there was a large neighbor woman with puffy scars covering her meaty arms who would go at several carloads of police officers almost every weekend, it seemed, after they were called out and tried to wrestle her considerable mass into a paddy wagon that looked only half big enough. But that was a long time ago.

After all, since then I had gone off to college and gotten refined, and had been acting civilized and sophisticated for years. And I was hopelessly middle class, having come home from college to find my parents living in the suburbs. They had given up on living in the slums and watching the weekend shootouts. I joined them and found a house in the suburbs, too, pulling all the attendant suburban trappings around me and leaving the places where I had grown up far, far behind. Could I even speak the language of the streets anymore? Would my ear fail me? After all, it had been a while since I'd even been back to the old neighborhoods or any of the similar places around town, except on assignment, and even then, I didn't have to rub shoulders with the natives too much. It didn't seem to help me now, that I had been one of the cool cats who hung out in front of that little record shop downtown on Broad Street after school, leaning against the wall and talking trash to any girl who walked by: "Say, mama, I'm going your way, slow it down." But that was more than a dozen years ago. I used to know the key words to say to the niggers on the corner down at Capitol Avenue and Ormand Street, where they hung out, dressed to the bone, with their cases (knives) in their pockets. I was cool.

But what about now? I didn't even dance anymore. That was

something I had given up in favor of brooding over my job and my position in life. Almost everything had to take a back seat to getting ahead, biting off a big piece of that American pie everybody talked about so much. I was in full pursuit of the dream, so much so that I didn't have time to notice what had been happening to the people I'd left behind in the ghetto and in the poor backwoods communities. And the one thing I was sure was still true was that you couldn't run no bullshit by them folks. You had to be real or nothing. I just knew it wasn't going to work. The whole thing began to seem like such a foolish idea.

What the hell ever possessed them to come up with such tripe in the first place? I was thinking. Hell, it was easy for them — Minter, Rankin, Lott, and whoever else had a hand in it — to sit back and dream up this bullshit, because they didn't have to do it. They never had to leave the comfortable world of the offices where they lived each day, never had to give up anything, never had to expose themselves to God knows what. They didn't have to risk making fools of themselves. They had it made, could play it safe. If it didn't work, it would simply be my fault.

They had picked the wrong boy. I just wasn't up to the task. Nobody would blame them. I was the one who had to go out there and face all those people, try to make sure I didn't sound too intelligent, hold my temper around white folks, try to be handkerchief-headed. At that moment I was thinking about what a fool I was. Were they really trying to ruin me? Things hadn't changed any in the South. Just like in the old days, they send the nigger out to do the dirty work, and if he gets in a bind they just disavow any knowledge of the poor darky.

I ate breakfast with my wife and three daughters for what I knew would be our last morning together for a while. The older two went off to school. I hung around waiting for the mailman, to see if there would be anything for me, but nothing came. I tried not to let my wife see the fear in me. I had been able to tell for some time that she wasn't too pleased with the project. Finally, in the late morning, I could delay no longer. I packed the car with a single battered suitcase, and put work shoes and a heavy coat in the trunk. I was now more than a little angry, probably hoping the anger would help chase away the fear. I was determined to treat this as an assignment. I would not get too caught up in it. That seemed to me to be the only way I could get it over quickly and get back to my family. It was an assignment, nothing more.

North Carolina lay ahead. I am not absolutely sure why I chose to start there and work my way south. It has been suggested to me that somewhere in my subconscious I was convinced that North Carolina would be less racist, and that things would get worse the farther south I moved. Possibly that is true. But I had heard a lot about North Carolina being a tough place for blacks to live. I had a friend whose brother had been arrested in Lumberton, North Carolina, and sentenced to prison for allegedly committing an armed robbery. I had been amazed at some of the stories she told me about her efforts to find a competent lawyer in that area to help her brother. I felt drawn there, and it seemed logical to me to start at the top of the South and work my way down with the growing season.

After I kissed my wife good-by, petted the dog, and headed up Interstate 85 toward Charlotte, I felt a tremendous urge to just go to sleep and tune it all out. Maybe it would be over when I awoke. I turned on the radio and beat my palm against the steering wheel in time with the music, thinking about the days when I used to dance and talk jive. The days when I knew what to expect from poor folks.

•   •   •

As countless cars filled with indifferent strangers passed me, I thought of another southerner who, twenty years earlier, had set out on a journey to discover the world of the southern black.

John Howard Griffin, a Texan, was a white man with a black face, a man who wanted so desperately to understand the plight of America's second-class citizens that he underwent medical treatments so he could become one — temporarily.

I was very young when I first heard of John Griffin's sojourn in a black man's skin. I had been in a local movie house when the previews of coming attractions were shown and a movie called *Black Like Me* was advertised.

I remember that there seemed to be a lot of darkness: shadowy figures hanging around outside bathrooms, bus stations, and restaurants. The film had an ominous quality. It was seedy-looking, and I thought it was some kind of dirty movie, so I never went back to see it.

Years later, I got around to reading the book, and it angered me and made me wonder if the South would ever change; if people like me were just born at the wrong time or in the wrong place; if I and my brethren weren't forever doomed to be the white man's mules in America, the eternal beasts of burden.

While preparing for my own journey into the heart of the region I loved, I reread Griffin's book and realized the courage it must have taken for him to attempt such a thing.

He had gone out into the land of bigots and Klansmen before the Montgomery bus boycott, before the racial consciousness of this country was raised by the civil-rights movement, before the voting-rights act, before John Kennedy and Lyndon Johnson had exerted themselves, before Bull Connor and George Wallace had been pushed aside and replaced by more moderate leaders.

In a way, I was going back, walking some of the same ground to see what had changed in twenty years. When I thought of the danger he'd faced, my own seemed smaller, and I was a bit relieved. I was glad John Howard Griffin had gone before me, because the effect his journey had had on the hearts and minds of people in this country, blacks and whites, was making my job a little easier.

2

Breaking In

CHARLOTTE is a tough town — so tough on the day I arrived that as soon as I hit the city limits snow started falling and the temperature dropped nearly fifteen degrees in the next couple of hours. This city is in a county with a funny-sounding name — Mecklenburg. It always tickles me to think of that name — Mecklenburg, the way it rolls on the tongue after you get past the "Meck" part. One of those in-between towns, not real big and by no means small, spunky and still growing, flexing its muscles.

Having lived most of my life in the South, I have always had the feeling that Charlotte and Atlanta were both chasing the distinction of being the queen city of the South. In many ways Charlotte has more charm than Atlanta, the latter having given up much of its gentle naiveté to lust after the money of conventioneers: sweaty-palmed Shriners in silly hats; proctologists from the cold-weather states; swarming hordes of sewing-machine-bobbin manufacturers and sellers; and ear, nose, and throat men who rush to the strip clubs along Peachtree Street to gawk at other parts of the female anatomy.

Thus, over the past few years, as hotel after hotel sprang up in Atlanta, each a more curious monstrosity than the preceding one, with lakes in the lobbies, revolving restaurants, and other novelties, the Belle of the South has become less and less a city for its residents. She has lifted high her skirt and bared her privates for the conventioneers waving their greenbacks.

Charlotte, it seems, has moved at a slower pace, preferring to tease the money men, flirt with them a bit, leaving herself more time to decide whether or not to throw caution to wind and go whole hog.

There is a bustling downtown and central-business district, but not too many tall buildings. Also, a sparkling civic center, where, in 1976, I met California Governor Jerry Brown at a caucus of black Democrats. At the time, Brown was just one of those seeking the Democratic nomination for president. And I was but one of the reporters who "met" him as he waltzed around the place in a dark suit that looked a little worn. I'll never forget the frayed cuffs on the white shirt he wore. Brown dodged questions beautifully, was quite interesting, and made jokes about the pope and other sacred institutions. Jimmy Carter and the others were there, too, but Brown got most of the attention, at least outside the back rooms.

As I said, Charlotte seems to be a city still trying to make up its mind about the future. It bustles during the day, but virtually dies at night. It seems a nice enough place to raise kids, but a little tame for those used to big-city thrills.

One thing Charlotte seems to have more than its share of is fast-food joints. Just about every chain is represented; so, after driving around awhile and casing the place, I filled up on hamburgers and fries at a McDonald's. As I ate, I watched the parade of people in and out and tried to figure out what kind of person each was, what line of work he was in just from the way he looked. It was impossible; I knew I was guessing them wrong, which made me wonder what people thought about me on first sight. I know I felt odd. I kept trying to run my fingers through my beard — a habit I have — but found only my bare chin, which felt much like the skin of a plucked baking hen.

It doesn't take long for the loneliness to set in. Though I'd been there in 1976 to cover the caucus for the *Journal*, I had only spent three days, so it was still a strange city. I had made a couple of friends then — people I'd met at various caucus functions — but I wanted to see how close I could get to the inside of the city before I called on them.

In Charlotte's northwest corner sits Johnson C. Smith University, a predominately black liberal-arts institution with much of the city's black community branching out from it. I parked the car on Beatties Ford Road and wandered through the campus, which has an incredible number of buildings packed together on a relatively small piece of ground. The students eyed me as they passed. I spoke, and occasionally they spoke too. It was odd, for they seemed so young, so small. I had been out of college six years, and as I observed them going about campus with books clutched in their arms, some of the men and women holding hands, they did not strike me as adults at all, but as children. Children with clean faces and combed hair. They seemed so well behaved, so civilized. These were the "best" of us, many of them middle class and the rest soon to be. For these were the people with a chance. What did they think of me as they passed? Probably that I was one of the new maintenance men or grounds-keepers or something, me in my work clothes and faded hat. These were privileged ones just as I had been, seeking an education, the ticket that led to acceptance in the larger society, the white man's society. I would not spend any more time here. These were the wrong people.

•　•　•

I searched the streets on the black side of town, watching the people who inhabited the area. I saw them move about, congregate, enter their houses, linger in doorways — black people moving in their slinking way. Mothers towing small children. Young girls and boys strutting. There is something musical about black communities everywhere. Something unexplainable, but you feel it in the air. It shares the atmosphere with a tension that is like a coiled spring, ready to erupt into quick and lethal violence, a rush of madness, before calm prevails again. A kind of tension that exists side-by-side with the music of black life, the music the poor move to. I could feel the connection, feel the tug under my skin. Some things never change. I was beginning to feel more comfortable, a bit more confident that it was going to be all right, that I could pull it off, until I saw them gathered outside the chicken joint — some leaning against the wall, others standing above those sitting on the walk.

They were practicing the old ritual. This was the corner, alive and well and just as tough-looking as ever, to an outsider. I drove around the block several times, knowing that eventually I would have to stop and approach them. These were some of the people I had come to see. I was shaky as I got out of the car a couple of blocks away and walked toward the mini shopping center, with its fried-chicken place, washerette, and convenience store. Two or three young girls sashayed about the parking lot, and there was no doubt this was where the dudes hung out. A couple of fellows were engaged in a kind of slow, half-hearted courting ritual with two of the girls. The girls would come up and whisper something into their ears. They would all laugh. One of the girls would shout "uhn-uhn!" Then the girls would hit at the two boys and run, stopping to look back when they realized they weren't being chased. The fellows would just sit there, calling them back with their fingers. None of them was as old as I, though some were undoubtedly in their twenties. I got closer. What would I say? They were watching me now, checking me out. I could hear their minds come to attention, grind a little. Or was that mine making all that noise?

"What's happ'ning," I said lazily to anybody interested.

"You got it," one of them said.

"You what's happenin'," a short, stocky guy with pressed curls on his head said. They were really eyeing me now. My mind raced. I thought of the comedian Richard Pryor, and one of his albums that comes so close to describing black life in America. I remembered the routine where all these people try to crash an after-hours joint by asking for an apparently nonexistent person named Jesse.

"Y'all seen Jesse?" I asked.

"Jesse who?" the stocky dude with the fancy hair asked.

Jesse who? Damn. "Jesse Green," I said.

They were considering the name.

Most of them shook their heads no.

"I know Jesse Thomas," said a slender guy who seemed to be smiling even when he wasn't. "Live about four blocks over. But not no Jesse Green."

"What this Jesse Thomas look like?" I asked.

"Tall, ugly dude," the slender guy said. "He look a lot like you." He was smiling now. So were the others. "He's a funny man," the stocky dude said. "A real funny nigger."

"Bro', you left yourself open for that," Slender said. "Couldn't pass it up."

"You ain't never passed up nothing," Stocky said.

"Where you from?" Slender asked.

"Georgia," I said slowly, "but I been 'round a lot of places."

"Where this Jesse Green 'spose to live?" Slender asked.

I sat down on the curb of the sidewalk next to him. "'Round here," I said. "He told me I could ask anybody I see on any of these streets right through here and they'd know 'im. He said everybody know 'im."

"Well, we don't know 'im," Slender said.

"Shit," I said. "Nigger owe me some money. I needs my money." I tried to look disgusted, took my hat off. It was warmer outside now, and the snow had stopped hours ago.

"No wonder you can't find the nigger," Slender said. "Nigger owe you money. He don't mean for you to find 'im."

"Um gon' find that nigger or else," I said.

"How much he owe you?" Slender asked carefully. He wasn't sure how much of my business I would let him into. I hesitated a few moments before I answered.

"Fifty cent," I said. He looked at me funny. I wondered if I had blown it. Maybe it was no longer cool to say fifty cents on the corner when you meant fifty dollars.

"I'd find the nigger, too, for that kind of money," Slender said. The others didn't seem much interested in me and my search for the fictional Jesse Green. They had returned to whatever it was they were doing before, hollering at people in passing cars, telling jokes. Slender and I were sort of to ourselves.

"What's your name?" I asked him.

"Jesse," he said. "Jesse Green." He watched the stunned expression on my face. Holy shit, I was thinking. Then he broke into a smile. Fuck you nigger, I thought, your momma and the horse y'all rode in on. Nigger scared me.

"Prince," he said.

"Prince?"

"Prince."

"You live 'round here?"

"Three streets over."

"You sho' you don't know Jesse Green?"

"Not unless the nigger got another name."

"This really fucks me up. He said he'd have a place for me to stay until I could find me a gig."

Prince didn't respond.

"Nigger got me to come all the way up here for nothing. No money and no place to stay."

"You got his phone number?"

"Naw. But the next time I see that nigger, um gon' have his ass."

Prince laughed.

"You ain't got no money?" he asked carefully. He had a nice way of easing into things that might be sensitive, but you could tell he was going to ask anyway, hoping his easy manner would cover for him.

"Just a couple of bucks," I said. "But how long can you git by on that?"

He shook his head.

"Any boarding houses 'round here, or people who take in roomers?"

"People ain't doing much of that no more, these days, all this shit going on," he said. "Niggers knocking folks in the head."

"Anybody 'round here hiring? Um gon' have to git a job quick."

"Ain't much," he said. "The shit is bad. Just about everybody I know working one of them CETA jobs or on unemployment. I had a CETA job up until 'bout two months ago."

"You quit?"

"Naw, they just let me go. I think it was 'cause of all this mess in the CETA program [pronounced pro-*gram*]. I don't think everything was right up there at the office. I'd had my job almost two years. Nobody 'spose to work on them jobs more than a year."

"What you doing now?"

"I been looking," he said with a smile. "But not too hard. I git by."

"Any cheap motels?"

"Yeah, plenty. I would let you stay with me. I got a one-bedroom place, but my ol' lady coming in tonight from Durham. She in school up there. You know how that is . . ."

"Yeah," I said, " 'preciate it anyway. You all right, you know."

We sat there awhile watching cars go by and people pass. Late afternoon had arrived, and darkness was creeping in. I longed for the days ahead when the sun would stick around past 9:00 P.M., and children would play baseball in the streets until dark.

"I got to find a room," I said, getting up.

"Days Inn," Prince said. "They kinda cheap and they clean. It's one not too far from here, 'cross the expressway."

"Well, y'all be chilly," I said, leaving. Prince smiled.

"Later," Prince said as I moved away.

As I walked to the car, I wondered if they were talking about me behind my back. And, if they were, what they were saying. I was moving easy. I felt pretty good. They had accepted me. I searched for the Days Inn.

• • •

Charlotte got old fast. Days of going through the papers searching for work. Nothing for unskilled people like me. Walking the sidewalks, hanging out in the cafés, watching those who had jobs go to and from work.

By the time I met Oliver Blue, I was emotionally on a roller coaster going down. Charlotte had depressed me. I hadn't made much progress, if any. Jobs eluded me, and the misery of all those others who were out of work, and those still fighting for a few CETA jobs, didn't do much to lift my spirits. I was doubting myself again, doubting that this assignment would ever amount to more than a travel piece. And something else was beginning to happen. I felt as if I were somehow fading away. The change had been subtle at first, but after a few days it was shocking in its clarity. Things were different now when I moved about town. Dressed in suit and tie, traveling as a newspaper reporter, I commanded a certain amount of respect from blacks as well as whites. People would often say "yes sir" and "no sir."

In my new guise, gas-station attendants, cashiers in grocery stores and cafeterias, people all over seemed to look at me differently, as if they were not really seeing me. Not as many smiles were beamed my way, and nobody seemed to do anything extra to make sure I was satisfied. Once it dawned on me that this was happening, I began to look for it everywhere I went, and there was no mistake about it.

A friend I'd met during the caucus of black Democrats in Charlotte in 1976 set up the meeting with Blue. A tall, dark man walked through the door of my friend's house. He was about thirty, athletic, with plenty of spring in his step. A successful financial consultant and aspiring entrepreneur, Blue had been born and raised in Clarkton, North Carolina, a tiny town in the southeastern part of the state that had the distinction of being the home of the current lieutenant governor. Clarkton, one of a cluster of small towns that once thrived on agriculture in the Cape Fear area of North Carolina, lies less than thirty miles from Lumberton, a city I had already decided to visit. On the basis of the background Blue gave me on his home town and others in the immediate vicinity, I knew that that was the area where I would spend most of my time in North Carolina.

He had grown up poor, one of eight children of John Henry and Myrtle Blue. They had tried to make a living by farming, mainly raising tobacco. The house they lived in sat up off the ground on bricks, like the others near it, and all but two of the walls inside were unfinished.

"We owned our own house," Blue said. "Of course we owned it along with whoever we'd borrowed money from, 'cause most of the time it stayed tied up in debt. I don't know of any black people back home who made money farming.

"They'd make a little money, but they always had to go into debt before winter was over with to buy food," he said, stretching out in the chair. He had the long legs of a basketball player, which he had been in high school, the army, and college. Basketball had helped him get out of Clarkton and the paralyzing poverty that still plagues many of those there. My stomach flinched a little when he told me that things hadn't changed much even today.

"I don't remember my father ever being out of debt," he said. "I could tell it used to worry him. My brother and I would ride to town with him in the wagon. We went everywhere in a mule-drawn wagon. My father and mother never had a car.

"We used to go with him to this place in town where he would get this little piece of yellow paper. It was a hardware store on one side, and on the other side there was an office part.

"We'd go in there and talk to this little man at the counter, and he'd write on this yellow piece of paper and give my father one, and he'd keep one. That's what we used to get groceries with.

"My father would have to stand around in there and wait; explain to this man why he didn't have no money, why he hadn't made no money . . .

"My father died in 'seventy-three. We had just finished tearing down the old house and building a new one. He didn't get to spend much time in the new house. You know," he said, "I used to work side by side with my father in the fields all day, from sunup to sundown, and I didn't get to know him until he was in the hospital sick and dying.

"The hard times and the debt killed him. I don't ever remember my father hunting or fishing or anything like that. He was always working. He did nothing but work. And we still stayed in debt. And we didn't have anything to show for it . . ."

Many of the things he talked about happened in the late sixties and early seventies. I found it amazing that they were still going on that late, after the civil-rights struggles and after all the laws passed to guarantee people their rights as citizens of this country. I was so taken by his account of the place he came from that I immediately took him into my confidence and told him what I was really up to. When I told him I would soon be heading for his hometown and the area in which he grew up, Blue called his mother and told her a friend of his, who was looking for work, would probably be coming through shortly and might drop in on her. He gave her no more explanation than that, and she didn't ask for more.

We spent most of the afternoon and evening talking. When I left, sadness accompanied me back to my motel room. The things he had said about his father nearly made me cry, and I stayed awake into the early hours of morning thinking about my own father, who had refused to quit working after two heart attacks, but who had had to give in with the third. My father, who gets out of breath now doing simple chores, who spends his days gardening but refuses to believe he is retired. My father, waiting for the day when he will feel better, when he will feel "good enough" to go back to work, maybe do a few odd jobs, remodeling jobs. My father, who has thrived on hard work all his life, though it never gave him anything but an enlarged heart and three heart attacks. My father, a tall, muscular, once-stern man, now mellowed by sickness and a body that is wearing out. A man who sang to us sometimes at night, when I was young. I remember working beside him in the blazing sun during the summers, digging footings (foundations for houses) or pouring concrete — blistering work that made muscles ripple in our backs and covered our hands with callouses. My father continually badmouthed the kind of work he did, his own skills, and put himself down as an uneducated man — he went only to the third grade in school — who had lost his chance to be somebody when, as a child, he was forced to stay out of school and work in the fields whenever the white man who owned the land the family farmed came around and told my grandfather to keep the children home to work. While we were knee-deep in ditches, slinging those picks into the hard ground, my father would tell us, "The day some white man comes to my house to tell me to keep my children home from school is the day I go to jail. 'Cause that white man dead. No two ways about it." He pushed me out of the ditch and into books. He was determined I was going to get a college education and a "desk job." The kind of work he did wasn't fit for his children as a life's work, he said. We had to do better.

He was a man torn by the burdens life sometimes loads on us all. He really wanted to show us how proud he was of his skills, how he was a self-made man. He wanted to teach us all the things he'd learned the best way he could, yet he didn't want to make such a strong impression that we might stray from the path he was determined we'd take, the path to jobs in suits and ties, telling other people what to do.

"Don't end up like me and your mama," he'd say. "We can't do no better. Don't work hard all your life and have nothin' to show for it."

When he spent Saturdays and Sundays in the back yard with the family car spread out in a zillion parts around him on the ground, like pieces of a greasy puzzle, I was right there, watching and helping him reassemble it so he could go to work on Monday mornings. I was drawn to him like steel filings to a magnet. Though he tried to make what he did, and the things he knew, seem unimportant, I could tell he was really proud and glad that I was always around taking it all in. Deep down, there was nothing he wanted more than to pass on everything he knew.

3

After Dark

EVEN IN my darkest moments of dread, I had not imagined a situation so filled with the possibility of nightmarish horror and true evil as the one I found myself in about five miles north of Salisbury, North Carolina. Darkness had fallen hard, and my car had died on Interstate 85, so I let it coast onto the shoulder and got out with my flashlight to see if I could find the problem. I thought the fuel pump had gone, or that something had happened to the gas line, but after examining them both — as best I could in the dark, with cars whizzing by at high speeds — I could see nothing wrong with either. It was puzzling. The last time there had been trouble, the car had gone into a fit of coughing and hissing before shutting down; but this time it had gone out like a mallard caught by buckshot.

Pulling my jacket around me, I set out, with lighted flashlight in hand, walking the mile and a half to the next exit, hoping to find a service station with a tow truck and a mechanic.

I had never realized how eerie it is to be alone on a superhighway with fast, indifferent cars zooming past so close that you can feel the wind from their passing, seconds after they're gone; the headlights making weird patterns of light on the road signs, the billboards advertising resorts, amusement parks, and the exorbitant price of diesel fuel. I had to walk almost sideways, because the shoulder was cut on a slope which made me feel that one of my legs was longer than the other. The ditch between the shoulder and the banks that rose above the roadway was invariably dark and seemingly bottomless. I felt small, compared to the huge billboard signs and the cars speeding past, the road itself huge and stretching out as far as I could see into the darkness. I was utterly alone, one man by himself with a weak flashlight.

I knew nobody was going to stop. Besides, I was afraid that if anyone did, with my luck he would be a robber. No one stopped, so I continued to walk toward the exit, looking back occasionally at the dead car, which was growing smaller and smaller. I knew in my heart I did not want to return to it alone.

I reached the service station at the exit on the north side of the road and described my situation to the man who sat reared back in the chair inside. He pointed to the lot outside, shaking his knit-cap-covered head.

"No tow truck," he said. "Sorry. Try the one across the bridge." He shrugged and went back to watching the tiny TV set that squatted on the dusty counter. I was really worried now. Even the bridge was scary. In the dark, it looked like a drawbridge stretched across an eerie moat, and the lights from the cars passing below looked like evil beasts moving in the murky waters of the moat. I tried to force this image from my mind as I crossed, the wind from the cars whistling against my face. The station on the other side, almost hidden from the highway by a tall bank of grass, was semidark, but I could make out several cars and — thank God — a tow truck, in the parking lot. Drawling laughter spilled from the place and made me even more uneasy as I approached. When I opened the door and looked inside, I knew my nightmare was being acted out. I thought of the stories my paper had carried some two years before, about a black man in a south Georgia town who was found floating in a river. He had been castrated, beaten, and left for dead, but he lived. He supposedly got in that condition because some good old boys — allegedly including the sheriff of the county — suspected him of informing the feds about a local moonshine operation. My balls began to ache something fierce.

There were about six men inside, most of them squatting on their haunches around the space heater, chewing tobacco, rubbing their hands together slowly. A fuzzy-faced man, scrawny, with dirt smudges on his hands and face, wearing greasy overalls, was at the counter, and a redfaced man in camouflaged hunting coveralls, cap, and rubber boots, who was almost as wide as the door, leaned against the wall. When I stuck my head in the door, all conversation and laughter halted immediately. There was total silence for at least ten seconds. They all looked at me in amazement, then looked at one another. I knew they were all saying to themselves: "Well goddamn. Am I seeing things or did a nigger just stick his head in here?" The ache in my balls got more severe. I wanted to turn and run. Damn if I hadn't walked right into the den of the toughest-looking bunch of rednecks this side of Billy Carter's service station in Plains. There was one consolation — in my mind, anyway. I knew that if I survived, I'd probably have a helluva story, because I was sure I was about to catch more hell than I'd ever bargained for.

"My car broke down a couple miles down the road," I said in a voice I realized after the words came out was much too loud. "I saw the tow truck outside." I hesitated. Only then did I smell the pungent odor of liquor. Oh Lord, they had been drinking. It was classic, my mind was saying. Just like in all the Burt Reynolds redneck movies. I was soon to be a dead nigger, or, worse, a nigger wishing he was dead.

Nobody spoke for a while. Then the guy in greasy overalls and cap said, "I can tow you, but we ain't got no mechanic heah now."

I didn't say anything.

"He at our other place," he said slowly. "We got another station in Salsberry [Salisbury]."

"Could you tow me there?"

"I reckon I could."

"How much you charge me?"

" 'Bout ten dollars. First I got to call and see if he still there. He might be done knocked off by now." He went to the phone. I stood just inside the door. The others were watching me as if they still couldn't believe I was actually standing there. Chills ran over my body when I heard the attendant say softly into the phone, "It's a black fellow." He looked over his shoulder at me with unmistakable evil in his unshaven face. His eyes roamed about in his head like a mad man's, and there seemed to be a smirk on his narrow lips. The others who weren't chewing tobacco chewed on cigars. One of them, a fat man in a dusty felt hat, vinyl coat, and plaid shirt, balanced an enormous belly between his legs as he sat back on his haunches. His skin had the look of a pink lizard, and he was so thick he had deep creases in his neck. He stared at me when I wasn't looking directly at him.

"What's wrong with it?" the attendant asked, turning away from the phone.

"I don't know," I said. "Maybe the fuel pump."

"He don't know," the scrawny man said into the phone. "Bring him down? Awright." He hung up the phone. "I'll haul you down there. He'll look at it."

He put on a pair of gloves and told me to wait for him out in the truck. He took his time about joining me out there. As he left, he said something I couldn't hear to the men inside. They all laughed and were still laughing as we drove away. I had picked out a spot on the side of his face — at the temple, just below where his cap stopped — where I was going to hit him as hard as I could when the time came and the shit started. I watched the road carefully, to see if he was going back toward my car or heading in some other direction. To reach the car, we had to go past it, exit, cross the expressway, and come back north. When we reached the car, he carefully hitched it, hoisted the front wheels off the ground, and remarked that there was barely any tread left on the tires.

We started again and were halfway to Salisbury before he broke the heavy silence that had filled the cab of the rough-riding truck. "Hope it ain't too serious," he said slowly. "I don't reckon you'd wanna be stuck heah a day or two . . ."

It wasn't really a question, but it seemed to hang in the air the way a question does. His voice rose, then fell, as if it couldn't make up its mind. I was reminded of my ride in Minter's pickup a few weeks earlier. That ride had been something of a break-through. It had not mattered then that we were not the same color. That was not the case this time around, for it mattered greatly to me that I was black, that it was dark, that the driver was white, and that I didn't trust him as far as I could throw his scrawny carcass after busting his skull with the heel of my hand — which is what I planned to do to defend myself, if anything went awry. Here I was, building up hate for this man; enough hate so I could harm him and be convinced that it was right and just, that he had it coming. Here I was, letting the savage part of me take over; for when the time came, I was prepared to let loose the wildest ass-kicking display of battle this hick had ever seen. But in the back of my mind, I kept wondering what the hell I was doing here in the first place, in the dark, in the cab of a truck on this highway, probably about to get castrated or worse.

"Naw," I said, "I wouldn't wanna be stuck here."

"Then ag'in," he said with a sinister smile, "this heah ain't such a bad little place. You might like it heah."

"I doubt it."

"Never kin tell."

"I really don't think so." We rode on in silence with nothing but the occasional sound of a passing car filtering into the truck, along with the hum of the truck's engine, which sounded badly in need of a tune-up.

"I been heah all my life," he said.

I didn't say anything.

"You got Georgia plates," he said, "things hard in Georgia for blacks, ain't it?"

"It's hard everywhere."

"Yeah, but they did more against black people in Georgia and Alabama than anywhere else, didn't they? That there's the way I understand it."

"South Carolina, North Carolina, Mississippi, they all bad," I said, wondering what he was getting at.

"Don't sound like you like no place."

"I like a lot of places. Just ain't found no place special, yet."

"Yeah," he said shaking his head. "Really, this heah's a right nice place. Maybe you'll stay a while, see it."

"Nope," I said, "don't think so."

There was a long silence until we reached the Salisbury exit and pulled off the highway. In town, there were more cars on the streets, which made me feel a little safer. The service station was just a few blocks from the exit, and we were there quickly, once we got off the highway.

"Yeah," he said, "we do pretty good with this'n and the udden up the road. You wait in the truck. Um gon' talk to the man fixes the cars."

This station, like the other, was a little darker than I'd expected it to be — menacing, in a shadowy way. There were three men inside, before the driver joined them. He shifted his weight from one leg to the other as he talked to them, gesturing strongly with his arms and hands. The listeners, as if on cue, would turn their heads in my direction and look toward the tow truck, and I knew they were discussing me. I eased down out of the truck and stood in the narrow light next to it. The light was a mixture of moonlight, which filtered through thick clouds, and two outside lights. I stood there in the chill air with my hands in my jacket pockets, considering the lanes of escape I could use if and when they decided to come after me with blood in their eyes. In my mind, I measured the number of strides to the next corner, building, business, house, anything that might be helpful. Cars continued to pass intermittently, which gave me some consolation. If I ran into the street shouting for help, maybe some kind soul would stop and rescue me. Finally, the driver and a short plug of a man, who seemed to be mainly one piece with arms attached, started toward me. The others remained inside rubbing their hands together and holding them close to the fire of the space heater. They sat and watched through the glass as their partners approached me.

The short man walked as if he had no knees, his legs straight and powerful. The hams that were his forearms bore tattoos — a bad sign, I thought.

"What's the problem?" the short man asked. His voice was strong, tough.

"Said he b'leeves it's the fuel pump," the skinny driver said.

"I don't know," I said. "Fuel pump . . . something . . . It just stopped, all of a sudden, just cut off."

"Right on the 'spressway," the driver added.

The short man pursed his lips as he walked around the car inspecting it.

"Nineteen sixty-nine, ain't it?" the short man asked.

"Uh-huh," I said, shaking my head.

"Them's some good automobiles," he said, kicking one of the front tires. "Ones they making now ain't worth a shit. All that pollution horseshit on 'em, got all that horsepower, big ole engines and won't run worth a damn."

I shook my head in agreement. What was he getting at? Why didn't they just get on with it, whatever they were going to do?

"You buy this car new?" the short man asked.

"No. I ain't had it but a couple years," I said. "It's been good, though," I added quickly, feeling something else was needed.

"I bet it is," he said, "I bet it is. I bet you wouldn't take nothing for it. I know I wouldn't if I had it. Take that truck," he told the driver, "and push it up in that stall there. You," he said to me, "git in there and guide it in right there."

He walked back inside while the two of us managed to get the car straight in the stall. When this was done, the driver started to leave. "You ain't leaving?" I asked, as he backed up and began to pull away. "What about what I owe you for the towing?"

"Pay him," he said, pointing toward the office, where the short man was bent over in a fit of laughter with the others inside. "He's gon' take care of you now." The skinny driver double-clutched the big tow truck and pulled away.

The short man was still laughing when he came through the service door of the station and entered the pit where I was waiting with the car.

"So you think it's the fuel pump," he said, lifting the hood. He was so short that he just stepped right up onto the bumper and into the engine, at the same time taking a long-bladed screwdriver from the back pocket of his greasy pants. He lifted a metal flap on the distributor cap — I was watching him very closely — and found a small screw there, which he turned lightly with the screwdriver. He seemed to freeze there under the hood for a moment, as if trying to decide what to do next. Then he backed out of the engine and stood next to me smiling.

"Try her now," he said.

"Huh?"

"Try her now. Start 'er up."

I got in the car and turned the key in the ignition. It cranked right up. I was amazed. The short man was really beaming now.

"The points was stuck is all," he said smiling. "You thought it was the fuel pump. I thought it might've been the points all along. The way it just stopped and all." The smile was so broad it now covered his whole face. "I could've cheated you sho' as the world. I coulda put on a new fuel pump, a whole bunch of stuff, and you woulda paid for all that shit you didn't need."

What is this? I was thinking. Is he being nice to me? What?

"You said yourself you thought it was the fuel pump. I coulda stuck you with a hunnerd-fifty, two hunnerd-dollar bill easy. People always talking 'bout gas stations rippin' them off. I coulda ripped you off something bad, but no, it's the points. They was stuck. You didn't know that. I'm gon' tell you. You can go on with them points, but they gon' stick agin. I could put another set in there for you."

"How much?" I asked.

"Eight dollars."

"That's all?"

"See there," he said. "We honest folks here."

"Put the points on."

When he was finished, I cranked the car again. It sounded even better now.

"How much I owe you?"

"Eight dollars for the points and ten dollars for the towing."

I gave him the money. We were inside the office now.

"You tell anybody we honest here. Do good work and we don't cheat nobody. You hear." The men inside, who looked like they could have come straight out of the mind of a Hollywood casting agent conjuring up vicious southern rednecks, were still laughing and talking. They had looked up when we entered, but it hadn't seemed to bother them at all that I had entered their world.

"Sho' is cold tonight," one of them said, warming his calloused hands at the heater.

Another reached inside the several layers of shirts he wore and pulled out a rumpled pack of Winstons. "A smoke?" he asked me.

"No thank you," I said.

"You don't smoke?" he asked.

"Never picked up the habit," I said.

"You is lucky," he said with a smile. "I been smoking since I was eight or nine. And I 'on't even like it."

The others laughed. "Don't you start now," he said. "I know I already got two or three cancers. Sometimes my breath git so short, I git tired taking out my cigarettes tryin' to git 'em to my lips."

"That's why I chew 'bacca," another one said. "Ain't never smoked but one cigarette in my life. It was one of them Home-run cigarettes. I 'on't know if they make 'em anymore. Anyhow. That blasted thang make me so damn drunk, my head spinning, I thought I'd died and gone straight to hell. Ain't smoked another'n since."

The short man had written out the receipt, and he handed it to me.

"Well," I said, reaching for the door, "y'all keep warm." They nodded as I left. The wind had gotten even stronger, so I rushed to the car and started the engine. I looked back as I pulled away. They were still sitting around the heater, a couple of them resting on their haunches with their backs to the counter for support.

Watching them through the glass walls of the service station was like watching fish in an aquarium. Outside was darkness, and in the midst of that darkness was this lighted room, where the men sat dressed as if they were getting ready to shoot a scene from *Deliverance* or *The Beverly Hillbillies*. All they did was sit by the heater, warm their hands, tell jokes and stories, and comfort each other, passing the night hours before going home to bed. And I had been so afraid of them. I had heard all those warnings from friends anytime I was about to take a trip anywhere in the South — particularly through Alabama or Mississippi — that "you better take your stuff [gun]. Man, you stop at some of these filling stations without your stuff, in some of these small towns, these crackers liable to do anything." I had always refused to carry a gun with me on trips, thinking that worse things might happen with a gun than without, but I would never forget the warnings and the stories about those unfortunate black souls who had been without their "stuff" while traveling, and ended up terrorized or killed by "hateful crackers."

Such stories were legend in the black community. But that night in North Carolina, when I walked into that service station for help, I felt for the first time that I needed a gun, because I knew I was in grave danger. During all the time they waited on me and fixed my car, I was terrified, because I knew the moment they made the slightest suspicious move I was going to start kicking and swinging. And it was all in my mind. Those people were nice to me, and all the while I was thinking horrible thoughts, my mind assigning them the worst possible intentions.

Back on the interstate heading north to whatever awaited me in Greensboro, Lumberton, and, later, Bladen County — the rural, close-knit community where Oliver Blue had been raised — I felt foolish for having been so afraid. I had been frightened because of the way they looked, because they fit the stereotype of the low-life redneck crackers I had grown up fearing and hating. In all the stories I'd been raised on, these ghastly figures were continually raping, lynching, castrating, or killing poor, unsuspecting black men and women — even children — and never having to pay for their dirty deeds. When I saw them there in those two service stations, in their hillbilly get-ups and work shoes — the soles covered with caked-on red mud — I was seeing depraved villains who slobbered as they fondled some innocent young black maiden while her man was tied to a nearby tree and beaten. All the legends raced in my head. Tales of black men who disappeared while driving through the South in their fancy new cars, after stopping for gas or food in a small town where white folks didn't "cotton to niggers with new cars." What if I had been wielding a gun? I might have hurt somebody, thinking they were out to get me. I had to have more control over myself from now on. Everybody knew that things are not always as they seem. But the truth is that even though I felt foolish for being afraid, and felt a deep sickness in the pit of my stomach because of the fear that had been inside me, I could have acted in no other way. Even in 1978 — after the civil-rights movement, the black movement, voting rights; after all the things that were supposed to help remove the veil of ignorance and darkness from the South — I still did not feel safe traveling alone in a car in my native region. And no other black person I knew felt any safer.

4

The Way Some People Live

I, black, come to my prime
In the section of the niggers
Where a nickel costs a dime.
— Langston Hughes, "Prime"

I HAD already been on the road for more than a week when I
arrived in Bladen County, and thoughts of the assignment, fears,
anxieties, and the hodgepodge of events and experiences I had
been through up to that point were swirling inside me like
jagged pieces of a puzzle, refusing to be shaped together into a
sensible picture that I could fully understand. I had spent several
weeks planning the project before I took to the road, but it was
the kind of undertaking that almost defies planning. How does
one prepare for such a task — leaving comfortable things behind
to seek out the mysteries of other worlds, the marrow of other
people's lives? Up to that point, I had been trying to get my
bearings. Frequently, I found myself in strange places where I
did not know the codes, the signals, the things that are known
only to those who live around one another. The incidents at the
service stations outside Salisbury stayed on my mind. I thought
over and over about the fear that had engulfed me that night.
Another incident stood out in my mind — something that oc-

curred in Greensboro my second day there. I had gone down to Ashboro Street, which is in the city's black community, to look for a room in a boarding house. I wasn't even sure I was going to spend much time in Greensboro. I was anxious to get on to the Cape Fear region of North Carolina — the area Blue had described to me so vividly in Charlotte — because, after talking to him, I had felt drawn there as if the small towns he described were sirens; my thoughts drifted toward southeastern North Carolina and Bladen County.

An acquaintance had told me that I might be able to get a room at one of the boarding houses on Ashboro Street. "It's pretty rough down there," he had warned.

Using his directions, I had no trouble finding the place. After several turns around the neighborhood, I parked my car on a side street and walked up and down Ashboro, inspecting the huge boarding houses with signs out front advertising vacancies. Most of them were in pretty bad shape, with rotting wood porches and peeling paint. Farther up the street, I had seen children playing on the porches and in the yards of dilapidated houses that had paper tags nailed beside the front doors announcing that the houses had been condemned by the city. Despite the signs, people continued to live there. The children smiled at me as I walked past. One smooth-faced girl of about eight waved as I went by the porch she was standing on. I stopped and turned toward her. "How long has that sign been up there?" I asked.

"Long time," she said with a smile.

"Real long?" I asked. "Longer than a year?"

"Yeah," she said.

"You and your family going to move soon?"

"No."

"You know why?"

She shrugged her shoulders and shook her head. "What's your name?"

"Chester," I said.

She giggled.

"Why is that funny?"

"The man live in that house 'cross the street dog name Chester," she said. "He got three legs. And I got to go." She turned and ran to the other side of the porch, where other children were playing. As I walked away, I heard her telling the others that my name was Chester. They all laughed.

A sign on one of the boarding houses directed me just down the block to the house where the landlady lived. I knocked on the door and was greeted by a dark, husky woman with a broad, red-lipped smile. She was wearing a multicolored print dress under a thick wool sweater. The dress was rimmed by a faded slip, which was too long and hung below the hem. She had been eating breakfast on the sofa in front of a gas space heater in the small living room. She wiped grease from her mouth with a handkerchief she kept balled up in her hand.

"Yes?" she said in a friendly voice.

"I come 'bout the room," I said. "I didn't know you was eatin'."

"Aw shucks, honey, don't mind that. Come, let me git that key, I'll show you the room. It's real nice."

"How much is it?"

"Twenty dollars a week in advance. Wait just a minute. Come on in."

I stood just inside the door. The house had the smell of camphor, the way my father's aunt's house had always smelled when we visited her. I recognized that pungent sweetness right off.

She emerged from a back room with a string of keys. "Honey, you gon' love this room," she said, reaching inside her dress at the shoulders and adjusting the strap that held up the slip. The bottom edge of the slip moved up her leg and disappeared under the multicolored flowers and designs of the dress. "It's the best room on this street. The best one I got." As we walked the few blocks up to the boarding house, she told more about the room: there was a gas heater, a good mattress ("not all pissed up like you find in a lot of places"), and good floors ("solid floors, and I allow privacy. A man oughta have his privacy").

The room was at the back of a bleak hallway. There were several other rooms that opened onto the hall, and each door bore two or more padlocks and numerous scars where fittings for locks had once been. The room was dismal, dank, and eerie. When she closed the door to search for the light switch that was behind it, I felt strangely lonesome in the darkness, as if I had just entered my death cell. There was something heavy in the air, something besides the odor of dirty toes and mold.

"You lucky this room vacant," she said with a smile. "The previous roomer just moved out yestiddy."

"Why'd he leave?"

"Two boys who live upstairs there broke into his room and stole some of his possessions," she said calmly. "They busted the damn lock slamp off."

"Are they in jail?" I asked.

"Naw, they upstairs," she said.

"No thank you," I told her and left.

After I left Greensboro, I saw that landlady again and again in my mind, smiling grotesquely, waving me into that dungeon of a room, and I knew that sooner or later somebody was going to take the room, because he would not have the choices I had. What would happen to him? I wanted to know. Would the "damn lock be busted slamp off" again? All the while I had been on Ashboro Street, I had had the double-edged sense that something was waiting to pounce. The grocery store on the corner was barred and caged to keep robbers out, and I knew that almost anything could happen on those streets, where some people lived in houses that had been condemned, where burglaries were as common as rats, where locks were torn "slamp off" doors, where police protection was lax, and where those poor people trying to live quiet lives were easy victims for thugs. And there was no place for them to go; the low-rent housing projects were no better. Security and police protection cost money, and they didn't have it.

Somehow I knew Bladen County was going to change things for me. After being there only a couple of hours, I already felt a new kind of movement inside my psyche: I felt that I was a camera just beginning to focus on something that had been vague for a long time. Something was being formed, though I didn't know exactly what. I felt something for the stooped people who walked the muddy streets here, who looked up passively at my car as I drove by, who seemed to be so bent by life and so heavy with despair.

Elizabethtown, the county seat of Bladen, with its wide main street and one block of shops that looked as if they had been brought in off the back lot of Warner Brothers and set in place, seemed a relic of the old West, a vision of Dodge City from all the Westerns I had absorbed as a child. As I cruised down the main street, I almost expected to turn the corner and find that the buildings had no sides or backs, only long pieces of lumber propping up the storefronts. But this was the East, southeastern North Carolina in the twentieth century, and tobacco and farming were king, not cattle and gunfighters.

There seemed to be people all around, walking or sitting in front of the stores on the few side streets of the business district. A stone's throw from downtown, I found the narrow dirt roads, rutted and muddy, that served the black community. The houses were dismal, small, and oddly shaped, with tiny rooms that jutted out from the main structures at odd angles, as if they were afterthoughts. In a few of the yards, there were beat-up cars resting on flat tires or bare rims. These people seemed to have very little hope, or else they didn't show it for fear it might count against them to want too much. You didn't even have to get out of the car to see it. Many of the old people seemed to be waiting to die. They talked a lot about God and about meeting Him, His kingdom and power. They had given up on man.

I thought of old people in urban settings. In high-rise apartments in Atlanta where the elderly are herded together, they complain about the weird environment they find when surrounded by old people like themselves — all fighting the same battle, the same loneliness. Their surroundings constantly remind them of their own ailments (because they see them in others), their own mortality (because death is widespread in such places), and their own longings.

Country people, by contrast, are probably a bit better off than the old folks I see so often around Atlanta. In the country, there are no gleaming towers for the aged that serve to imprison them in the miseries of advancing age. At least these rural people are still with their families. Even though life in the country is tough — especially in the boondocks, where there is no running water or central heat — these people have made some kind of peace with the hardships of their lives, and they hang on until God calls.

I needed a place to stay. While out walking, I asked some of the people — mostly elderly men in felt hats and thick suits shiny from wear, who were sitting in front of one of the stores near downtown, a couple of them leaning forward on their canes — if people around there took in roomers.

"Nobody got room 'nough," said a white-haired man with sunken cheeks and a white stubble covering his face. " 'Sides that. Hit'd be hard ter find anybody'd trust ya', a stranger, ya' know."

One of the others mentioned the only motel in town, something called Coles, a few blocks away. And then there was a boarding house just downtown — but "you won't like it," the white-haired man said.

"How come?"

"Just won't," he said, smiling and shaking his head. The others were shaking their heads, too.

"Is it white?" I asked.

"Yep."

"Anybody can stay anywhere now, you know," I said. "Right?"

They kept smiling and shaking their heads. They obviously thought I was very funny. I had seen the establishment they were referring to, when I first rode into town. It was on the main street, a large brick house with a wide porch and a neat sign in the yard. I decided to try it. I took the steps to the porch.

Through the glass pane, an old lady looked up at me from a wheelchair. Her eyes avoided mine. She was terrified: I could feel her trembling. She was a tall woman, but the chair and her disability made her seem small. I felt sorry for her. It was not my intention to frighten her, but I could tell that nothing I could say would put her at ease.

A young woman holding a baby was standing above her. Another small child romped about the room, which I assumed was the lobby–sitting room. They didn't notice me at the door until I knocked. The old woman, confronted with this absolute horror, slowly wheeled herself to the door.

"Yes?" she asked in a small voice that cracked. Her pale white face seemed to fade into her white hair. She made no motion to open the door. The pane glass was her protection.

"I'd like to rent one of your rooms," I said, in what I hoped was a kind enough voice. She began shaking her head "no" before I finished the sentence. At the same time, her hands snaked up from her lap and straightened her sweater, then pulled it closed across her chest.

"I'm not renting any rooms today," she said, avoiding my eyes.

"I could come back tomorrow."

"No. I'm not going to rent any then, either. Not any this week."

"Thank you," I said, "sorry I bothered you." She still wouldn't look at me. As I turned and walked down the steps to my car, I looked back and saw her pull the curtain closed. But she kept peeking out at me until I drove away.

I headed for Coles, the only other option. Again the landlady was an elderly white woman — this time short and a little plump, with graying hair. She told me she did have a vacant room, and that there were a few others who lived in other towns but worked nearby and stayed at her motel during the week. The rent for a week, she said, would be $31.20 in advance. I paid her, and she pointed out the room. It was on the second floor, the top level.

Though on the top floor, the room was by no means a penthouse. The first thing I noticed after unlocking and opening the door was the mouse staring at me from the bed. When I dropped my suitcase to the floor, he darted across the bed and out of the room through a hole in the wall next to the windowsill. I sat down a minute and surveyed the room. It was a dump: there were cracks in the plaster walls, and the bed was lumpy and smelled a bit strange. An aged air-conditioning unit sat in the window as if it were some kind of strange fungus growing there. It was covered with dust and dirt, and there were cracks around it where wind could squeeze into the room. A tiny black-and-white TV set rested in a chair. The pungent smell of decay was everywhere, and an army of bold red ants continuously marched across the stained sink in the bathroom. When I complained about the mouse to the landlady, she told me that nobody had ever complained of rats in the room before, and gave me a mousetrap.

* * *

It was early afternoon, so after I got settled into my new "home," I made a few entries in the journal I was keeping for this project. Ever since I started, I had been rushing back to wherever I was staying at night, to write down everything I could remember from the day. I was trying to get on paper whatever it was I felt happening inside me. I was losing some of my professional distance. Up to that point, the project had been mysterious and loosely organized, because it was hard to put into words exactly what I was looking for. I knew in an abstract sense that I wanted to find out what progress had or had not been made in the South since the civil-rights movement of the fifties and sixties, and how blacks and poor people were living now. But these phrases were just jargon easily tossed out from the comfort of a cozy downtown office, by men with lofty ideas. What was the connection between this jargon and real life?

I had confidence now that the project would unfold as I went along, and I decided to follow my guts and my heart. I understood now that what I was looking for did not have a specific name, but was something that encompassed a way of life; it cut deeper, hurt more, and was truer. I was moving closer to the people in this land of plenty who trudged through life at the lower end of the American dream. I wanted to get close to their souls, their fears, the kind of shit that made them sweat in the night or shiver in the daytime, the gods they prayed to and the demons they fought. And I realized that the things that had happened to me so far had been small indoctrinations. I was getting closer to the flames now, and the heat was against my face.

* * *

A woman in one of the offices in the Bladen County Courthouse told me I could find Janice Blue in the basement, where she worked in the county's manpower office. I peeked in and saw her behind the desk. She was a petite, delicate woman of twenty-two, who looked no older than sixteen or seventeen. I waited in the hallway outside her office while a number of sullen-looking people went inside one at a time to talk to her about jobs. Those waiting in line sat beside me on the bench outside. They were silent in the manner of people used to living inside their own heads. When I tried to make small talk, they seemed annoyed. Most of them were fairly young, though several were middle-aged. A few eyed me suspiciously, but they did not speak.

After fifteen or so interviews, I was the only one left, so I entered the office and introduced myself. "I'm a friend of Oliver's," I said. "He told me you work here."

"Yeah," she sighed, rubbing her eyes. It had been a long day.

"Is it like this all the time?"

She looked at the stack of folders and applications on her desk and shook her head. "It's pitiful," she said. "So many of them, and only a few jobs. A lot of people have never had real jobs before, you know, outside the farm. Since this is government-funded, they have to list incomes, how long they've been unemployed, things like that. Just about all of them come from families below the poverty level. That's the way it is around here . . . You looking for a job?"

"Sho' am. You know where I can find one?"

"I spent four years in college, to get out of the tobacco fields," she replied, "and this was the only job I could find, and it's so hard, facing all these people who can't find work. I mean, they've got so many problems. When I go home in the evening, I'm worn out. I guess, when you think about it, I was lucky to get this job, if you wanna call this job luck."

"There's no need for me to pretend with you," I said. She looked puzzled. "Didn't Oliver tell you what I was doing?"

"No."

"He didn't tell you I was a writer?"

"No. What are you doing?" She seemed the least bit frightened, like maybe I was crazy or something.

"You off now? I'll walk you to your car and try to explain. It's kind of a long story."

At first she thought I was joking, my story sounded so far-fetched, but I assured her it was the truth, that my assignment was exactly as I had described it. I told her Oliver knew all about it. Finally, she seemed to believe me.

"If this is going to work," I told her, "I've got to be very careful to keep my true identity a secret." She shook her head, indicating that she understood. "I'm asking that you don't tell anybody, okay?" She promised to keep my secret, and we left for her hometown.

● ● ●

Clarkton, where the Blues lived, was only ten miles from Elizabethtown, down Highway 701. I followed Janice in my car. The town itself seemed incredibly small to me, but there was a block or so of downtown: a laundromat, a feed and farm equipment store, a grocery store, a couple of tobacco warehouses, and three or four mills and manufacturing plants. It was notable because, as the sign at the city limits said, it was the home of then North Carolina Lieutenant Governor James "Jimmy" Green. We passed by his large white house with its American flag over the front door, blowing in the February breeze like a red, white, and blue guardian.

When we turned onto Old Brown Marsh Road, Oliver was in my mind. I imagined the cradle that had rocked him, the folks who had raised him, the fields he had walked through, the tall trees where he had often chopped wood by moonlight until midnight or beyond, to keep enough firewood on hand for the tin-barrel heater. I thought of how chopping wood had made him strong, and, along with the plowing and tobacco cropping, had made his legs tough and springy for basketball. How he had sharpened his eye by shooting rocks, balls, anything, into a peach basket nailed to a tree. How his father, John Henry, was always working. How John Henry left home in the late sixties and went to Greensboro to work on a public job for the first time in his life, because he was hopelessly in debt, and, with his farm land shrinking in size because of predatory creditors, he felt he could never dig his way out otherwise.

"We didn't want him to leave home," Blue had told me, "but he figured it was the only way. He started out working at North Carolina A & T [University] as a cook, but they let him off. He was getting up in age then. But he took a job digging ditches — hard work. It was all he could find. He didn't have but a fourth- or fifth-grade education. I don't think he ever adjusted to working on a public job, after farming all his life.

"My father had a stroke. It partially paralyzed him. He had only minor use of one side of his body. Then he seemed to be getting better. He asked me to take him home. There, after about two days, he began hemorrhaging, and he had some kidney trouble, too, and he died. All those years I worked beside my daddy, and I didn't get to know him until he was dying. It was sad. He didn't have time to know me before then.

"He was always working. Driven by that debt. He just worked until it was time to sleep. And I don't think he ever slept that well. Debt chased him even there . . . You know, my daddy lived and died without ever owning a car. He went everywhere in a wagon. We didn't get electricity until the sixties."

What was John Henry Blue's greatest dream? To be free of debt? Whatever it was, he apparently died without realizing it. All the hard work, the stroke, the aching body that broke down under the tremendous strain. His story was so close to that of my own father, who was born to a family of dirt-poor sharecroppers in Monroe County, Georgia, about sixty miles southeast of Atlanta. When he was just a boy, they moved to Griffin under cover of darkness, because my grandfather — Mr. Ches, as he was called — had killed a white man; shot him in the stomach with a single-barreled shotgun. According to my father, who is also named Chester, the man and his two brothers, who were known as roughnecks throughout the county, one night had ridden their horses out to the house where my grandparents lived. Earlier, they had had a dispute with my grandfather over some corn liquor he had made for them. They claimed he had held some back for himself.

They had told Granddaddy that they were going to come after him later that night. He waited outside the house next to the chimney, and had his shotgun ready when they rode up with their guns. They told him they were going to kill him and burn his house down. One of the brothers got down off his horse slowly and came toward Granddaddy with his gun drawn. Granddaddy cocked the shotgun and fired, hitting the man in the stomach. The others were incredulous. They hadn't believed Granddaddy would actually shoot — a black man shooting a white man! They gathered up their wounded brother and rode off. According to my father, the man died later at the hospital. "Poppa never said a word to us children," my father said, "he just gathered everything up, and we moved in the dark. We all knowed they'd be coming back."

When my father was fifteen, even though he "plowed mules in the ground in the field" he was not treated like a man. Two things spurred him to run away from home. One happened a year or so before he decided to leave.

"The white man who owned the land we was sharecropping came by one morning and told Poppa to keep us, the children, out of school to work in the fields.

"It made me mad as hell. I couldn't read, 'cause I was only able to go to school when it rained, and never could git nowhere in school, so I said loud enough for them to hear me, 'When I git grown, ain't gon' let *no* white man tell me what to do with my own children.'

"Poppa said, 'What you say boy?'

"I knowed I was gon' git a whuppin', so I said it ag'in, louder. The white man said, 'Ches, you oughta whup that boy.'

"Mama had to git daddy off me, he beat me so bad. It really hurt him for me to say that."

The other incident happened the evening before he ran away. Daddy had plowed hard all that day and thought for sure Granddaddy would let him go to a dance at the church that night, but Mr. Ches refused.

"It was September of 1929, the beginning of the Great Depression. That night I went to bed wit' my clothes on. Late over in the night I left, walkin'."

He eventually made it on foot all the way to Key West, Florida, in an incredible odyssey that made what I was doing seem like a walk in the park on Sunday afternoon. He slept in graveyards and churches. Hired himself out as a farm hand when he could, plowing all day and sleeping in people's barns with their livestock at night.

"When I got to Key West, I couldn't go no further," he told me. "Wasn't nothing but water. All that damn water."

The journey nearly killed him several times.

"One night, I was somewhere in south Georgia. Churches used to leave their doors open, and I would go in 'em and sleep. I went in this church, and as I went up the aisle, I stepped on something. It was somebody on the floor asleep. Hoboes and tramps was everywhere then. And they was mean as snakes. They'd kill you for a nickel. People was desperate. A lot of 'em ain't have nothin'. They was even crazed-looking in the eyes. So many people was hungry, including me.

"When I got to the pulpit, I stepped on another body. They got up chasing me. I b'leeve they thought I had money or somethin'. I ran, but they caught me. They was beatin' me. I took out the old knife I carried, and stuck one of 'em. He turned me loose. I stuck the knife in the other one and ran. I ran 'til I nearly fell out, 'til I didn't hear nobody coming no more."

He told me there were times he was so hungry that he would "stop where I saw horses and eat the kernels of corn in horseshit. That's right. It was that bad, but I wanted to live.

"Then it got so bad my feet was swollen, my stomach swollen and hurting. Hurting all the time. I was dizzy, aching all the time," he told me.

"I jus' laid down in the road in front of a trailer. I didn't care no more. But the man stopped the truck, got out and hoped [helped] me. He took me to a place and bought me a drink and fed me. I had been plannin' how I was gon' knock him in the head and take his money when I got the chance, but after he was so nice, well, I jus' couldn't do it."

He started the long walk back. When he got home, he had been away — walking — for three years. It was then 1932. He was eighteen.

"When I walked up, Poppa was working in the yard. He saw me. I walked up to 'im. Neither one of us said nothin'. I took out some tobacco I had in my shirt, and rolled a cigarette. Took a match and lit it. Drew on it. He watched me, quiet. Then he came up to me. He was frowning. He said, 'Welcome home son.' We shook hands. And right then I knowed I was a man."

This was the man I came from. The man whose name is my name.

• • •

It was a strange meeting. I — all of six feet three inches tall and 220 pounds — and this kind-faced, diminutive woman, Mrs. Myrtle Blue, eyeballed each other through the doorway. It was as if I already knew her, had known her all my life. This smooth-faced, slightly plump, dark-skinned woman, who must have been in her late fifties at least, though she looked fortyish, made me feel comfortable and safe. And I guess I did already know her, for in spirit she was the same woman who had stood watch over us from her porch, in the neighborhood where I grew up, while we played childish games. She watched like a hawk, to make sure we kept out of the street, out of the path of passing cars. She was the woman who would invite us in for cookies. One of those kindly black women who was somebody's aunt, mother, or grandmother, who seemed so wise and friendly, so motherly, so easy to love.

Janice told her I was Oliver's friend, and she welcomed me immediately, motioning me into the kitchen where she was preparing dinner, talking to me as she worked. The house was cool and dimly lighted, but comfortable; modest, but nice. With central heat, three bedrooms, living room, kitchen, and eating area, it was a far cry from the house it had replaced — the one Oliver had described as having unfinished inside walls, drafty windows, and brick pillars to hold it above the hard ground. Across the open kitchen was a window that looked out on the tall trees in the back yard. A portable TV with a rapidly fading picture rested on a stand near the dining table. Pale images crossed the screen, blinking and rolling, fading out more and more the longer I looked at it, but the sound was clear. Mrs. Blue had been "watching," or, more appropriately, listening, to the afternoon soap operas.

"That thing's just about to give out," she said when she noticed me eyeing it, "but I keep it in here anyhow." There was a console color TV in the living room.

"Why you leaving home?" she asked.

"Got tired of it," I said, "wanted to move on. I always wanted to own some land. If I can find a place I like, get a job, I'm gon' buy me a few acres, start over."

"You got bad memories in Georgia?"

"That's all I got there now."

"You ain't running from nobody?" Her voice rose, indicating the high level of her curiosity and the seriousness of the question.

"No."

"Well, all right," she said, "just checking."

"I guess I'm trying to find myself something better." She was busy with the meal — chicken, collards, dressing, cornbread, potato salad. The wonderful scent in the kitchen reminded me of the homes of all those ladies I remembered from my childhood. They were always cooking, it seemed; always sending up those heavenly aromas.

"What kind of work you interested in?"

"Most anything," I said. "I just need work."

"I know a woman works down the mill here, in the office," she said. "I'll talk with her tomorrow, see if that'll help. Other than that, there ain't too much work 'round here now. Too early yet for anybody to be farming: ground too wet for breaking and planting. It may be after Good Friday before anybody's planting. Then they don't hardly pay no money."

Somebody was at the door. A young man Mrs. Blue introduced as Neville, her grandson, walked in. He and Janice were the only ones left at home with her now. And Neville would soon be leaving, too, for he would graduate from high school later that spring and, like many other kids from the area, would head north, away from the tobacco fields and the small-town way of life, to a land of more money and more opportunity. In the short time I'd been in the area, I had already learned that there was virtually nothing for young people to do there. It was almost as if the town had been set up to run them off as soon as they had wings to fly.

I shook hands with Nev (as Mrs. Blue called him). He was short and athletic-looking. Mrs. Blue told him I was a friend of Oliver's.

During dinner, Nev told me he was undecided whether to join a branch of the armed services or the Job Corps, when he was finished with school. "I know guys who say good and bad things about all of 'em," he said.

"You don't have too much time left to make up your mind," I told him.

We watched TV until around eleven. Then I left their house and drove ten miles through thick fog back to my room in Elizabethtown. The motel looked eerie as I approached it. It was the first time I'd noticed how odd it was, how it didn't fit in with the rest of the town. The building was a two-story stucco, with palmetto trees out front. It seemed to me that it would have been more appropriately located in California or Florida. The front desk was on the first floor, just off the street, and attached to the left of it was a boutique and, farther down, a hair salon. During the entire time I stayed there, I never saw anybody shopping in the boutique.

That night, I showered and got into bed quickly. There was a lot to be done the following morning. I would have to start looking for work. In bed, I made entries in my journal about the Blues and about other things that had happened during the day. The Blues reminded me of my own family — my wife, my daughters. I became melancholy. I wanted to see them. I would have called, but there was no phone in the room, and the front desk was closed. I thought about them until I fell off to sleep. I slept better that night than I had in many nights.

•   •   •

The next morning, I tried the Mt. Vernon Mills. The woman in the office said they had no openings, and wouldn't even let me fill out an application.

At Clarkton Mills, the woman in the personnel office gave me an application. When I turned it in, she said: "Oh, you're the one Myrtle Blue called about."

"Yes ma'am."

"You're from Griffin. Georgia."

"Yes ma'am." She was going over the application.

"You ever worked in a cotton mill before?"

"No ma'am, but I'm a good worker. I'll do anything."

"We don't have anything right now," she said, "but something could turn up in the next week or so. I'll get in touch with you. Can I reach you through Myrtle Blue?"

"Yes ma'am."

"Okey-dokey."

"Thank you."

"Uh-huh."

• • •

I next tried an outfit called Sport Tee, Inc., manufacturers of casual clothing, but was told there were no openings. I filled out an application in Elizabethtown at a company called Veeder Root, Inc., a manufacturing plant, but no job resulted. Then I went to a couple of stores, to see if they needed clerks or janitors, anything; but no luck. Later I drove to a town called Whiteville, about fifteen miles from Clarkton, to apply at the Blue Jean Factory, but was told the company was laying off help, not hiring. Finding a job was not going to be easy. Then it occurred to me: If all those people who filed into the county manpower office every day couldn't find work, how the hell was I — a stranger in the area — going to walk right in and get a job? I would just have to be patient and see what developed.

• • •

"These mills 'round here a closed shop," Mrs. Blue said that night during dinner. "You got to know somebody with influence to get on."

"That lady at Clarkton Mills told me she had talked to you," I said.

"She promised to look after you if she can. I don't know if she gon' be able to do anything. Where else you look today?"

"Everywhere," I said. "I went to the blue-jean place in Whiteville. Something called Veeder Root; Sport Tee —"

"They hire mostly women up there," Janice said.

"At Sport Tee?"

"Uh-huh. They make shirts. It involves sewing."

"To tell you the truth," Mrs. Blue said, "I don't know if you gon' be able find anything 'round here. So many wanting to find work already and can't."

"I don't guess I'll ever be able to buy no land," I said sadly.

"Child, folks 'round here can't hold on to the land they got. The black people can't."

"How come?"

"White folks take it away from them," Janice said.

"One way or another," Nev added.

"That's been going on a long time," Mrs. Blue said, "a long time." A car passed by on Old Brown Marsh Road, and, though the house sat far back from the road, the car seemed to be passing right by the windows. Its engine seemed loud and close.

"Why don't somebody do something about it?"

"Who gon' do something?" Mrs. Blue asked. "Child, we lucky to have this little two acres we got left. At one time, my husband owned more than forty acres of land. It got away."

"The young people," Janice said, "don't care about land anymore. They just want to get away, get good jobs and have nice things. The last thing they want to do now is farm. They don't want to see no farm."

"Right!" Nev said. "Especially no tobacco."

"A lot of these people are older people," said Mrs. Blue, "with nobody to help 'em." She looked at Janice and Nev. "You hear 'bout it a lot 'round here. I hear 'bout it in church. People always talking 'bout it. So-and-so lost her land, or the boss of Clarkton done got somebody else. People get in debt and they go to two white men 'round here for help. They helps 'em out, but pretty soon they foreclosing on 'em."

"Tell him about the lady who goes to our church," Janice said.

"Oh. There was some land had been in her family a long time. Belonged to her mama who give it to her. Now she live in a trailer in her daughter's yard. A white man got the land.

"Lord, she so sad. You oughta see her. It would break your heart. Don't nothing else matter to her but that land. And where she staying in her daughter's yard, she can see the land. She got to look at it every day and be miserable."

I could still see Mrs. Blue shaking her head in sorrow when I got back to my room that night. It was my birthday, and I had forgotten about it until I started to write in my journal. Sadness came over me in cold waves. It was March 1, the first birthday I'd spent away from my family since I'd gotten married nine years before. I stopped writing, put my jacket back on, and walked across the street to the phone booth. It was late, but I would wake them up. I had to talk.

5

Living Off the Land

I SPENT the mornings looking for work — an increasingly point-less endeavor — and in the evenings I ate with and talked with the Blues. No matter what we started out discussing, before the evening was done we always got around to talking about the poor souls who sat helplessly by while their only possession — the land they owned — was pulled from under their feet. And we talked about those who really had it hard, the tenant farmers. Today there are still tenant farmers and sharecroppers pouring their blood and sweat into somebody else's land. These people are caught on an endless merry-go-round of borrowing from the landowner to make ends meet during winter, working like dogs all summer, and turning all their earnings over to the land-owner in the fall. Working hard just to stay in the same rut. It is life on a conveyor belt to nowhere.

Whenever we talked about the elderly and their land problems, or about tenant farmers — subjects that began to interest me more, the more we touched on them — the names of Savannah Temple and Pilgrim Hill, two small communities a few miles out-side Clarkton, came up. One night, a farmer named Kinsey Ross was mentioned. He had supposedly sharecropped or tenant farmed a patch of land owned by Lieutenant Governor Jimmy Green and was rumored to be dissatisfied with the way the deal had turned out. I decided to set out for Savannah Temple and environs.

The next morning I followed the directions Mrs. Blue had given me. "I got relatives up in there," she had said. " 'Course just about everybody there kin to one another somehow."

Remembering my experience in Charlotte, I decided that the device of pretending to be looking for someone was a good way to break the ice and get people talking. But I realized I would have to be careful, because country people have a deep distrust of outsiders and a strong tendency to protect neighbors who might not want to be located. I guess it didn't really matter whether I found Kinsey Ross or not. I just wanted people to talk to me. In fact, I hoped I wouldn't find him too soon.

Savannah Temple is a tiny impoverished community that grew up around a church. It mainly consists of a string of small, nearly dilapidated old houses along the road to Lisbon, in the midst of some of this country's choice farm land. Years ago, the main occupations for the people there were sharecropping and tenant farming, but over the years farming has rapidly declined. The young people — those fortunate enough to find work in the surrounding towns — have taken jobs in the factories and plants, while the older people mainly survive on social-security payments. Many of those unable to find work subsist on welfare.

There are a few small family farmers who still manage to scratch out a living from their own land. Some sharecroppers still struggle to hang on, but their number shrinks with each growing season.

Not many people were stirring the morning I drove down the road toward Lisbon, past the old church that had been the anchor of the community in the old days. It was a quiet morning, and no cars passed me on the road. I decided to just pick out one of the houses, knock on the door, and begin my search for Kinsey Ross. I settled on a small, timeworn house, which had narrow concrete steps leading up to a porch so narrow that there was barely room for one person to stand at the door.

I knocked. A stocky young black man in his middle twenties, bare-chested and with sleep in his eyes, came to the door.

"I'm looking for a fellow name Kinsey Ross," I said. He looked me over. I could see he was not fully awake. "I'm sorry if I woke you up," I said. "I'd better go and let you get back to sleep."

"No, it's okay," he said with a yawn that made his broad, dark face seem even wider.

"You see, I'm trying to find work," I said, "farm work, whatever I can. I was told in town Kinsey Ross was the man to see. They said he live 'round Savannah Temple somewhere. I been riding 'round here trying to find him." He was still checking me out. A small girl with short plaits on her head and dried mucus above her top lip came up behind him. She peeped around him, looking up at me.

"You say you looking for who?" he said, wiping his face with a meaty hand. His shoulders were thick, his back broad. I could tell he was used to hard work. "You have'ta 'scuse me," he said. "I was 'sleep. I work at night."

"I'm sorry, I —"

"Who you looking for?"

"Kinsey Ross." His eyes seemed to be brightening a bit now, as if his head was clearing.

"Yeah," he said. "He live back down the road there about two miles or so. You passed right by his place."

"You see, I'm from Georgia," I said, "Griffin, Georgia. I'm trying to find work. They wouldn't be hiring nobody where you work, would they?"

"I work at the paper plant about thirty miles from here," he said. "Come on in. Ain't no use in us standing in the door like this."

Most of the small rooms were covered with cheap wood paneling, which made the house dark and glum. Breakfast dishes were still on the round, plastic-topped table in the kitchen.

"My name Chester," I said, reaching out to shake his hand.

Pointing toward the sofa where his rumpled white shirt was bunched against one arm, he said, "Sit down. You welcome to sit down." I did.

"If you looking for a job share farming," he said, "don't waste your time."

"I'm looking for whatever I can find," I said.

"You can't make no money share farming. People barely making a living 'round here farming they own land, much less farming for somebody else."

"Are there still many people share farming?"

"There's some," he said. "Not many as it used to be. You were asking about Kinsey Ross. He was share farming. I don't know if he is now. I works at night and be sleeping through the day," he said. "I don't get much chance to see people 'round here. Besides," he said, "it's not quite time for the farmers to be getting started. In another month you'll see more people about, clearing land and stuff."

I felt confined in my conversation with him. I didn't think I could ask him all the questions I wanted to about the way he and others lived, while I was under the guise of a drifter looking for work. I decided to take a chance and tell him what I was really doing. I didn't think it would hurt the project. I would probably never run into him again, anyway, and he wouldn't know where I was headed once I left him.

"Listen," I said. "I'm gon' tell you the truth." He perked up noticeably. "I'm really a writer from Atlanta," I said. He looked at me curiously.

"I'm trying to do a piece on the South, black people in the South. To find out if things have changed much in the past ten years or so. Is life any better . . . ?"

He crossed his thick legs and scratched his face along the jawbone.

"I don't think things are a whole lot better, may not ever get that good for black people," he said. "Black people always on the bottom of the list. Catching hell like always. Those people you can still find 'round here share farming," he said, "they be really catching hell. Everything they make out of the ground, they got to give it right to the white man who owns the land.

"They might as well be slaves," he said. "It's the exact same thing, far as I'm concerned. Used to be a whole lot more people doing it. But now there's just some who can't help themselves. They can't find nothing else."

"What kind of work did you say you do?" I asked.

"I work on the wood yard at the paper company about thirty miles from here," he said. A car moved past slowly outside, squeaking on its springs like a child's noisy wagon.

"I been there six years," he said. "I guess I'm lucky. I used to farm with my father. He still doing it, but ain't making much money.

"Out there where I work, the pay is pretty good, 'cause we got a union. They start out somewhere 'round five thirty-five an hour.

"Most places — mills, factories, farms — you make right 'round two dollars and something an hour. Ain't no unions.

"I'm twenty-five," he said, punching himself in the chest while gesturing with his other hand. "My wife works in Elizabethtown. We git by all right, 'cause this her grandmother's house and we stay here rent free. Most people 'round here ain't so lucky.

"We're putting our money together so we can move out of here to someplace nice. Most of the people here are stuck here. They been here all their life, and they gon' be here. There ain't nothing else but Savannah Temple for them."

"All this pretty farm land around here," I said, "who owns it?"

"Man, black people used to own it," he said. "All you see, they used to own it." He moved to the small window that looked out onto the road to Lisbon. I could see the tops of the depressing little shacks across the road. And there was some kind of little store whose outside walls seemed in danger of caving in at any moment. The front of this dismal building seemed to be made of scrap lumber and old doors pieced together, and there were rolls of rusted chicken wire lying on the ground around it.

"But so many people were tricked out of they land," he said, "or they got in debt dealing with these crooked white folks and lost it. It's pitiful. Around here, you hear 'bout that kind of thing all the time . . . And it's so hard for black folks to get ahead, everything going up so high. I guess I just blew it," he said sadly, apparently reflecting on some missed opportunity.

"I blew my chance. My brother tried to git me to go on to school, and I didn't. Now I got a family and everything. I finished high school and started working. My brother went on to

A & T [North Carolina A & T University in Greensboro] and Harvard. He's a lawyer now.

"I was tired of school. I guess I might move back down home. My father has thirty-some acres. He's growing tobacco, corn, raising hogs. It's hard for him to make a living. I guess I could try to help him out.

"My brother," he said with a smile, "he's some kind of lawyer. He got outta here, but he didn't forgit who he is. He tried to help me, but I just couldn't see it then."

"You're only twenty-five," I said. "It can't be too late yet."

"Every year," he said, "it gets harder and harder to go back to school. It takes more and more money to live. How can you give that up to go to school?"

"You could make it," I said.

"I don't know."

"Man, you and your brother could have your own law firm."

He laughed and looked past me. His mind wasn't really in the room now. I could tell. It was away in that land where dreams are real and everything is fine.

"Wouldn't that be something. I bet we could tear up the world."

"Tear it up," I said.

• • •

I left there feeling glad that I had met him, hoping that one day — somehow — I would run into him again and find him no longer a worker in the wood yard of a paper company but an enterprising young lawyer. I also thought about the startling contrasts that abound in the world of the less fortunate. This man lived in a pocket of poverty and saw his future as bleak, but had a brother who was a successful, Harvard-trained lawyer.

Some people will not be defeated. I wanted somehow to explore further that capacity to survive — the drive that had sustained my own parents, had carried them through the hardest times, and had pushed me to strive for what I wanted out of life. My parents suffered many setbacks while trying to raise my brothers and me, but they were never defeated. They always rose to face the world, always tried harder.

I wanted to articulate that will to trudge on, that determination to survive even under wretched circumstances. I looked back from the road and saw the young man I had just talked with and his small daughter, waving at me from their window. Though there had been a note of melancholy in his voice when he talked of his failure to go on to school, I felt that it was just a fleeting despair. I could sense that he would one day succeed at something, for he and his wife were working hard and saving almost every penny of their earnings. They desperately wanted to improve their lives, and as I got into my car, I had no doubt they would.

I had sensed in him, in just those few moments of conversation, a quiet strength underlying the feeling I took to be temporary sadness. And though he seemed to regret not following his brother's lead, I could not consider him a failure. He would have another kind of success, I believed, because he seemed a hard worker and he was willing to live frugally now so that he might live better later on. That willingness to sacrifice made me like him and respect him very much.

He made me think of sad people, burdened by life, who can still get up to dance, whose souls can still fly when life moves them, even if the joy only lasts a little while. That was something I was deeply interested in, and I wanted to capture it on this journey if I could.

•   •   •

I stopped at several houses along the road and talked with people, before I reached Kinsey Ross's place. Ross wasn't home, but I spoke with a stout young woman who said she was his daughter. She was carrying a small child on her hip and looking after other little ones. Children seemed to be everywhere. She told me that her father was no longer share farming. She did, however, mention a woman whose name many others had brought up when I asked them to suggest somebody who was tenant farming. Everyone mentioned this woman — they said she was probably in her late thirties or early forties — who was said to be tenant farming a place owned by "Mr. Green," the lieutenant governor.

Because this woman's name came up so often, I decided to try to find her; but it was hard to locate anyone who knew exactly where she lived. It seemed that tenant farmers were forced to move about frequently, in order to find a situation that better suited them each growing season. Finally, an elderly woman, whose gray-white hair was covered with a brilliant orange and red scarf knotted below her bony chin, pointed me in the right direction.

"You see yonder," she said slowly, almost out of breath from walking out to the edge of the road to show me the way. "Pass the church there, see? That fork in the road yonder — I 'as born right in there — turn right. That's the Elkton Road. Jes' keep a'goin', follow hit. Hit'll take you to 'er house." She stopped a moment to catch her breath again. It was a crisp morning, the sun climbing in the North Carolina sky like the red ball on a thermometer. "By the railroad," she added. I thanked her and, as I left, watched her move her wizened bones toward the lopsided little house where she spent her life.

I found Mrs. Rouse's home a few miles outside Elkton, next to the railroad track with its rusting rails. First I saw the sprawling front yard, a muddy wasteland of puddles and rotting cornstalks bent over like sick children hugging the ground. When I saw the house, I decided to play it straight with these people. If they were living like this, I wanted their story. I didn't want to blow it with a ruse that might backfire, and I wanted to make it clear that I was not making fun of them or parodying them in any way.

Far back from the road, in the midst of a muddy expanse of land, sat the house — big, awkward, something out of an earlier time, with faded white paint peeling like diseased skin. I thought of my parents' descriptions of the Great Depression of the 1930s, a time of mass despair.

The entire area surrounding the house — the road, the tracks, the leaning trees — projected the sense of things breaking down, of rot and decay. But forty-one-year-old Vivian Nadine Rouse and five of her six children lived there as tenant farmers.

Mrs. Rouse greeted me at the door with a smile. The floors creaked when I entered the house. It was a certainty that one day soon the tired floorboards would give way and somebody would wind up on the cold ground under this rickety house. It was cold on the March morning I found the Rouses, so the whole family was crowded into what I guess should be called the living room. This was the room where the Rouse family did most of its living, since it was the only heated room in the house. Heat was furnished by a large tin barrel filled with burning wood. This makeshift heater sat up off the floor on bricks and had a flue that carried the smoke out through the roof.

Their living room was filled with odd pieces of furniture — old, but holding. Plaster had fallen from the walls, which were painted pink. The holes in the plaster were covered with cardboard, which had also been painted pink. There were no panes in the large windows, but sheets of thick plastic had been stretched across the openings like animal skins, to ward off the chill wind. When the wind blew, the plastic crackled. A thin linoleum rug almost covered the creaky floor. There were numerous spots where the rug had either worn away or had been torn, and I could see the ground through the cracks in the floorboards. It made my flesh crawl. I thought of all the vermin that probably entered the house through these cracks. My wife would not have spent even one night here. I knew she would have forever complained about things crawling on her. But these people lived here every day. Though they were tenant farmers, their story differs from those of their fellow farmers. Seven years earlier, they had come to the area from the North, to escape a dreadful existence in a public-housing project in a New Jersey slum.

Mrs. Rouse, a friendly, heavyset woman with smooth brown skin, said her children ranged in age from five to twenty-one. Her marriage had broken up and her husband had left them years before she moved her family south. They had recently moved to their present house from a house that belonged to Lieutenant Governor Jimmy Green, where they had lived the preceding year and tenant farmed the land. They had moved in January, she said, because "Mr. Green said he was going to remodel the house and we had to git out.

"We had to find some place to go fast," she said. She was dressing the youngest child, who sat in her lap still wiping sleep from drowsy eyes. The other children were gathered in the room, except for the second-oldest, Theodore, who was outside chopping wood for the heater. "We looked around and found this place," she said.

I told her I was researching a news story, and she said she didn't mind my small tape recorder. My eyes were still panning the house, trying to take it all in. It was an ugly, depressing house, yet this woman was not depressed. "The owner said we welcome to make any improvements we able to," she said with a smile. The house had no bathroom, not even an outhouse. To get to the kitchen and one of the three bedrooms, you had to go outside. Inside the house, there were no passages to these rooms. The roof leaked, and the only water came from a pump outside the front door. Yet Mrs. Rouse and her children insisted they were happier here in the backwoods of North Carolina than they had been in New Jersey.

"We were living in the projects in Newark," she said, as the sound of Theodore chopping wood outside filtered into the room. I could feel the hard blows of the ax jar the log. "And I was working day and night," she said, "trying to take care of young children, you know.

"It began to be a lot of dope around the projects." The children were listening intently, as if they had never heard their mother speak about their old neighborhood before. "If you were waiting on the elevator, all you would see was a lot of young men and women just hanging, you know, standing there.

"The way I was working, I was afraid for the children," she said, "afraid they would get into the same thing." The child in her lap had big brown eyes, clear, free of sadness.

"You know, I was afraid every time I left my 'partment, and afraid to stay home, too. It was that bad, really."

In the summer of 1971, she brought the children to North Carolina to visit her mother and stepfather, she said. "After we got here, the children just got out running in the woods. It was the first time they'd ever seen such wide open spaces. They were just running and screaming, 'We free! We free!' I didn't have the heart to take them back to Jersey after that.

"When we first moved down here," she said, "we lived in Robeson County in this lady's home. They owned this house and we lived there rent-free, but I had to take care of her crippled sisters.

"The three of them were all invalids. She was the only well one. I was seeing after them from seven in the morning to six in the evening, and they had told me it would only be three days a week. But I wound up going six and a half days, even taking my Sundays, and I was making only five dollars a day.

"I had four children with me then. One of my children is in California, and my mother was keeping another," she said. "I just couldn't make it with four children on five dollars a day, even though the rent was free, so I applied for food stamps, and that came through."

It was these hard times, she said, that made her turn to tenant farming.

"We moved over with a man named Marvin Britt, which was tenant farming. He was paying twelve dollars a day, six weeks out of the year, and the rent was free.

"We stayed with him about three years. It was good," she said. "He was nice to us, nice in his way. You could go to him and borrow money whenever you needed it, to git you through the winter when there wasn't no work. But by the time you worked and paid him back, you still was just as broke as you were before you borrowed, you know."

Theodore, nineteen, who had the thick shoulders of an athlete, entered with an armload of wood, which he began feeding to the flames in the heater, one piece at a time. Suddenly a little more heat entered the drafty room.

"If we'd stayed in Jersey," Mrs. Rouse said, "Theodore wouldn't be graduating this spring. He was kept back a year there, because he was playing hooky from school. I was putting him in the front door and he was scooting out the back door.

"In the North, he would've been with the wrong group of boys, and they would've been saying, 'Man you nineteen years old and still in school? You better come on out here with us.' I know. I've seen it happen to so many boys in the projects.

"In Jersey, if children fail in school it's like a crime, a shame held over your head. Here it's not so bad, not as much finger pointing. And my children are happier with school here."

"I like the South much better," said Theodore, in the sturdy voice of a Marine drill sergeant. "When I was in the North, I worked at stores bagging groceries, you know, and every time I got paid off I had to run, because there would be a gang of boys waiting to take my money.

"It ain't like that here. I don't have to fight all the time."

I told him that was truer of southern small towns than of the big cities, where you still might have to run on payday.

"Though we have fewer material things and less money here than we had in Jersey," Mrs. Rouse said, "I feel freer here. I have more peace of mind. I can leave my house and not have to worry about anybody breaking in.

"In fact," she said, "last summer I left here and spent two weeks in Chicago. I didn't even lock my doors. When I got back, just what I left in my house was still here. Nobody had touched a thing. The mailman had laid the mail inside the door on the floor every day."

Though small-town life offered some advantages for the Rouses, life there was still hard enough to break a person up, crush him. The rigors of tenant farming had broken many strong men and women there. Change comes slowly in rural areas far away from the big cities.

"I still don't see why we had to move from our previous house so it could be renovated," she said. "Not a valid reason why.

"My stepfather was sharecropping with Jimmy Green. This was Jimmy Green's house. He's got farms that black people live on from time to time and sharecrop. Me and my children lived in the house and worked the land.

"My stepfather and Jimmy Green was supposed to share the profit half and half . . . He pay his labor and Jimmy Green supply the fertilizer and the land, the worm poison. They were going to halfen the oil for curing the tobacco, and whatever it cost for the lights and for running the stringer, they were to halfen that also . . .

"Anyway, me and my children lived in the house rent-free and helped with the farming. But Jimmy Green decided he wanted to repair the house. He said he couldn't repair the house with us living in it. We had to move. And if we wanted to move back in, maybe we could, but we'd have to pay rent," she said, hot under the collar, gesturing vividly with her hands.

"It seemed to me like a runaround, you know. I know there's a house in Clarkton he did renovate with the white family living in it, so why the black family have to move out? All this be running through my mind. The black family have to move out, but the white family could stay there and he could still fix it. Why?"

She looked at me, her shoulders raised to emphasize the question. I shook my head. "I don't know," I said. "Racism, I guess." She stared at me, then down at one of the cracks in the floor, as if she might find the answer there. When she looked up again, her mind had turned to another problem. The children were quiet, except for the oldest daughter, Rosalind, who was sniffling a bit from the beginnings of a cold.

"Ain't much work here for blacks, unless it's farming," she said. "Farm hands. That's the way it's always been. If you want to farm, all right. But after the season's over, there's nothing to do, so you go to welfare for help.

"Vern here, he's twenty-one, had been searching for a job for two years after returning from the Job Corps," she said. "A few weeks ago, he finally got on at the Hardee's in Elizabethtown.

"The money ain't much, but we need it. Before he got that job, we went everywhere. Everywhere, looking for work. They would say come back in three weeks. When we went back, they'd say come back in six weeks, come back Monday, come back, come back, come back.

"We went to the mills, same thing. Everywhere the same thing. Yet and still, the white children were getting jobs, and a few of the black children, too. But they had relatives already working at the mills, or knew somebody white in these places."

As we talked, as I sat there looking at this family, at this scene of privation, and as I heard them insist that they were happy, it was impossible for me to deny my feelings. I felt shame that they had to live like this, these warm, unpretentious people.

When I first started working at the *Journal* six years before, an idealistic kid right out of college, I believed that I could have some hand in changing the world — a world I thought could stand a hell of a lot of change. And there were many more like me, for we were the protest generation raised on civil rights and voter registration, nourished by antiwar demonstrations, shocked by racial strife and violence in the streets, our brains fried by assassinations, our minds dulled, hopes shattered, dreams dimmed, voices silenced by endless TV reruns of the nightmares of our lives — the bombings, the assassinations, the battles between police and students, and the dead counts in Vietnam, all the horrible black death that came to us in color over the tube, all the rot and stinkingfuckingdeathshit spewing from the screen as we dropped acid, smoked our brains, and shivered in corners, wondering what had gone wrong with the world, with people, with us. And how the hell could we escape this crusted napalm dream that was our inheritance, with our elders saying, "Here, take it. It's yours, kid."

Anyway, I still believed America could be wonderful and the world could be set right again. I started out as a sportswriter. My first week on the job, Lewis Grizzard, then executive sports editor of the *Journal*, sent me to Warm Springs, Georgia, to cover an amputee golf tournament. I think he knew I was going to blow it.

The long drive down there was pleasant, but I was terrified. I didn't know how I was going to act once I got there. When I arrived at the clubhouse, I couldn't believe what I saw. All around me, men and women were laughing, joking, talking. I was damn near the only person there with two arms and two legs. A man balancing on one leg was putting on one of the greens. The other leg was gone, lopped off just below the hip. A woman on another green made a short putt. She and the woman she was playing with put their hands together — they only had two between them — and clapped. It tore me up. Guilt and shame poured over me. I could barely interview the winners. How the hell could I write about this? I felt so afraid of offending them, so guilty for having two arms and two legs, for being healthy. I wanted to make sure not to feel superior or show any pity toward those courageous people. Worse still, every last one of them acted natural, as if there wasn't a single handicapped person on the field — except maybe me; because by the time it was over I was feeling mighty handicapped. When I got back to Atlanta, I blew the story. I couldn't write it. I spent pages backing into it, describing the scenery, the drive down there, everything except what happened. I couldn't see the beauty of it then, couldn't get past my feelings of inadequacy and guilt, or past feeling sorry for myself for having been there.

Sitting there with the Rouse family, I felt the shame and guilt again, and I wanted to fight it. But guilt is a powerful emotion. I didn't like what it had come to mean to me during the years I had been reporting. Guilt had become something that I attributed solely to the liberal whites who flocked to the South in droves during the civil-rights movement, or who sat back in New York or Boston and said "Oh, what a pity" in faggotty tones, whenever some young Mississippi black kid was put on trial for murder-rape-looking-at-a-white-woman-too-hard, or was sentenced to forty years of hard labor for stealing a head of lettuce, or was gunned down in the streets by cops who just couldn't abide niggers running away from them. At first, it seemed that there was something deep behind this guilt, something human and meaningful, but with each succeeding act of horror, the cry was the same, never changing, and you knew it was hollow: "Oh dear, the poor, poor darkies. Why does man have to be so mean to his fellow man?" Guilt was so predictable that it made you sick. It was dropping a dime in a blind man's cup and moving on quickly before he could reach out and touch your hand. No, I didn't want to feel that bullshit, all that wringing of hands.

And here I was, twisted inside, feeling many emotions at the same time, wanting to reach out and touch this woman and say *keep on mama, keep moving, you're strong. You've come this far, goddamn!* I wanted to sweep up the whole family and kick that house to the ground; take them off to another land just across town, where there were good houses that people like them deserved.

"As soon as the rains stop and the land dries out some," she said, "the landlord is going to get us an outhouse, and the boys will dig the hole for it."

"That'll be a welcome relief," added Theodore. "Dumping that bucket gets to be a drag."

We had come out onto the rickety porch. Mrs. Rouse and the children had to straddle the holes in the porch floor as we talked. The weather had warmed up a bit, and the sun was shining brightly.

She shook her head and looked out across the yard, her eyes roaming the landscape. In the summer, the ground would be broken by their toil, and crops would spring forth from their sweat. People would be fed from the labor of this family.

"What's the matter?" I asked.

"Just always something to worry about," she said sadly. "How do you ever get all the things that broke down during the winter repaired before summer? Because you know then, in the summer, things gon' break down. You know what I mean?"

"Yeah." My response was dry, and I looked away.

"You have to repair these things when you're working, if you're working. But by the time you pay for the things that tore up during the winter, the summer money is gone again. What d'ya live on then?

"You're always robbing Peter to pay Paul," she sighed. "I'm hoping we don't have to stay here more than a year, maybe a year and a half.

"I just want me an acre of land. One acre, that's all. One acre. Maybe put up a cinder-block place on it. That would cost about fifteen hundred dollars, I been told. It's probably gone up some now. The land, if you can git it cheap, costs about four hundred to five hundred dollars for an acre.

"God, I don't know if I'll ever save that kind of money. But if I could just git the land. If I had to put up two sticks and hang a sheet on 'em, I'd be happy. It would be mine."

When I tried to leave, my car got stuck in the muddy yard. Vern and Theodore planted their feet deep in the mud and pushed me out, the car spraying them with mud from head to toe. I thought about giving them a few dollars for helping, but decided against it. Somehow it didn't seem appropriate.

As I drove back to my motel room, I looked out over the barren fields that would soon hold tobacco and other crops, and I thought about what Mrs. Rouse had said when I asked her if she didn't see hope in the fact that for the first time several blacks were running for public office in the two counties around her.

"One thing I've learned about black people in my forty-one years," she said, "is that when a black person gits in office or gits ahead, they forgit their brothers that's down below.

"If we could just stick together, and they was to stick with us and raise one up, so he could reach back down and raise one up . . .

"But that first one forgets about the rest no sooner than he gits up there, and walks away and leaves us. He don't want nobody to know this is where he comes from."

I knew exactly what she meant.

6

On the Verge

FROM THE BEGINNING, Myrtle Blue regarded me as somewhat mysterious and was a bit suspicious. Her doubts about me didn't prevent her from extending the full hospitality of her home and friendship, however, and she was too considerate to come right out and question me. Then one day not long after I had visited the Rouse family again, I went by to see her. It was in the middle of the day, and she was home alone, in the kitchen. When she opened the door, she had the look of someone who had been wrestling with troubling thoughts during the night. I knew something was up; questions covered her face.

"How you this morning?" she asked.

"Fine," I said, "what about yourself?"

"Oh, I'll do." We were quiet for a minute. She seemed to be searching for something, a way to get around to what she wanted to bring up.

"You gon' be 'round here for dinner tonight, ain't you? I'm gon' cook some fish. I been had a taste for fried fish for two or three days now. You like fish, don't you?"

"You bet I like fish, especially fried."

"Just a minute," she said, disappearing into the back of the house. When she returned, she had a small purse in her hands and was fishing inside it for folded dollar bills.

"Would you mind ridin' over to the fish market in Bladenboro and gettin' the fish?"

"No ma'am," I said.

"Get two-three pounds of spots," she said, handing me the money. "Make sure they fresh."

• • •

Bladenboro was only a few miles away. When I returned with the fish, I knocked on the door. Mrs. Blue, with an impish grin on her plump face, opened it slowly.

"You with the gov'ment?" she asked quickly.

"No," I said softly, stepping into the warm kitchen. The grin on her face spread into a broad smile.

"You not with the gov'ment down here to see about how black folks treated 'round here?"

"I ain't with the government," I said. She sat in the chair next to the phone on the wall, near the back door.

"Who you with?"

"I'm just trying to find a job, find a place I'd like to settle down in. Maybe buy some land 'round here, if I could get a job."

"You sure you ain't with the gov'ment?"

"Yes."

"Why you ask so many questions then? Why you wanna know 'bout everybody's problems? I been watching the way you be listening when we be talking about somebody's problems, how things are 'round here. What things been happening to folks. You be taking it all in. I been noticin'."

"Honestly," I said. "I guarantee you I'm not with the government." I didn't tell her the truth right away, because I wanted to see how long it would take her to figure things out.

"There's some more to this than you been telling," she said. "And Oliver ain't told me what he know 'bout this either. I'm gon' drop it now. But I want you to know I know. I figure you'll tell it when you ready. Now let me see this fish you bought."

Later, when I told her the whole story, she just smiled and said, "I knew it all the time. I could tell it. You be careful, 'cause a lot of folks won't like what you doin'. "

• • •

No matter what you talk about with farmers around Bladen County, the conversation eventually turns to the land. They have worked it all their lives. They love it as they love themselves. To them it is almost holy. It is collateral for loans they must get every winter to see their families through; it is the provider of food and cash crops; it is mother and mistress. They cling to it for dear life, for it has never let them down the way their fellow men have.

I spent days talking and listening to farmers, often walking with them out to their fields to look over the dirt, as they thought about the groundbreaking and planting to come. They are sad men, in a way, because they are laboring at something their children care little about. Many of them have already lost their children to colleges and jobs in northern cities. They are both happy and sad: happy to see them move on to better lives, but sad that they have left the land, the only thing that has taken care of their predecessors.

Some of them talked about the problem of trying to compete with the big tobacco growers for the good prices that usually come early in the bidding season.

"We don't have the heavy 'quipment to git our crops out the field and into the warehouse like they do," one of them told me. "By the time we git there, the price done dropped."

And even if they manage to get to the warehouse early, there are still problems, they told me. "There've been times, plenty of times," one farmer told me, "when warehouse workers would put rotten tobacco on your crops in the warehouse there while it's waiting to be graded, and the federal inspector will grade it low. Once you git a low grade, you have to sell it for little or nothing. The warehouse owner buys it, removes the rotten layer, and gets the crop reinspected, then sells it for more.

"Ain't nothing you can do, neither. You sho' can't be 'round that warehouse watching your crop all night," he said, "and you got to take it to the warehouse to sell it.

"In some places, after closing, warehouse workers are told to go 'round and steal a few pounds of tobacco off everybody's pile," he said. "It adds up to a good bit for the house. I know it goes on, 'cause I know somebody used to work for one of 'em."

Another farmer, who has pulled enough money out of the

soil in the past two decades to send four children to college, build himself a modest brick house, and keep a fairly late-model pickup truck in his driveway, said that it had been a real struggle for him since the very beginning, when he had to fight with a white man over rights to the land he now farms — land that had belonged to his father, who was on the verge of losing it because of heavy debt.

"I wasn't gon' let him take my land," he said one day, screwing his long-billed cap onto his bony head. "I got me a lawyer and got my land square. You can't git out there with no talk when these people trying to take your land, you got to git out there with some money and fight."

He talked about the strange relationship that exists there, in the backwoods, between white merchants and the poor black families who must trade with them.

"These guys in business to make money," he said. "They let these poor people live during the winter when they don't have nothing, which is good in a way. It costs them in the end, though.

"Ain't none of 'em really your friend, you know, but they give you credit. And some of 'em add on to the bill, run it up, and if you don't keep your receipts, you can forgit about it. You'll never stop owing them.

"I seen so many people washed out like that," he said sadly. "They was too trusting and didn't tend to their business right. You got to watch these whites. Now don't git me wrong. I'm not talking about being no militant or nothing, 'cause you got to live with these people. But you got to stick up for yourself so they won't run over you."

He said he thought blacks in Bladen County were missing a golden opportunity for change, for real improvement.

"We got more black people than white people in Bladen County," he said, "and this year we got a lot of blacks running for office — sheriff, school board. This would be our chance to really vote our people in and change things. But even though black voting-age folks outnumber the white, there's more white people registered to vote. So many of our people who registered back in the sixties just let it go, after it didn't look like it was doing no good.

"A lot of us 'round here now trying to get people registered, but it's hard," he said, "especially the young people. You'd think they'd be leading this thing. You go to some of our meetings and you see a lot of old people and hardly no young folks. These young folks got to bear down. You see, that's one thing 'bout our race of people, we do a lot of talking, a lot of talking.

"And so many people say the vote ain't done us a damn bit of good," he said. "'Course it ain't, since we ain't used it."

•   •   •

The conversations were often long and winding, touching on a multitude of life's problems, but they always came full circle — back to the land. And more often than not, they touched on Mrs. Ola Davis, a sixty-two-year-old woman whose story moved the hearts of even the toughest old fleabitten farmers — men who normally weren't given to tears. But more than a few of them came close whenever we talked about the troubles of "that poor woman."

•   •   •

Pilgrim Hill. The house wasn't much to look at, but it was in the shade. The porch sagged, its weather-bleached boards seemingly ready to crumble under the weight of the next foot that touched them. Two roosters crowed as they and a passel of hens and biddies ran under the house and out again, staring back at my car as I pulled into the yard. Some of the chickens had hidden behind the aging brick pillars that held this tired house above the ground. The rest were in an uproar.

The house had been built thirty-five years before by the woman who now lived there and her husband, now dead. This had once been a happy place, years ago when things were different, when new beginnings were possible, when dreams seemed only one good crop away, when advancing age and declining health were only phantoms in that enormous, faceless thing called the future. It was not a happy place I approached on that March day. Across the creaking porch, behind the wooden door that rested cockeyed in the crooked doorway, sat a woman who had sixty-two years of hard living behind her, sixty-two years of fighting unrelenting pressures, the demons that eventually chase us all to the grave. On the wall above her head was a picture of the Last Supper, painted on cloth. The house was dark. The door would not open all the way, because the house had shifted over the years. The woman's eyes were sad, heavy. She was confused, but still placed her faith in God. She only had one dream left, and she wanted to see it come true before she was dead and gone. She wanted her land back.

"Ola Davis my name," she said. I told her who I was and described my mission. A small, round-eyed boy clung to her. He was curled in her lap atop the many skirts she wore to keep warm.

"I 'dopted him," she said of the boy. "He came to my house since he was eighteen months old. I got a boy and a girl of my own. My girl live in New York."

This lady's pain was so deep, so total, it seeped out of her, filled the room with a fourth presence, clung to me like wet leaves. I couldn't shake it.

"Do you think things have gotten any better for blacks here?" I asked.

"No," she said, "seem like they got worse to me. This sixteen acres of land we sitting on right here. This used to be my land. Me and my husband, Avant, bought it thirty-five years ago. We worked it. Now it ain't mine. We built this house our self, my husband and me . . . It ain't mine no more. It belong to a white man, now, and he say I got to pay 'im rent to stay here. And I made this house — made it! Wasn't nothing here . . . made it!"

"How did you lose this land?"

"I don't exactly, hardly know," she said. "This man took up the note on it, then call hisself closing it out.

"We bought the land thirty-five years ago, when we got married, from Mr. Jimmy Clark. He dead now, too. Somewhere 'long the line in the last few years before my husband died, we got in debt. My husband died five years ago . . ."

"How much was the debt?"

"I don't really know. My husband handled the business. It was one thousand dollars or fifteen hundred dollars — no, I just don't know." She was rubbing her hands together. "We was farming, and he borrowed the money to git 'quipment, fertilizer.

"He owed the money to Mr. Clark. Then this other man took up the note, 'cause when my husband died I ain't have no money to pay it," she said. "I have a son, but during that time he wasn't working, but now he's working and he trying to help me git my land back. When the man come to close us out, he say we didn't have no time."

"How much is the debt now?"

"My son got a statement or something on it," she said, turning her head away, then looking at her hands. "I b'leeve it's fifteen thousand dollars. We trying to git a loan through FHA [Farmers Home Administration] to git the land back."

Although the new owner of the property was charging her rent, she didn't know how much it was supposed to be. "He never told me how much," she said. "He closed us out in January. If we git the loan through, I guess we'll pay the rent, too. Whatever it is.

"We been farming every year. We still plant 'bacca, beans, and stuff. My son have to do most the farming," she said, "'cause I'm sixty-two and I can't git out there in the sun like I used to. I got high blood.

"He [the new owner] don't never bother me 'bout the rent, 'cause whatever come out the farm go right to him automatically."

"How much do you generally make farming?"

"I imagine 'round two thousand dollars. We have to pay for our gas and stuff. We pay him at least twelve hundred or thirteen hundred dollars. Year before last, we paid him more than sixteen hundred dollars, but he didn't count none of that on the pay pad. He say that all goes for fertilizer, so forth. But it ain't that. He just a man ain't doing right. So we don't git no money out the farm, still we owe him fifteen thousand dollars, and it keep going up."

"How do you eat?"

"We works at other farms some times, raise chickens, some

food. We got a piece of heir property right down yonder side the road. It ain't but a few acres. My husband' daddy left it to 'im. We farms on that. The man trying to take that, too. We don't owe him nothing on that, that's ours, but he trying to take it, 'cause we owe 'im for this."

She pointed through the half-open door. "I was born right down there at that intersection, that white house," she said. "Lived 'round in here all my life. I want that land back 'fore I die. I want it. And I b'leeve the Lord will make a way for me to get it. My son talked to a lawyer 'bout it. I don't know what come of it.

"You know," she said, "it's hard to live, so hard to live. I git my little money, social security. I couldn't make it without that." She was crying silently now, but the tears were there, coming down her weathered face slowly, painfully slowly. I tried not to watch them, but my eyes kept turning to her face.

"When I first lost my land, it hurt me to my heart; to my heart! You hear me! To my heart!"

The chickens were quiet now. We sat silently. I was about to explode. The top of my head felt like it would blow right off, but I tried to sit still. There was nothing to say.

• • •

Eventually I managed to leave Ola Davis sitting in the darkness. After talking to her sister-in-law, who lived down a winding road nearby, I drove back to Clarkton, passing the trailer of the elderly black woman from Mrs. Blue's church. The trailer sits in the yard of the woman's daughter. From the trailer, she can see the eight acres of land that used to belong to her, that had belonged to her mother, that had been in the family for decades. The house she had spent much of her life in was rotting away, falling in on itself, as if dying because she was gone. Ragged grass and stubborn weeds grew through the doors and the cracks in the floor, overrunning the deteriorating carcass. The woman's fondest memories were in that house, amid the decaying wood and bricks. I think her spirit will always remain there. She and the house will die together.

A few years back, the property had been sold at public auction for one hundred and ten dollars. It had been taken from her by the county, because of delinquent taxes. A sheriff's deed was issued and the property sold. It was bought by the same man who now owned Ola Davis's farm.

•　•　•

I went to the county courthouse to examine land transactions involving some of the blacks, to see if I could find any significant patterns during the last few generations.

Sitting in the hot, dusty deed room with the heavy, musty volumes of official records open in front of me, my despair solidified. All the legal records of the land were there — the sheriff's deeds, the notations of property auctioned, the tax liens, the deeds to secure debts, the foreclosures.

These records were the terse, cold annals of the poor, and the human stories behind them leaped out at me. I saw the painfully made X's of black folks who couldn't write their names, and the crabbed signatures of those who could write at least a little bit.

Beneath the dry legal language of the documents, I could see the poor, elderly woman who, as recorded there, had borrowed $615 to buy heating oil for winter, and had been forced to put up as collateral her interest in eighty-seven acres of inherited land. Any single acre, I knew, was worth more than twice the $615 she was borrowing.

That tiny room was full of people's lives — lives of ache and suffering, privation and hunger, and lost human dignity. It was also full of the meanest kind of exploitation and the cruelest extortion.

I sat there no longer seeing the pages before me, remembering other lives, other miseries.

I remembered Oliver Blue's description of how a white man had come to their house one day after his father had left to seek a public job in Greensboro. Oliver, his mother, brothers, and sisters were trying to carry on the farming. As usual, they were sinking in debt.

They were using the back porch of the old house to store tobacco. One day, a man came with a truck. They owed him some money. He would wait no longer. "He was just going to take the tobacco," Blue said. "My mama was trying to stop him from coming in. He was just going to push her aside and force his way in. Didn't respect her in the least. Didn't respect none of us. He was going to take that tobacco. Me and my brother decided we were going to kill him. We had gotten a gun. We were going to kill him. We'd made up our minds. We were tired of all the mess. We were going to kill him . . . But it never came to that. Even now, I know we would have . . ."

And I recalled the story my mother had told me a year or so earlier, when she and Daddy took me to her birthplace — the plantation near Griffin, Georgia, where she and my father had lived and sharecropped when they were first married. She showed me the house she'd grown up in. The weeds had reclaimed it. And then, almost with tears in her eyes, she told me about the car her father had bought before 1920 with money he had worked for and saved. It was a convertible — beautiful, sleek, dark, and shiny. When he drove it home to the plantation, the white man who owned the land, and damn near owned the family, made my grandfather park that car. He falsely claimed that Granddaddy Jester owed him money, and that as long as he did, he sure as hell wasn't going to ride around in a shiny car. Granddaddy never drove the car again. It sat out in front of the house and rotted. The children used it to play in, lying in its rag top as if it were a hammock. Slowly it rusted and rotted. Granddaddy couldn't bear to see it. He moved, to get away from it. She pointed out the spot where the car had been. It was gone now, but it seemed that scars the rims had cut into the ground were still there. I don't know if it was in my mind, or if they were really there. It sure seemed like they were.

I had to get out of that tiny, stifling deed room, out of that courthouse, out of town, out of North Carolina. I looked at the two other people in the room: a lawyer-type and a middle-aged white woman who worked there. I didn't want them to touch me. They spoke. I said nothing, only hurried past them and out the door, sweat dripping down my face. I ran for the hall, for the outside door, for my car, trying to find a way to escape the clutches of my own evil feelings.

7

Asylum

THE BLUES saved me.

When I entered the quiet house standing in the shade of tall trees, with Mrs. Blue greeting me with a warm smile, and the rich smell of chicken cooking, it was as if I had been pulled from the cold, murky depths of some sinister lake at just the point when my lungs were about to explode and my life float away. The Blues kept me together, kept me from exploding. That night I told them about the tragic case of Ola Davis. They listened attentively and were kind, often shaking their heads in pity and consternation. When I left that night I felt almost whole again. The fire that had raged inside me was only simmering now, but I knew it could blaze up again at any moment. It was good to have the Blues nearby. They were my family here. They made North Carolina bearable.

When I dropped by the next day, Myrtle Blue told me about her own close brush with disaster. When her husband, John Henry, died in 1973, she had gotten Jimmy Green to take up the mortgage on the house they had just built, so she wouldn't lose it. A couple of years back, with all her children home to help, she had gone to "settle up" with Green, so her house would be free and clear.

"At first, he wouldn't even talk to us," she said. We were sitting in the warm kitchen, the scene of most of our conversations. A comfortable, radiant piece of sunlight illuminated the room. "He told us he was going to take a nap and didn't have time to talk. He didn't want to settle with us. When he finally did talk to us," she said, "he tried to say we still owed him two thousand dollars, but I wasn't going for that.

"I had saved all my receipts where I had been paying him. They came to seven hundred dollars. I showed 'em to him. He was stunned. He said he couldn't find the receipt book they came out of and doubted they were his.

"But he couldn't deny his signature on 'em. He had said he was just gon' take the land, that we didn't have the right to settle with him. But he had to give us credit for that seven hundred dollars, and with my children's help, we paid 'im off and kept our land," she said proudly. "We couldn't let anybody take this. We just couldn't."

"I know," I said. "Believe me. I know."

• • •

It was hard to leave them. I had come to know the Blue family so well in the few short weeks I had spent with them that leaving them was like cutting out a part of myself and burying it someplace I knew I'd never go again. The day I told them I was leaving, I had bought some new spark plugs for the car and was installing them when Janice came home. Later Nev came. When they were all there, I told them I had to move on to Wilmington for a few days, and then on down to South Carolina. I told them I was going to set out for Wilmington early the next morning.

"I reckon you got to go sometime," said Mrs. Blue, trying to sound cheerful. "It's your job. We enjoyed having you."

"Come back," Janice said. "I bet we won't see you again."

"You'll see me again," I said. "I don't know when, but you will. I'll be back."

It was a quiet meal. Nobody had much to talk about. After dinner, we watched most of the NCAA basketball semifinals on TV. Mrs. Blue and Janice went to bed early, to get the good-bys over with quickly, I believe. After sitting in silence for several minutes, I told Nev I'd better go so I could get an early start the next morning. We shook hands. He wished me luck. It was tar black outside. He told me he still hadn't made up his mind whether to try the armed services or the Job Corps after graduation. I wanted to get it over quickly. I moved through the door without looking back. I heard the door close behind me. The slicing night wind cut through my jacket. I started the car and drove off slowly, looking back through the window until the house was gone and the rear window was filled with blackness. No other cars were on the road. I knew I would see them again. It might take years, but I would see them again. They had adopted me, and they were mine.

•　•　•

Wilmington was a silky smooth Johnny Mathis love song. The Cape Fear River flowing right next to the heart of downtown. Big ships going by so close that from Water Street you could nearly touch them with your fingers. These huge vessels dwarfing the cars, riding on currents of dreams, not bound by the ugly realities of those of us on shore. On side streets, quaint bars and shops like relics from waterfront towns of bygone eras. Magnificent old houses like gentle, elderly matrons, brightly painted and restored to their former glory. And trees rising into the blue canopy that is the sky. For me, it was love at first sight.

Unfortunately, the city did not feel the same way about me. She was selfish, standoffish. It was unrequited love. I was an outsider, a stranger with no invitation.

"Beautiful, my ass," the black dude at the recreation center said. "Pretty? This is a racist town, brother. Remember The Ten? It might look pretty from the outside, but it's some nasty shit going down here."

The Ten. The Wilmington Ten. Nine black men and one white woman convicted in 1972 of arson and conspiracy in connection with the firebombing of a white grocery store during a racial disorder in 1971. After a much-publicized trial, The Ten were sentenced to a total maximum of 232 years in prison. Since then, however, a confusing, ugly, and politically vicious battle has been waged in this country and abroad over whether The Ten were really guilty of the crimes they were tried for, or were, in the words of Amnesty International, a London-based human-rights organization, "prisoners of conscience," not "arrested for the crimes for which they were charged, but because of their political work."

All the defendants have now been released from prison on parole, including Reverend Ben Chavis, who has steadfastly insisted he was framed, and for a long time refused to accept anything less than a complete pardon. Since the trial, a key witness has changed his story several times, alternately affirming and denying that he lied during the trial. (In November of 1978, the U.S. Justice Department took the unprecedented legal step of asking a federal judge in North Carolina to overturn the state court convictions of The Wilmington Ten, arguing that a review of the case had uncovered evidence that the defendants' rights to a fair trial had been denied. According to the government, the defendants' rights were violated because the state prosecutor and the judge suppressed a statement that raised doubts about the testimony of Allen Hall, the pivotal prosecution witness.)

So much has happened, and so many charges of racism and impropriety have been thrown at both sides — the state and the defense — in the years since the trial, that it now seems almost impossible that the truth about what happened on February 4, 1971, will ever surface. One thing is certain, though. The case serves as yet another indication of the serious problems this town has, the lesions under the skin, the racial hatred and mistrust that began long before any of The Wilmington Ten was born or even thought of.

In the late 1890s, incensed by the gains blacks had made during Reconstruction, angry whites swarmed through the city's streets, gunning down blacks in what later became known as the Wilmington Massacre.

In the 1970s, after the city had finally desegregated its public schools, open hostility lingered. This was heightened when black students organized a boycott of the schools, demanding observance of Martin Luther King Day and respect for black courses and black identity. At the request of a local minister, Chavis, an organizer for the United Church of Christ's Commission on Racial Justice, came to Wilmington to take charge of the boycott.

As I moved about Wilmington, I could sense an undercurrent

of hostility, a tenseness invisible to the eye, an ill will in the air. It seeps into the waking mind, somehow, like dreams move in and out of the sleeping mind. You feel uncomfortable on the street. You rarely see blacks and whites talking together. Such a beautiful city. I could never reconcile all that beauty with the ugliness surrounding The Ten. They didn't fit into the same picture, didn't belong in the same town. But they were there.

Some things will never make sense.

I couldn't find a job, and I began to tire of seeing the unemployed move about Wilmington like zombies. There they were, the flesh and blood behind the government's statistics. There were even those who had stopped looking for work and were no longer counted. It was depressing to see them hang around the street corners in the black community. The unemployment office was depressing. The people were hard to talk to, they were cold. I hung out in my hotel room a lot, reading, thinking, being consumed by restlessness. I was like a criminal hiding out, waiting for the law to come in the night so we could shoot it out and end it once and for all.

I thought about how my emotions had been on a roller-coaster ride ever since I began this assignment. One day I would be way up, happy, with a strong sense of well-being, and the next day I would be angry, desperate, feeling violent, as if I could kill randomly. I felt I was getting more and more violent — that is, having thoughts more violent than I could ever remember having before this assignment, before North Carolina, before Ola Davis and Vivian Rouse, before the cotton mills and the factories, before Wilmington. It was wearing me down.

One day during my stay, I drove out to a shopping mall to eat lunch at a hamburger restaurant. It was part of a small fast-food chain. I noticed a sign in the window seeking counter help, so I applied within. I wanted to pick up the sign and take it in with me, like those guys used to do in the movies, but it was taped to the inside of the window.

"I'm your man," I told the lanky, handsome white woman who managed the place.

"How old are you?" she asked, looking me over carefully.

"Twenty-eight," I said, "but I've got lots of restaurant experience."

She was silent, still looking me over. Then she moved from behind the counter and told one of the girls in the back to stay by the cash register. There were only a few customers in the place. She led me to a booth in the back. "Sit down," she said kindly.

"Thank you," I said.

"You married?" she asked.

"Not anymore," I said.

"Listen, I'm gonna be honest with you. I would love to give you this job —"

"Good," I said, interrupting, knowing bad news was on the way. "When do I start?"

"You didn't let me finish." I had at first thought she was in her forties, but on closer inspection she looked early-to-mid-thirties. It was her eyes that had thrown me off at first. They were tired, dark, in need of sleep.

"How long would you stay at a job like this?"

"I'd try," I said. "I need the money badly. I'm a good worker."

"You know, I use mostly high school students. Some of them are flaky, but I can usually count on 'em for a couple of years. A man your age ain't gonna want to be fixing hamburgers next to some teenyboppers for long. You'll split inside a week."

"Why don't you give me a chance?"

"It's for your sake as well as mine that I'm not gonna give you the job. Believe me. I can look at you and know you wouldn't like it."

As much as I wanted not to, I kind of liked her, though I could have done without the free analysis.

"I need money," I said.

"Yeah, and a job is a job, right?"

"Right," I said.

"Wrong. It would be demeaning to you. I can't let you do it. I won't give it to you. That's that."

"Thank you," I said. I got up and began walking away. The

few customers at the tables looked up from their cheeseburgers and fries and glanced at me curiously as I walked past.

"Don't be mad," she called from the door. "You'll find something."

•   •   •

Back in my room that night, everything was caving in on me. I was tired of being nobody, a faceless slob who couldn't even get a job cutting lettuce for hamburgers. In the weeks I had been on the road, I had sat helpless while countless personnel managers or their assistants or their secretaries stared down their noses at me. They had all turned me down. I had been rejected over and over. All that rejection had begun to work on my mind. I was doubting myself. Was I really a successful middle-class journalist pretending to be a poor slob, or was it the other way around? After all, I had come out of poverty; but maybe I'd never *really* come out. Maybe I would always be one of those uncouth niggers from the ghetto. Maybe my job with the paper and my status in the suburbs were *really* the act. Maybe seeing the bottom of life again was jarring me back to reality. Wilmington was no good. I was living too much inside myself, in that realm deep in the unconscious where scary things grow, that inner darkness where we first begin to understand who we *really* are.

I moved on to South Carolina, but before I left that room, I came to understand something that I had probably sensed all my life but had never fully realized: Without a job in America (unless you're filthy rich), you are nothing. Absolutely nothing.

II

The Fire
Behind the Face

The only genuine, long-range solution for what has happened lies in an attack — mounted at every level upon the conditions that breed despair and violence. All of us know what those conditions are: ignorance, discrimination, slums, poverty, disease, not enough jobs. We should attack these conditions — not because we are frightened by conflict, but because we are fired by conscience. We should attack them because there is simply no other way to achieve a decent and orderly society in America . . .

— Lyndon Baines Johnson,
    from an address to the nation, July 27,
    1967, during a summer of racial unrest.

8

Days Without Grace

IT WAS the crowning blow. I stood there in the tiny backroom kitchen of that oyster bar in Charleston, South Carolina, with a small knife and a couple of wet oysters in my hands. I had applied for the job as oyster shucker that I had seen advertised in the morning paper. The man had looked me over and led me across the gritty wood floor to the kitchen, where a huge bucket of oysters sat on the floor.

"Let me see you handle them," he said. I took the small knife he gave me and began to open the little beasts as best I could. It was not as easy as I had imagined. Two or three times, I had to use such force to pry the shells open that they flew out of my grasp and onto the floor. The man looked at me, shaking his head.

"Can't use you," he said.

I spent the rest of the day touring "historic Charleston" — the Dock Street Theater, the old slave market — ending up outside the glitter of downtown in a section I thought must be the renowned Catfish Row of *Porgy and Bess* fame. The tight dirt streets lined with tiny row houses and littered with mangy-looking dogs served to depress me even more.

I had trouble finding a hotel room for the night. Everything was filled, I was told, until I tried the Holiday Inn downtown. I hoped I would finally get a good night's sleep there. That would help chase away my blues. It didn't work. Lying in that room, I was alone with my depression. I thought back over the day. I had been turned down for a job as an oyster shucker. I mean how low could I go?

I lay there in the dark feeling absolutely alone. I knew that when I awoke the next morning — if I ever got to sleep — I would have nowhere to go; no one was expecting me anywhere. I was reminded of the Edward Albee play called *A Delicate Balance,* which had been performed by the theater group at my college when I was a student.

In the play, a middle-aged husband and wife are struck by terror while at home. They don't understand it. They only know that suddenly they are afraid of the very room they are sitting in; they are afraid of the house they have lived in for years. They cannot stay there any longer. They cannot bear to be alone in the house anymore.

The couple — Harry and Edna — flee to the home of their best friends, Tobias and Agnes, and ask if they can spend the night. They are embarrassed to tell their friends what their trouble is, but they try to explain. Tobias and Agnes allow them to stay, hoping they will soon be told the full story of this terror that drove their friends away from home. But of course the nature of this terror is such that it cannot really be explained, for it is a terror of the unknown, a fear of nothingness.

Being unemployed holds the same sort of undefined terror. You sink into it, and it obliterates your feelings of self-worth. If you remain unemployed long enough, I thought, the world begins to seem distorted. You get the feeling that you're walking backward, away from all the things the rest of the world is moving toward. People look at you differently when they pass you on the street corner. In their eyes, you can see the assumptions they have made about you. You are relegated to the same category as the winos who lean helplessly against lampposts, thirsting after nickels and dimes to pay for another day of alcoholic bliss. People walk by you carefully, as if they don't want to touch you; as if you are pocked with sores oozing pus and disease.

I had been watching the unemployed. They seemed to move in slow motion, out of step with the working world. Many pretended it didn't hurt that they couldn't find a job, but I knew better. I knew the hurt. Some of them had stopped looking for work and told themselves they didn't really want a job anyway. This was a psyche job designed to protect them from the erosion of self-worth that comes after many rejections. "Me want a job?" one guy said to me outside a restaurant where we'd both been passed over. "Me slave? Sheee-it! My mama died going to work and my old man died coming from work. And you better b'leeve I ain't going neither way." I had heard that before.

Many of these people had to force themselves to feel they were *not* constantly being screwed by society. Somehow they had to convince themselves that they were in control. When you have a job, you at least have the illusion of controlling your own destiny. Without a job or wealth (which is power), you have no control, and everyone knows it. You feel that you're in limbo or are being manipulated by those with money and power.

I did something extremely dangerous in that motel room, considering the state of mind I was in. I opened a novel by Alice Walker entitled *The Third Life of Grange Copeland* and began reading. This book deals with the very things I was trying to describe on this journey — the brutalities suffered by the poor. It is a book about a family of black sharecroppers, and it has much to say about the history of black people in this country.

When I read the passages that deal with the mental and social awakening of the main character, Brownfield Copeland, I immediately recognized that the author was describing exactly what I had seen. She laid bare the struggles of the lowly sharecroppers, and the pains and hopelessness of the downtrodden. She was writing about the past, the twenties and thirties, but what she described was the same thing I was seeing in the 1970s.

Describing Brownfield's awakening thoughts about his daughter, Walker wrote:

> That pickaninny was Brownfield's oldest child, Daphne, and that year of awakening roused him not from sleep but from hope that someday she would be a fine lady and carry parasols and wear light silks. That was the year he first saw

how his own life was becoming a repetition of his father's. He could not save his children from slavery; they did not belong to him.

His indebtedness depressed him. Year after year the amount he owed continued to climb. He thought of suicide and never forgot it, even in Mem's [his wife's] arms. He prayed for help, for a caring President, for a listening Jesus. He prayed for a decent job in Mem's arms. But like all prayers sent up from there, it turned into another mouth to feed, another body to enslave to pay his debts. He felt himself destined to become no more than overseer, on the white man's plantation, of his own children.

It seemed to me that little had changed since Brownfield's time. So many without hope. So many whose debts continued to pile on top of them, smothering them. So many who believed that it was their fate to be caught under the feet of those in power. So many who could turn to me and ask, "What civil-rights movement? What war on poverty?"

After a night of fitful sleep, I left Charleston for Anderson, where, if nothing else, I could see two old friends of mine. At that moment, I was badly in need of friends.

•   •   •

Anderson County, situated in the South Carolina Piedmont about thirty miles south of Greenville, is a burgeoning area of more than 120,000 people, a mixture of farmland, vast recreation sites, and numerous industries. The county seat is also named Anderson. It is a city of some 35,000. Both the town and the county were named after General Robert Anderson, a hero of the Revolutionary War.

According to its chamber of commerce, Anderson has "made history in scores of ways" since its founding in 1828. Nearly seventy years ago, according to chamber literature, it was christened "The Electric City," because it was the first town in the South to have an unlimited supply of hydroelectric power available for general usage – a fact that certainly must have contributed to its development as one of the boom industrial areas of South Carolina.

The chamber is also proud of the fact that "one of the earliest cotton mills in Dixie was located at LaFrance [a nearby community] in 1838 and has run continuously since that time." And according to the chamber, the world's first electric cotton gin was operated in Anderson County in 1897.

Principal industries in the county are textiles, clothing, electrical appliances, fiberglass, and fishing tackle. In and around the city, there are businesses of all kinds — shops, factories, mills, gas stations, eating establishments, and others. My first impression was that there would be jobs there for everybody wanting to work.

But that was not the case. The job-service office on Whitner Street was crowded with people poring over the huge computer printouts that listed available jobs in the area. For semiskilled and unskilled workers, there was hardly anything at all. The competition was fierce for bottom-level jobs — jobs that are shrinking in number daily, because of automation and other technical advances. Not only must the havenots battle the haves, I was thinking as I looked around the crowded room; they must also fight one another for the crumbs the haves cast aside. So many sullen people left the office just as they had come — jobless and disgusted.

I could not find anything I was qualified for, so I left, deciding to just go to the factories, mills, dairies, and other businesses I had spotted, and ask for work.

After leaving the job-service center, I first tried the Biltmore Dairy on Clemson Boulevard. The woman in the personnel office was quick and precise with her answer to my request for work.

"We haven't had an opening in a year and a half," she said sharply. "Stopped taking applications two months ago. It was a waste of everybody's time."

Coble Dairy Products Company was next. No luck. Abney Mills — no. At Orr-Lyons Mills, makers of Wamsutta products, the middle-aged white woman behind the counter in the main office first asked if I wanted to talk with the personnel manager. But that was before I finished filling out the application form. A young black woman was waiting to be interviewed for a job. She had mentioned a man's name to the woman, and said the man had suggested she apply. The white woman smiled and left, disappearing into a room off the main office. When she returned, she told the black woman to go across the parking lot to an adjoining building and ask to see a certain supervisor. I did not hear the name or job title.

Then she turned to me, with my completed application form in hand.

"Well, Chester," she said in a syrupy voice.

"I'm willin' to do 'bout anything, ma'am," I said, hating myself for talking that way, but feeling it was necessary.

She stood there for a moment, looking at the application. "I know you need something bad," she said, "but there's really no need for you to talk to him [the personnel manager] now. He's said we don't really have anything open."

I didn't say anything. She seemed uncomfortable, as if it bothered her for me to stand there looking down at her. I tried to look more subservient.

"Like I said, I'll do 'most anything," I said. "I need work in the worse way. I'd 'preciate anything you can do for me."

She smiled. "I'm sorry," she said. "I really am."

I said nothing, just tried to look pitiful.

As I walked through the door and back into the parking lot, she spoke just before the door swung shut. "Good luck," she said.

I quickened my pace to the car. I had not seen a single black face behind the counters in any of the offices of the companies I had visited. Not one. Apparently, the civil-rights movement hadn't quite made it into the offices I'd seen. Sure, it had helped more blacks get jobs in the bowels of the plants, maybe even in positions as high as line supervisor or shift supervisor, but in the offices where the big decisions were made, it had not had much impact at all. The niggers are still working in the fields, or in the stomachs of these mills and factories. Still working in the dust, dirt, and filth, just like always. People have been too quick to speak of the New South. They have been influenced by the sight of a few black faces in elective office. But that is not power, only the illusion of power, and until black people fully understand that, no progress will be made. Well-dressed black politicians in fancy cars will continue to ride around waving their hands in the air while the needs of their constituents go unserved. Power in the South has not passed from white hands to black hands. Economics is still the great controller. Economics is *money* is *power* is *white*. Blacks are still being controlled as much as ever, although the means of control are a bit more sophisticated now. In the old days, blacks were kept in check through laws that mandated segregation. They were lynched, whipped, burned out, held at bay by vicious police dogs and water hoses. Today the weapons are economics, money, and employment. The paycheck (which can be given and taken away at will) is a more powerful controller than a hundred vicious dogs. Whites, through their economic might, their control over the means of production in this country, still have the power to strangle us or let us breathe.

•   •   •

I was beaten down. Weary. I needed help. I headed the car toward Townsend Hills. I knew I could find comfort there.

The Townsend Hills subdivision is about two miles outside of town, off the road that goes to Belton. Built about a decade ago in an area cleared of pine trees and thick underbrush, the clusters of modest brick houses were laid out along two or three snaking blacktop roads and were immediately snapped up by middle-class blue-collar and professional blacks eager to move out of deteriorating in-town neighborhoods. For many of them, this was their first opportunity to own the houses they lived in.

The neighborhood quickly became Anderson's version of suburbia, for the mainly young, upwardly mobile black families drawn toward it by the sense of progress it offered.

One such young family back in 1970 was that of my wife's sister, Gracie, and her husband of two years, William Floyd. The Floyds, in their twenties at the time, were both professional people, both teachers in Anderson schools. William, known as Sank to friends and relatives, was also a football and track coach at what was then the city's largest black high school, Westside High. The two had met and fallen in love while both were students at Allen University in Columbia, Gracie's hometown.

Sank had been born and raised in Laurens, a small town between Greenville and Columbia. It was to the Floyds' home that I went seeking comfort. I had come to know them well since we met nearly eleven years before. Not only are they two of the best friends I have in the world; they are family, and I was badly in need of family by the time I left Charleston.

The Floyds are open, unpretentious people. Gracie was surprised to see me at the door that warm March day. She had known I was working on some kind of special assignment that involved a lot of traveling and close-up research, but she had not been told the full details of the project. It was like going home for me when she opened that door, reached out and embraced me as if I were a lost child finally returned from years of wandering in the wilderness. It made me tremble inside with joy. I felt better the moment I entered the house.

It is not a fancy house, but comfortable, bought for less than $20,000 in 1970 but now worth at least twice that much, given the spiraling costs of housing in this country. They have made it stand out from the surrounding houses by adding a glorious wood deck on the back, which overlooks a smooth expanse of green lawn dotted by colorful flower arrangements.

Much has happened to this family since the days when I first met them and they were living in a concrete-block two-bedroom house on South Towers Street, in the black community near the high school where Sank taught and coached. Two sons have been born to them; they have both gained advanced degrees in education; school integration has changed their lives and profession; and they, like most of us in middle-class American life, have struggled to keep afloat in a world of rising costs and declining purchasing power.

Observing the Floyds over the years, I have come to understand the changes for the better that have taken place in my own life and in the lives of the people around me — my neighbors, my friends — because the small neighborhood where the Floyds live is so representative of suburban America. Watching them, I have come to see more clearly the isolation of suburbia. I have seen the Floyds move from young adulthood into their thirties; out of their old neighborhood in the city's black community, and into the mezzanine of the American social structure. In the old neighborhood, before the children came, they had been carefree, always entertaining friends. The years have changed that.

Most of the people who were close to the Floyds followed them out of the old neighborhood and into the suburbs, but the relationships are not the same. Something has been lost. Though the couples live within shouting distance of one another, they rarely visit any more. These people used to visit each other constantly. Now they mainly converse while mowing the lawn or taking out the garbage.

I think it has a lot to do with suburban space. The yards are bigger in suburbia, there is more room. You can stretch out, and your elbows don't have to touch your neighbor's any more. There is not the same sense of neighborhood that existed in the city, where you lived close out of necessity. The doctrine seems to be every man for himself.

It is the same where I live in the suburbs of Atlanta. Moving up in life spreads you out, and the hustling you must do to maintain that house in the suburbs keeps you running, leaving less and less time for you to know your neighbors. We easily fall into this kind of lifestyle and find it hard to break out, even when we realize what is happening.

In Townsend Hills, as in other suburbs, people speak politely to one another, but the conversation is generally hollow. There is no time for substance. The children have time to enjoy one another, but even they do not escape entirely, because they grow up witnessing the peculiar estrangement of the adults.

With the advent of school integration in Anderson in the early seventies, district lines were redrawn and Sank was dispatched from Westside to T. L. Hanna, formerly an all-white high school. In 1972, he was given the head coaching job in basketball and became the first black to head a varsity squad at the school. Then his troubles really started.

When I first began visiting Anderson in 1969, I noticed something about the town that surprised me. Though a kind of redneck attitude seemed to pervade the whole area, there was apparently a good rapport between the races. It was rather refreshing. But after watching what happened to Sank Floyd during the years after he became head basketball coach at Hanna, I have come to believe that the rapport was not genuine and that the truer, deeper feelings were more vicious.

After a few mediocre seasons when Sank was handicapped by a lack of talented players, things began to fall totally apart. From the beginning, white parents didn't give him the kind of co-operation and support his predecessors had received. And the local paper began taking shots at him, constantly criticizing his coaching, ignoring the fact that he was operating with minimal talent at best. He took a beating, but he kept going.

Over the years, Sank put everything he had into practice sessions. He read basketball, ate and slept basketball, trying to find a way to improve his teams. His teams often played above their ability, winning games they normally would have lost — a tribute to his talent and determination. During all the attacks, friends and fellow coaches told him privately that they knew he was being treated unfairly; but they never came to his defense in public. In the end, I think that hurt him more than anything else.

Sank has since given up the head coaching job, after seven years of battling against the odds. The former girls' varsity coach at the school, a white guy, has been given the job, and Floyd's detractors seem pleased.

On the day I arrived (this was before Sank decided to give up coaching basketball), he was down and out and probably as much in need of loving care as I was. We talked nonstop until two in the morning — about my project, about the troubles he was having, and about the pros and cons of life in Anderson, Atlanta, and other places. We were like spiritual brothers and sisters separated early in life and finally reunited after years of searching. When we finally got to sleep, I fell into the most peaceful state of rest I had experienced in weeks. I had found Hemingway's clean, well-lighted place.

•   •   •

I spent the mornings looking for work and the rest of the day wandering around Anderson, talking to people and watching the city go about its business. I became obsessed with watching those who had jobs — watching them go to those jobs, watching them on the job, if possible, and watching them arrive home in the evenings after work.

For some reason, I was particularly attracted to the crew at Perx Car Wash on McDuffie Street, near downtown — the women and teenagers in coverall uniforms sitting on the wall in the sun with their drying cloths, waiting for another chrome-and-steel monster with beads of water on its gleaming back to emerge from the mechanical washer. Their motions — elbows pumping quickly, several of them on each car going as if polishing a huge apple — intrigued me. The workers sweating, wiping their brows with their sleeves, some whistling, some humming, some cursing to themselves, swearing that this would be their last day washing cars.

Dried, the cars slipped into the afternoon parade of traffic, as clean as new formica. And the workers went back to their wall to await the next client.

When I tired of watching the crew at the car wash, I would drive or walk around the inner-city neighborhoods, particularly in the southside, where many of the poor live. Walking along, passing houses so dilapidated that many of them looked as if they could easily collapse and bury their occupants, I felt as if I were inside a surrealistic painting, maybe a Salvador Dali. (I thought of his painting of the soft watches, which gave the sense of time distorted.)

These houses gave me the same eerie feeling of surrealism. The house on South Towers where the Floyds used to live was totally different from the way I remembered it from 1969. It badly needed painting now. The yard had eroded and decayed over the years. It was a disaster.

And deeper in the interior of the black community, near Westside High, which was now silent like a retarded child, the houses were even worse. They leaned so much that they seemed to lack proper form. They seemed to sag inward on themselves, soft like the watches in the Dali painting, giving a distorted sense of the world, a feeling of insecurity.

On the porches amidst the dust from the dusty streets, people sat waiting for the return of those who had jobs. I watched tired souls get out of cars and sit down on the porches, putting their feet up on bannisters that seemed as tired as they were. When I couldn't stand to watch any longer, I'd close my eyes and slowly walk away from the scene. After a few steps, I'd open them again and look back over my shoulder. It was all still there. Maybe it will never go away.

•   •   •

"I don't know quite how to explain it," I said during dinner one night, after I'd been at the Floyd's several days. "It's disturbing, though.

"It's an incredible difference. When I was in the small towns of North Carolina, the kids couldn't wait to get out. Go anywhere. Many of them went to college, and the others, who couldn't afford it or couldn't get in, went into the army or moved north to get jobs. But here in Anderson, the kids seem to find what they want right here. It's alarming how so many of them leave high school and head straight for the mills," I said.

"Into the mills, a new car, debt, and marriage," Gracie replied.

"That's the cycle they choose?" I asked.

Gracie and Sank nodded their heads.

"How can they have so little ambition?" I asked.

"I think they get spoiled," Sank said, "by getting these jobs in the mills while they're still in school. With money in their pockets already, higher education isn't so important any more."

"At least that's the way *they* feel," said Gracie.

"It doesn't hit 'em that they might have made a mistake," Sank said, "until they've been in the same boring job at the mill for years, while their friends who went on to school are doing all kinds of things. They get very dissatisfied then," he added. "It tears you up as a teacher."

"It's so unfair for them to end up like that, but what can you do?" said Gracie. "It's their choice. And a lot of the parents don't push."

"Well, so many of them never got beyond the mill themselves," Sank said. "They don't see anything wrong with it."

"Let's talk about something else," Gracie said. "This is so depressing . . ."

We shook our heads in agreement. Then I said, "I think I might have a good line on a job."

"Really?" Gracie asked. "Where?"

"I saw it in the paper this afternoon. I'm going for an interview tomorrow. I'll tell you about it when I get back."

9

Three-Dollar People

THE RATHER LARGE waitress/cashier in the tight white dress, blue smock, and sagging white stockings asked if she could help me.

"I'm here for the job," I said. "The one in the paper." She handed me an application form and pencil and directed me to the straight-backed chairs lining the wall.

When I had finished filling out the form and was waiting to be interviewed, a middle-aged white man with heavily greased hair came in, along with two thirtyish women. The man was seeking the same utility position I was.

He sat pitifully hunched over, scratching across the application form slowly. The marks left where he had raked a comb through his thinning black hair made his head look like a newly-plowed field ready for planting.

Seeing him made me think of a small raccoon I had once seen crouched under a tree pawing food with its tiny hands. The man's thin shoulders were deeply rounded, and his long, blotchy neck goosed forward.

I did not want to compete with this man for a job. I told myself that maybe there were two positions open, but I really knew there was only one. I started to turn and walk out, leave the job for him, but I couldn't do that either — not after all the rejections I'd piled up so far. Besides, it was my responsibility to the project to try for this job.

The interviewer, a short, dark-haired man in black-rimmed glasses, came out and led me to a booth in the dining room. After looking over my application and asking a few questions, he told me that the job would be six days a week, Monday through Saturday, 8:00 A.M. until "three or so."

"Your salary — if you get the job — will be about one hundred dollars a week, to start," he said. "We start you at two dollars and eighty-five cents an hour. Of course we don't mind giving raises to keep a person, once they learn the job and do good work for us."

He looked up at me carefully, much concern in his face.

"I want to ask if it will bother you to bus tables," he said. He looked down, then back up at me. "It bothers some people."

"No. It doesn't bother me," I lied.

"What exactly does a day utility person do?" I asked.

"First of all," he said, "in the mornings, you clean the bathrooms in the front here, mop the floors in the galley and all the dining rooms, ready two hundred to four hundred pounds of potatoes for baking. During lunch, you bus tables and wash the dishes, keep tea at the stations and ice in the boxes, and there are other light duties. Then in the afternoon, before you go home each day, we'd like for you to pick up the parking lot, the areas outside. Pick up the paper, trash, beer cans. Once you learn where everything is, it'll get to be pretty routine.

"If you get the job, you'll have to have a white short-sleeved shirt, black pants, a black bow tie, and black leather shoes."

I had none of these things, and my money was dangerously low. Since I had just paid Gracie Floyd for my room for the week, I had only ten bucks to my name. When the interview was over, the interviewer shook my hand and said he'd be in contact if I was chosen.

About three days later, he called and said the job was mine, if I still wanted it. I immediately thought of the sad-looking man who had applied the same day I did. Nevertheless, I told the interviewer, who was an assistant manager at the restaurant, that I would take the job.

Then the problem. Where was I going to get the money to buy

the necessary clothing? It was a cruel joke. I needed a job, because I didn't have any money; yet in order to take the job, I would have to borrow enough money to buy the uniform.

I decided against calling Jim Rankin, my contact at the *Journal,* and asking him to wire the money. That would have been too easy. What would I do if I were indeed the person I was portraying? I asked myself. I would have to turn to family or friends.

My mother-in-law, Mrs. Maria Williams, lives in Columbia, about a hundred miles from Anderson. I knew I would be able to borrow the money from her. I drove down the weekend before I was to begin the job and borrowed fifty dollars. I decided to stay over and leave Columbia before daylight that Monday morning, so I could get to The Red Lobster Restaurant in Anderson by eight.

• • •

It was one minute before eight when I rushed through the front door of the restaurant. The assistant manager was waiting. He showed me where I could change clothes and quickly introduced me to my duties. They seemed to consist of endless mopping, bending, and lifting.

By the end of the day, I was exhausted. I had started at eight, and it was nearly five before I was told I could go home. All the while I had been working steadily, without even one ten-minute break. I worked there for three days before I got a lunch break, and that was only after I mentioned the problem to the management. No wonder the job had been open, I thought. Slavery lives! The first couple of days nearly killed me.

I've had a wide range of demanding jobs in my life, including construction work, pouring and finishing concrete, working in restaurant kitchens, and digging foundations for houses. I am convinced that certain restaurant jobs come close to being the hardest work in the world. This utility job was one of them. It was a back-breaker, and for $2.85 an hour — twenty cents above the minimum wage.

When I got home after the first day's work, I could barely walk. I got out my journal and began writing: "March 27. I am so tired tonight I can barely write. My fingers keep collapsing together. I can't control my hand. It is threatening to quit on me. My back aches from that mop. My feet and legs are sore from the walking, the standing, and the stooping and bending. On this job, you are in constant motion. There is no idle time. This is the kind of job that — in real life — I wouldn't think twice about. If someone offered it to me, I would probably insult them . . ."

At work, I tried to carry on as best I could, finishing one task as quickly as possible and then going on to the next. I had thought that if I worked fast during the morning and finished the morning chores ahead of time, there would be some slack periods when I could rest a few moments. But that didn't seem to work. Whenever I finished any particular job, somebody was always waiting, ready to assign me something else to do. It was usually late afternoon before I even had time to look up and see what was happening around me.

The assistant managers were giving me more compliments each day, bragging that the floors were cleaner since I had been doing them than they had been in months. This was little consolation to me, however, since most evenings I stumbled back to the Floyds' able only to eat and then fall across my bed to update my journal.

Journal excerpt, March 28:

> More hard work. It is hard to claim any dignity for yourself in this job. My head automatically lowers itself — I guess in shame — whenever black people come into the restaurant. They look at me queerly. I can feel their eyes on me, but they turn their heads quickly when our eyes meet. There is something unspoken, perhaps unspeakable, between us during those brief moments of eye contact. I think they feel sorry for me. I want to tell them it is not what they think. I am somebody. I am an educated man, graduated magna cum laude, all that good stuff. I am somebody. They don't have to feel sorry for me. But I say nothing; that would blow the cover. I shuffle past them in my black pants, white shirt, and black bow tie, with the required white apron around my waist, covering my pants from belt to mid-thigh.

They leave thinking I am as they see me. I wonder if they think about me in their cars on the way home. I can tell from the uneasiness in the air whenever a black person enters that I am a burden to him, especially if he is in a party of whites.

The whites who visited the restaurant treated me differently. In fact, they didn't notice me at all. As far as they were concerned, I was as much a part of the decor as the fishing nets that hung from the ceiling, and the paintings on the walls.

I was careful to use every opportunity I had to observe the relationships and interaction between the black and white employees. There was a lot of friendly banter, but it was hollow, merely polite conversation. Almost everybody there seemed to treat everyone else as if they existed only on the job.

There were no blacks in positions of power. All the managers and assistant managers were white. Blacks were servers, waiters, cooks, kitchen helpers, or dishwashers. There was one black guy who was kitchen manager, but his authority was unclear. The blacks didn't complain much, however. Most of them didn't seem to expect a lot out of life. There was one black waiter, though, who said that someday he would own the place, or at least manage it. He always dressed well, walked tall, arrogantly, shoulders back, head up, as if someday the whole world would be his.

And then there was the young black guy who worked "on the line" in the kitchen, preparing food. He came in one afternoon while I was busy wrestling the lunch dishes into the dishwasher and taking them out at the other end, scorching my hands in the process. He walked in as if he already owned the place. Said he'd been there for four years.

"Left once, but came back," he said. "Couldn't find nothing no better." He told me his name and stuck out his bony hand for me to shake. His black arms were pocked with scars where hot grease had stung them.

"I been burned, everything," he boasted, moving about on his toes like a prize fighter, a broad grin on his narrow face. "Don't bother me," he said. He told me he had started out as a dish-washer and worked his way up to the line. "'Course, whenever they shorthanded, I still have to fill in washing dishes," he added.

I was struggling with the hot dishes and at the same time try-ing to slosh the leftover food and filth from the plates and bowls into the huge, smelly garbage can beneath the counter.

The appearance of the area around the dishwasher would have made a neat person run out into the streets screaming. The floor was covered with water, and I had to slip and slide through it, trying to keep my balance while I pulled the nasty dishes along the counter. They were piled high. I had to separate the silver-ware, glasses, bowls, plates, and cups into different racks, and dump all the filth and mess — broken lobster claws, smashed baked potatoes, picked-over salads, bread, and wet cigarette butts — into the garbage barrel.

"You like this job?" I asked.

The former dishwasher was tall and straight, and he loved talking about his job. "I don't exactly dislike it," he said. "I don't think about it. I just work." He said he worked six days a week — Sunday through Friday.

He seemed to enjoy watching me work, though he looked as if he wanted to step right in there, amid all the swirling garbage and hot dishes, and show me how it was really done. He re-strained himself, but I could see a glimmer in his eyes, and I knew he was good at this work, better than I could ever hope to be.

"One thing I don't like," he said, "is working on Sundays. That's a day folks ought to be able to go to church, lay back at home, or visit. I *really* don't like working Sundays, but they schedule you like that."

As I listened to him, I knew this place was it for him. He was trapped. Ten years from the day we stood there talking while I wrestled with that pile of filthy dishes, I could return to Red Lobster and find him still on the line, with even more hot grease scars on his thin black arms. He would have that same proud walk, that stride which made you think that everything within those walls was his and his alone. He was easy to like.

Journal excerpt:

This job I do is degrading. What do they expect? I do the work of three people. No wonder they are happy to have me here. I am their good thing, and they are going to get everything out of me they can. People always give you that old saying about being the best of what you are. If you are a busboy, be the best darn busboy there is. That is pure bullshit. I think about that when I am cleaning toilets in the bathrooms at the restaurant.

Even if I wore a top hat, tuxedo, and cane, it would not change a thing. It is degrading. The fact would remain that what I am doing is cleaning a place for somebody to put his ass . . .

It will give me tremendous pleasure to leave this job at the end of this week or the next. I am judging this thing day by day. But I have decided not to take much shit . . .

It's hard. I've always had a complex about people in those professions where you wait on other people as if they were royalty. I find myself being overly nice to waiters and waitresses, even bad ones. I often tip more than necessary, or more than the service warrants.

When I first started working for the newspaper, I was startled by the way reporters screamed at copy carriers, calling for them to pick up their stories. I have never been able to do that. I think it is some sort of master-slave complex. Maybe it is because I've known too many domestics in my life.

One day in the middle of the week, it rained. It was morning, and I had mopped the dining rooms and the front lobby area. When I was just about to put the mop and buckets away, a couple of waitresses and one of the assistant managers walked in right across my newly mopped floor with mud all over their feet. I thought I was going to explode, and then everything would hit the fan.

I stared down at the red gritty trail they'd left on the damp floor. I stifled a scream. It was a monstrous scream that started between my ears and nearly tore off the top of my head, but I lowered my eyes and stood rigidly, hands at my sides, suppressing the rage, the urge to take that mop and break every white bone in their alabaster bodies.

I wanted to start with their maggoty heads, bash their skulls in, and then destroy the rest of their bodies. After that, I would run around outside in the mud, then come back in and track up all the floors and make the managers clean them up at gunpoint. There were several long seconds of near insanity before the rage passed and I was able to clean the floor again like a good little nigger boy. Somehow — and I don't know how — I managed to resist the urge to kill them all.

• • •

On the third day, after I had made up my mind to tell them I would be leaving at the end of the week, the managers called me into the small dining room and told me they had good news for me.

"We're going to raise you to three dollars an hour," one of them said. "You've been giving us a better job at two eighty-five than some of our three-dollar people, so starting Monday you get three dollars an hour."

They were all smiling. They seemed so happy for me. I felt it was a bad time to tell them I was quitting, so I thanked them for the raise and went back to my duties.

My fourth day there, I was put on the sign-changing detail, along with a young white guy I'd seen around quite a bit. He said he was from New Jersey, just north of Philadelphia. He and his wife — who was from Anderson — had come here in January with $350 in the bank.

"I was broke in two weeks," he said. "Saw the utility job in the paper just like you did. Did it for five weeks before moving up to production work. In Jersey, I drove a taxi."

He watched me closely as we worked, changing the letters on the big outside sign that advertised the specials for the coming week. He seemed to be searching me for some detail, a clue that would solve some question that was puzzling him.

"You really don't have too much of an accent like a southern boy," he said.

Uh-oh, I thought. "Born and raised in Georgia," I said. "Spent some time around Chicago and Minnesota a few years back," I added. He was obviously intelligent. I figured he had some college in his background, if he wasn't a graduate.

"You're pretty smart, too," he said. "I'm trying to see how far I can go in this business. You're a good worker. If you keep it up, you could get out of that utility slot and into something better. What about your family?"

"What about 'em?"

"They here with you?"

"No, still in Georgia with all those other bad memories," I said. "That's why I came here, to get away from all that."

"Yeah, I understand that," he said. "Indeed I do." We finished up in silence. I knew I couldn't stay much longer. He would ask too many questions.

I finally told the management that I would be leaving on Saturday, that I had found a job which paid more. I was lying. They said they hated to see me go, but wished me luck on my new job. They told me it would be three weeks before my pay check was ready. I had been told this when I first started.

As I left that day, I looked for the last time at the floors that had punished my back so severely. I smiled as the front door closed behind me, and I knew I never wanted to return again, certainly not as day utility person. When I finally did get my paycheck, it amounted to $122 before deductions, for 43 hours worked. After taxes, my take-home pay was a whopping $105.99. Somehow it just didn't seem fair that people should still have to work so hard for so little money in a country as rich as ours.

I hung around Anderson for a few more days, watching the people and their dilapidated houses, watching those work who had jobs. I drove outside of town to a nice subdivision that had really fine big houses, where some blacks were now moving. It was becoming the flashy new showcase spot, making Townsend Hills look like yesterday's beauty queen.

That night at dinner, I said good-by to Gracie and Sank. The next morning I rose early and left, glad to be Georgia-bound.

10

Georgia: A Song of You

Sometimes a wind in the Georgia dusk
scatters hate like seed
to sprout their bitter barriers
Where the sunsets bleed.
— Langston Hughes, "Georgia Dusk"

By THE TIME I reached the southwestern tip of Georgia where Americus lies, the joy I had felt upon leaving South Carolina was gone.

The long drive had been boring, with the predictable farm houses flying past the car windows, the cows grazing in the fields, and the warm sun burning through the windshield. Just past Butler, Georgia, on U.S. 19, something caught my interest, and I sat up straight to get a good look at it.

A small concrete-block building sat just a few feet off the road. It was a church. A huge neon sign outside its curtain-covered front doors announced in tall red letters: JESUS SAVES.

I pulled off the road and stopped the car near this odd-looking structure. It seemed hastily put together. Mortar was falling from the joints, the doors were ill-fitted in their casings, and the electric cord leading to the sign looked a little frayed. I peered inside.

No one was there, only a rickety-looking podium and a score of folding chairs. I stood there a moment beside the road. Not many cars went by. I don't know why, but a feeling of peace passed over me, and I began to feel a little more lively. My outlook suddenly brightened. I felt as if I would soon encounter something pleasant, and I took that feeling to be a good omen for the project. I was whistling when I got back into the car and drove away. I couldn't wait to see if there were, indeed, good things ahead.

Soon I entered Sumter County, home of Jimmy Carter, peanuts, and pecans. I had decided to hit Carter Country shortly before I left South Carolina. Thousands of people from all over the world had been attracted there since Carter was elected president, and I had never been in that part of the state before, so I figured I might as well see what the attraction was.

After riding around Americus, the county seat, for a while, I found a room for the week at the King Motel on U.S. 19. The room was hard to come by, because, as I later found out, the Shriners, with their well-known antics on those funny little motorcycles, were about to descend on the town for several days of convention.

I felt pretty good about the project now. I figured I no longer had to concentrate so much on getting a job, following my short stint at the Red Lobster in Anderson. I had experienced a job and felt that part of my assignment was taken care of. I decided to concentrate almost entirely on finding people who were having a hard time surviving. I would try to get them to tell me their stories.

Then I found Beale Street.

The community lay just a block or two off one of the main drags — the one with the decorative signs advising travelers that they were passing through the city's historic district. There were no signs, however, to advertise Beale Street and the community around it.

I figured it was a good bet that the city fathers hoped tourists who came through, making the pilgrimage to Carter's hometown of Plains, ten miles away, wouldn't stumble onto Beale Street and discover people living in poverty as devastating as any I had ever seen.

The stench of the outhouses on Beale Street will drive you to your knees. It attacked me. I did not want to open my mouth. I kept my teeth clinched tightly. The smell informed me that I was witnessing the underside of life in America. The more I moved about this neighborhood, however, the more I was able to live with the smell. It remained deeply offensive, but I was soon able to bear it.

Two or three scrawny dogs lay in the narrow street. They refused to move as I drove through. I veered around them. I wasn't sure whether they were just too mean to move, or whether they wanted me to hit them and take them out of their misery. From the looks of their lean flanks, it could have been either way.

Small children played in the street, oblivious to my passing, too young, yet, to realize that they ought to be filled with rage. Too young to know that they were considered disadvantaged by the larger society they lived within. Too young to know they were being dumped on every day of their lives.

The houses, with rusting tin roofs that made them ovens in the summer, looked like rows of barracks. They lined both sides of the street, with outhouses in between them. The faded wooden boards of each house were covered with asphalt sheets made to look like bricks.

These were shotgun houses. You could open the front and back doors and look straight through the houses into the back yards. There was no running water inside. Faucets in the front yards provided the water. They were double-tenant houses, except in rare cases where one family lived on both sides. Each side had three rooms.

I parked at the top of the hill. When I got out of the car, the small camera I occasionally used was hanging around my neck. I didn't even think about it until I had already walked several yards away from the car. When I did think about it, I decided to let it stay where it was.

A few women sat on the porches of some of the houses, but mostly I saw small children. At one house, I noticed a young man leaning against the bannister talking to an older woman.

"My name is Chester Fuller," I said, holding out my hand to

him. "How y'all gettin' along?" He was looking at the camera around my neck. The woman nodded.

"Fine," he said. "How 'bout yourself?"

"Pretty good," I said. Then, "It's mighty warm for April."

"Sho' is," the young man said. Then there was silence. I noticed that the two of them were half smiling. I took that as a good sign. I decided to go on.

"I'm from Atlanta," I said. "I'm interested in the way black people are living in the South now." They looked at each other, puzzled. "How much things have changed." Silence. "Y'all lived around here long?" I asked.

"I was born and raised in Sumter County," the woman said. "I'm fifty years old, lived here all my life."

"What's your name?"

"Lillie Ruth Harris."

"What's your name?" I asked the man.

"Fred Dennis," he said.

"You live here too?"

"No," he said, "I live 'cross the street, that house where the woman on the porch with those three kids. That's my wife. Two of them kids mine. The other'n she keeping for a neighbor."

"Y'all mind if I ask you some questions? It would help me in my research."

"No suh," Dennis said. Mrs. Harris shook her head no.

"Please, don't call me sir," I told Dennis. "Makes me nervous. You in your mid-twenties, right?"

"Yeah."

"Well, you're 'bout as old as I am, so don't call me sir."

They both laughed.

"Mrs. Harris, how long you been living here on Beale Street?" I asked.

"Nine years," she said. "I like Americus fine. This my home. I told you I was fifty, but actually I got two birth certificates. My sister say I was born in 'twenty-seven. My aunt say I was born in 'twenty-eight. I don't know which one it is, but I took the one that made me the oldest."

A small boy and two little girls darted across the street and began playing in the dirt at the edge of the yard. All three had their hair in braids that stood about their heads like small flags. Their little faces were ashy. Mucus dripped from the little boy's nose. They all seemed lost in their play, and they laughed and chased one another, tickling and hitting and then returning to dig in the dirt near the curb.

The children made the street pulse with life. Without their laughter, their tiny little high-pitched voices and the constant motion of their frolicking about, the street would have seemed dull. Except for the infrequent cars that went back and forth past the house where we talked, the children were the only things that moved.

"Y'all think things have gotten any better for black people in the past few years?"

"Where?" Dennis asked.

"Anywhere," I answered.

"What kind of research you doing?" Mrs. Harris asked.

"I'm a writer," I said. "I'm interested in black people and the way they live now in the seventies."

"Ain't got no better to me," she said. "What you compare it to?" she asked.

"The past, I guess."

"It's still hard," she said. "Same pains still hurting you, same bills, still live in the same kinda places. I know things 'sposed to be different, and maybe they is, but it sho' seem the same from where I sit."

"You know," I said, "the president is from around here. You think that makes any difference?"

"I ain't seen no difference," she said. "I liked the man, but I ain't seen no difference."

"Them kinda things don't make no difference," Dennis said. "Not to the ordinary people. It might make some difference to the mayor of Americus or the governor, but not to us. Grocery still going up every day, and ain't nobody gon' buy it for us. It's harder and harder to live. What difference it make?"

I shook my head. I had noticed that Mrs. Harris was holding her left arm close to her body, as if it pained her. She shifted her weight in the straight chair she was sitting in, moving very deliberately, as if it hurt to move.

"What's wrong?" I asked.

"My left arm and leg been partially paralyzed since 'sixty-nine," she said. "It started right here in my foot." She was pointing. "The stiffness, the soreness. When it wind up, right here in the arm and leg.

"I had to have an operation on the back of my neck in 'seventy-three, where something was wrong where the spine go into the neck," she said, rubbing the spot with her good hand. "The doctor said if I hadn't had the operation, the other side would've been paralyzed, too.

"Then, in 'seventy-four, I broke my knee. Had to have another operation last year. Stayed in the medical center fourteen days. Tomorrow'll be a year ago that I come out," she said. "I'm still under the doctor's care."

"How can you afford the treatment?"

"If I didn't have Medicaid, I couldn't afford it," she said. "I still don't know exactly what it is I got that cause my arm and leg to be stiff. I guess they've tried to tell me, but I never got a understanding of what they talking about."

"How do you make it?"

"I been on disability for 'bout four years," she said. "Everybody 'round here pay twenty-two fifty a month rent, unless they rent out both sides. Then it's forty-four dollars a month. I got a 'lectric stove. I try to keep that bill down. Gas was high this time, 'cause it was cold last month and the heat stayed on. I get by, but that's 'bout all."

"How do you make it, Fred?"

"I work hard," he said.

"Where?"

"I help deliver milk. Been on that job nine years. I have to git up early in the morning, but I'm finished most days by midday."

"You mind if I ask how much you make?"

"I draw one hundred and twenty-five dollars a week, but I make a little extra money, 'cause I play with a rock band on the side. We call ourselves Little Mickey and the Sticks of Dynamite.

We cut a record a while back, in a little studio in Warner Robbins," he said, beaming. "Cost us four hundred dollars. The record didn't sell. We still playing mostly on weekends in little bitty joints and things."

A tall dark-skinned man emerged from a path between the two houses directly in front of Mrs. Harris's. He approached us.

"How y'all doing?"

"All right, Pete," Dennis said. "What's going on with you?"

"Ain't nothin' shakin'," the man said. It was obvious to me that the three of them knew each other well. I stuck my hand out to the new man.

"My name is Fuller," I said, "Chester Fuller. I'm a writer. I'm doing research on how blacks are living in the South today."

"Oh yeah?" he said. "I'm Pete Evans. I live over on the next street. Glad to meet you."

Evans said he drove a sanitation truck for the city of Americus. "I've been doing it about eight months now," he said. "That's one thing that's changed for blacks. Used to be that a black man couldn't have the job I got. The only place for a black man was on the back of the garbage truck. Not in the cab. Shoot, he better not try to git in the cab. But now, if you got the qualifications, you can just about git any job a white man can git," he said. "If you got the qualifications."

"How do you feel about living here in this neighborhood?" I asked Evans.

Without a blink, he said: "The city oughta git the biggest bull-dozer they got down there and come in here and clean this whole area out. Ain't no sense in people living like this. But the rent is cheap. It's all some of these people can afford.

"The houses falling down. These outhouses ain't sanitary," he continued. "The city, nobody makes the landlord keep 'em up. They came through here years ago and started putting a sewer through here, but they just stopped. Why didn't somebody make 'em finish it? Cause don't nobody care."

"They put all them cesspool pipes in the ground down here 'round 'bout 'seventy-four," Mrs. Harris said. "Then they stopped. Now the house down there on the end, he has his own bath," she said, pointing. "But you know, most of the people don't complain about not having a bathroom."

"But what about that smell?" I asked.

"It ain't nothing now," Dennis said with a smile. Both Evans and Mrs. Harris shook their heads in agreement. "Wait 'til summer and it gits really hot," Dennis said. "You come back then."

"Me and my wife ain't gon' be 'round here much longer," Evans said. "We both working and saving our money so we can move out of this area. We want an acre or so of land, if we can git it cheap enough. My aunt knows a man who owns some land not too far from here. We want to buy some and put a mobile home on it.

"You can git some nice ones," he said. "I know one guy with a real fancy one, got two or three bedrooms and a stereo system that comes up out of the floor. I seen some guys have a brick mason lay bricks around their trailers, and boy, you can't hardly tell 'em from a regular house."

"I'd just settle for a bathroom in this house I got here," said Mrs. Harris. "You know, honest, you don't have to have no complete full bathroom," she added. "You don't have to have no tub. We just need a flush toilet and a sink. Those things out there just ain't sanitary."

Though Americus has a large number of blacks who are unemployed, Dennis and Evans had little sympathy for those who couldn't find work.

"Some of 'em just don't wanna work," said Dennis. "A lot of 'em looking for a certain kind of job. Take somebody wanna work, you take what you can git."

"The thing is," Evans said angrily, "they don't want to do no hard work. They'd rather hang around these wine bottles."

"Or smoke dope," Dennis added. "Ain't no job easy, or it wouldn't be a job. You just got to do it. Some days I don't wanna git out of my bed at two in the morning, and the cold wind is blowing outside. I have a lot of bad days like that, but I git on up and go, because I need that little change. I ain't never laid out in the nine years I've been on the job. I missed a few days, because I was sick or hurt or had to be off."

"That garbage truck kills me sometimes," Evans said. "I mean,

I be wore out when I git off, but I just keep thinking 'bout all the vacation time, sick leave, health insurance, and things I didn't have before I took that job."

Mrs. Harris had moved her chair out in the yard, to catch more of the afternoon sun. Suddenly it seemed to me that more children were about. Older children were hanging around the small grocery store up the block and talking together in the street a few houses up. There was more life on the street.

Still, as I looked at the houses and those tall, goose-necked faucets that rose out of the ground next to the front porches, I felt pity for the people who lived there.

I was reminded of the summers I had spent in Griffin, Georgia, with my cousins, when I was growing up. My grandmother (my mother's mother) was very old and lived in a rambling white house on East Solomon Street with several of my aunts, cousins, and their children. The house always seemed crowded. Children were everywhere, and there was never enough money to satisfy the needs of everyone under that roof, but my memories of the house are good ones. Those summers, my cousins and I all played together in streets like Beale Street. The houses on those streets had bathrooms attached, though. It seemed that all my brother and I did there was play. We played ball in the fields across from the house, we played in the creek a few miles away. We played everywhere, and we never thought about being poor or what it meant. We were just like the kids who were playing around me now in Beale Street.

Thinking about those long-ago days and watching these children play made me feel a kinship for them. It was as if they were my own children. They seemed so happy, yet I was sad to see them playing there. I wondered about their futures. What would happen to them? How many would leave Beale Street? One thing I knew for sure was that none of them would end up like another little boy who used to play in the road a few miles from there. None of them, I was certain, would grow up to be president.

As Dennis, Evans, and Mrs. Harris continued to talk, another disturbing aspect of this community surfaced. It didn't seem important to them, but it really stuck in my mind. Perhaps what added to my uneasiness was the casual way in which they seemed to regard this evil.

These were all nice, friendly people who had made me feel at home almost from the time we started talking. Yet their conversations were filled with tales of lurid violence. And their references to these acts of violence were quite casual, as if they were an accepted part of life on Beale Street.

Pete Evans told me about the time he spent several days in jail. When I asked him what he was in for, he replied, "Shot a dude."

"What for?"

"A little misunderstanding."

"Did you kill him?"

"No, he lived. I just shot 'im three times."

"Where?"

"All over. It was a shotgun." He and Dennis laughed.

"That ain't nothing," said Dennis. "A little while ago, the man up the street and the guy that live in that house right there had an argument, and they both went to git they shotguns." He was beaming as he moved into the story. Evans had a broad smile on his face too.

"While the man up the street was tipping 'round this man's house trying to surprise him, the man he was arguing with sneaked up behind him and let him have a load of buckshot," Dennis said. "Shot him right in the ass." Evans was bent over laughing now, slapping his knee.

"Yeah," Evans said, "a few weeks ago, a guy walked up to another man, stuck a pistol in the man's mouth, told him to bite down on the barrel, and shot him in the mouth. It's rough 'round here sometimes."

"Y'all ain't scared?"

"Who?" Evans said. "Niggers better not mess with me. I don't bother nobody, and they better not bother me."

"But it's some crazy niggers 'round here," Dennis said, "cutting and shooting each other. I ain't never seen nobody stay mad all the time like some of these folks 'round Americus. If you ain't careful you can git tore up."

"What about the police?" I asked.

"They all right," said Mrs. Harris. "They patrols over here every once and again. Been a lot of vandalizing churches and whatnot, stores. Every now and then you might hear of a burglary, but ain't nothing to complain for. You just give them they rights and let them give you yours. People kinda look out for they self."

Two of the bigger boys up the street were boxing now, moving out into the street, their fists flying like laser flashes. They had footwork worthy of Muhammad Ali. I had assumed they were playing until I heard one shout, "Uh-uh now nigger, I'm gon' knock your face back through your neck." The one who had shouted swung a vicious blow that just missed the taller boy's nose.

"Nigger, you crazy!" the taller boy yelled, kicking the other in the knee, then running up the street and darting between two houses, with the others in pursuit.

"Don't pay them no 'tention," Evans said. "They carry on like that all the time."

I continued to watch the chase. The taller boy emerged from an alley between two of the houses and was cut off by some of the others. He was held for the shorter boy. They dove into each other and tussled on the ground. He wound up on top, pounding the shorter boy with his fists.

"As long as they ain't got no knife or nothing," Evans said.

The shorter boy was crying now. The taller boy finally got off him and walked off up the street rubbing his hands. The others followed, leaving the short boy sitting on the ground crying. He got up minutes later and walked up the street alone, brushing the dust from his jeans.

"Mrs. Harris, is there anyplace else you'd prefer to live?" I asked.

"Uh-uh," she said, "but I'll live. If I had to live on another side of town, I'd make it."

"Well," Dennis said, "I'd like to have a better, more decent-looking house, but you know . . . rent so high."

"I could probably git one of these apartments 'round here,"

Mrs. Harris said. "You have to pay one hundred to one hundred and fifty dollars a month, and you don't have as much room as I got now. And they got so many rules, you can't even paint 'em or fix 'em up like you wanna."

I was getting hungry, and the conversation was running out. I told them I had to go, but promised I would stop by again while I was in Americus.

As I left, the small children were still playing in the street, and I had to blow my horn to make them move. My mind dwelled on them and the violence that surrounded them. To the grown-ups here, it was a way of life. The children would probably grow up thinking of it in the same way. Shotguns were something they'd know a lot about. Not from reading books, either; from experience. I drove away slowly.

11

A Tale of Two Brothers

I DID NOT understand what was happening.

As I recorded in my journal what I'd seen and heard on Beale Street, descriptions of the people I'd met, I noticed a tremendous difference in the way the words made their way onto the page. The process was almost totally mechanical. I didn't feel the suffering and passion I had felt all the other times, when I had painstakingly recorded in my journal the sorrows and recollections of each day.

There had been a change in me that I couldn't figure out. I stopped writing for a while and thought about this new development. It was as if I were on a plane of being different from the one I had been living on previously. The things I saw on Beale Street produced in me a feeling of disgrace and pity that people should live in such awful conditions in this country in the 1970s, but my response had somehow changed. It was as if I was already so filled up with the woes of the downtrodden, had absorbed so much of their lives and sorrow, that there was no more room.

I was beginning to feel numb. And this was not because of the return of my professional distance. It was something more, something deeper. Perhaps an inner safety mechanism was taking over. Maybe my subconscious mind was throwing out the lifeboat in the nick of time, because it knew I was sinking too deeply into despair. As I had learned already, it didn't take long for the despair of others to become your own.

This numbness occurred suddenly. I was like a man who had been drunk for several days and had suddenly awakened in bed in the middle of the night, cold sober.

It was kind of refreshing. I felt a bit lighter, as if I knew I could go the distance now. The load was no longer too heavy. But with this new freedom came a tinge of guilt, a tiny voice deep inside asking whether I might not be tuning too much out. I tried to ignore it, thinking that my subconscious was responsible for this sudden sense of peace and knew the best course for me to take. I decided to leave the matter in the hands of the responsible force.

I wrote in my journal, "Poverty is poverty. What else can I say about it? I mean, what can I do?"

I put down the pen and finished off a cold barbecue sandwich I had bought the night before. The French fries had become cold and greasy. I threw them away and, later, went to sleep thinking about a more immediate problem I had to solve before the end of the week.

• • •

Downtown Americus is small, with a central business district only a few blocks long and three or four blocks wide. The city is home for some 20,000 people. It was a sleepy southern town until the presidential candidacy of Jimmy Carter focused national attention there and attracted tourists from throughout the world, on their way to ogle the Carter homeplace ten miles away.

Americus residents seem to have taken it all in stride, however. As I walked along the downtown streets, people around me moved in the slow, deliberate fashion they had been accustomed to before all the publicity and the flood of tourists. Nobody was in a hurry except me.

I was desperate. My money had just about run out. I had $12.66 left, and the rent was due on my motel room for the coming week. I was about to be homeless.

I found the Western Union office across the street from the old brick building that housed city hall, the police, and other city offices. Though I had gotten the address from the phone book, I passed it several times before I figured out that the Western Union office was behind the army recruiting office, which was located at the same address.

I went inside. The sergeant who was sitting behind the big wooden desk smiled and rose to shake my hand as I entered. "I'm looking for the Western Union office," I offered quickly. I didn't want him to get the wrong idea. He looked deflated. Times were hard, apparently. Every time I had been in town, I had seen that recruiting office, and I'd never noticed anybody there except the sergeant, who sat patiently behind the desk or stood by the window, looking up and down the street.

He was clean-cut, neatly pressed. His clothes fit as if they had been sewn together with him in them. He could have been a poster propped in the chair behind the desk.

"Oh," he said, "right through there."

"Thank you."

At the end of the hallway, I found a cramped, dim office where a middle-aged man in glasses sat looking through a huge book. Electric cords seemed to be hanging from the ceiling all over the place, and desks and clutter were everywhere.

"My name is Fuller, Chester Fuller," I said. "I am expecting a moneygram from Atlanta."

"Fuller, Fuller. Let me see." He searched through the pile of debris on his desk and found another large book. "Fuller. Chester, did you say?"

"Yes."

"There's nothing here."

"There must be some mistake," I said. "Actually, it should have been here yesterday. Surely it arrived this morning."

"No. Nothing."

"Will you get in anything else today?"

"Maybe, maybe not. I have no way of knowing these things. Sorry."

"Thank you."

I was fit to be tied. What the hell was going on with Rankin in Atlanta? I had called several days before and told him that I needed a couple hundred dollars immediately, that I was fast running out of money. He had said he'd take care of it, but there was no money at the Western Union office.

I couldn't call him at the office, because there was a danger that whoever answered the phone would recognize my voice. I found a phone booth on a street corner and called my wife, Pearl. Because of the cars going by, I had to shout to her what the problem was. She said she would call Rankin and call me back. I waited by the phone.

Several minutes later, the phone rang. It was Pearl.

"Did you get him?" I asked.

"Yes, I got him," she replied.

"What did he say?" She was laughing. "What did he say?" I repeated.

"He was in a meeting when I called. He told me he was sitting there with the money in his shirt pocket. He had gotten the expense money but had completely forgotten about you."

"What?!"

"He said he had completely forgotten you were out there."

"How the fuck could he forget that?"

"He forgot. He said he was rushing out right then to wire the money."

• • •

I was in a state of shock. He had forgotten me. What if I were stuck away in a dungeon-jail in some rural south Georgia county and he had forgotten I was out here? It gave me the willies. Now I really felt vulnerable. It was one thing to suspect that I was all alone in the world, but now I knew I was, and that felt worse.

I had to get back to the King Motel and check out before noon. I hoped the money would arrive before the Western Union office closed that evening.

It did not. I searched until I found a cheaper motel, one that charged only $10.40, including tax, for the night, but I was shattered when I was told that there wouldn't be an available room until the following night. The Shriners were in town!

That night, I slept through three showings of a movie at the local movie house. Then I drove out of town a ways, parked the car in a deserted grassy area next to the railroad tracks, and napped off and on until morning.

When the sun came up, I got out of the car and stretched. My bones ached, and my neck felt as if somebody had been standing on it for hours. I drove back to the city and parked outside a fast-food joint and waited for it to open. When it did, I got a good cup of coffee that helped bring me back to life.

Finally, I walked over to the Western Union office. It was not open yet. Not even the recruiting office was open. I walked around, looked in the store windows, whistled, sat in the car.

When I went back to the office, the money was there — $188.35. The rest of the two hundred dollars had been eaten up by Western Union charges.

I felt better now. Money was my protection. I kept feeling it against my leg, kept putting my hand in my pocket to touch it. I didn't want to be without it ever again.

* * *

With my pocket replenished, I was ready to get on with the business of the project. I had been intrigued by a thin black guy I had seen several times on Beale Street. He was skinny to the point of looking unhealthy. His mannerisms were those of a kid, but face-on he looked older, perhaps in his twenties. It was hard to gauge his age.

One day I discreetly followed him after he left the cluster of teenagers he had been hanging out with on Beale Street. I watched him as he moved through Russell's Alley and entered a small house where a black woman, wearing many skirts, a sweater, and a coat, with a rag tied tightly around her head, sat on the wooden porch.

I passed the house, turned at the corner, and circled the block again. He had been standing on the porch talking to another youngster when I passed. I drove to the store across the street and parked behind it, so I could look back down Russell's Alley. Then I got out and walked toward the house.

The house looked like something out of a bad dream, but it

was his home. Outside, a pile of scrap wood rose almost to the roof of the dismal-looking house.

He was standing on the porch, still talking to the boy I had seen him with earlier. The old woman was sitting in a dark corner, next to the pile of wood.

"How y'all doing?" I said casually.

The two youths smiled. The woman nodded but said nothing.

"Fine," the two boys said.

"Mind if I come in and talk to y'all a minute? I'm interested in this area. The people who live around here . . ."

"Where you from?" the ageless young man asked.

"Atlanta," I said.

"Atlanta?" the other one said, with joy on his face. "You from Atlanta?"

I nodded my head.

"My name's Chet Fuller," I said. We shook hands all around.

"I'm Freddie Lee Mullins," the older-looking one said. "This my brother Eddie Lee, and that's my grandmama over there, Fannie Lee."

I found out Freddie Lee was seventeen and Eddie Lee sixteen.

"Can we go inside?" I asked.

"Yeah, come on in," Freddie Lee said. They led me into the front room, which was Freddie Lee's bedroom. The house was small and dark inside. Freddie Lee's room looked like something out of the black-lighted depths of a marijuana high. Though the room itself was dim, flashes of light shot out from the walls and ceiling. The faces of rock and rhythm-and-blues singers stared at me from every wall. These figures, on album covers attached to the walls, stood out from the darkness of the room like images in a 3-D movie.

"Why you talking to people?" Freddie Lee asked. "I seent you over on Beale Street."

"I want to find out what it's like for black people trying to live in the South today. If things have changed for the better."

"I don't know," he said. "How you tell?"

"Can you tell any difference in the way you live now against how you lived ten years ago, five years ago?"

"It's the same to me," he said.

"Me too," Eddie added.

"I got a lot of friends over there on Beale Street," Freddie Lee said. "They ain't got no bathrooms. They think 'cause we got a bathroom and I got my own room, they think we well off."

"Y'all tell me something about yourselves."

"I live here," Freddie Lee said. "My brother live with my mama a few streets over . . . I have lived in this room, here, at least twelve to fourteen years of my life. Right in this room."

He said he'd quit school when he was fourteen, because "I ain't have no clothes. Some people say that ain't no excuse. You see, I like to go somewhere nice, look halfway decent, you know, but they charge too much money for clothes now."

Somebody passed by outside and spoke to the boys' grandmother. She returned the pleasantry, and the man moved on.

"We ain't got that kind of money," Freddie Lee said. "I can't git no job. You got to go to school to git a job. Me and him don't go to school. I can't git no job, so I just forgit it."

Eddie said he'd quit school about a year ago, because he had to serve time in prison in Augusta.

"I was in prison for seven months," he said.

"What for?" I asked.

"Stealing. I stole this white man's car."

"They wouldn't have been so hard on him," said Freddie Lee, "if he hadn't tore up the man's car."

"Mashed in the front end," Eddie said, embarrassed. "I hit a cow."

Freddie Lee, who told me he wanted to join the Job Corps, claimed he had loved school when he was younger. "In elementary school," he boasted, "I got perfect attendance." He went to a nearby dresser and pulled out some certificates from a drawer and showed them to me. He was proud. Perfect attendance, they said.

"But in the eighth grade and the ninth grade," he said, "everything started changing, and look like I just couldn't hack it no more. I don't know what it was, everything . . . just went wrong. I couldn't do nothing right. And on top of that, we couldn't afford to buy no clothes, 'cause my grandmama just git a little check. She manage on social security. We have to pay thirty-five dollars rent a month. My grandmama been staying here since her mama died long, long years ago."

We were silent for a moment. I couldn't think of anything to say to get him talking again. I looked at the faces on the wall.

"I was 'shame to go to school after we couldn't buy no clothes," he said. "You don't wanna be raggedy all the time. People might not understand that, but I do. I know how I feel. You got to have some good clothes."

A noisy train passed on the tracks nearby, and the vibration it caused shook the house. "Sometimes it comes through here at five o'clock in the morning and stops, backs up," said Freddie Lee. "All that noise."

The sound of iron scraping iron. The train was stopping. High-pitched squeals. We sat there listening. After a while it was moving again and was gone.

"I had to walk to school all the time," Freddie Lee said. "When it rained, I would git to school all wet. People laughed at me, you know. Made me not wanna go over there . . .

"One time, I got my hand busted in the back of the door, and it was hurting something bad. Instead of them treating me for it, they just poured alcohol on it and turnt me back to my class. I told them then, if I ever got from over there that time, I wasn't never going back . . .

"Now, though, I think I might like to be back in school." His voice was sad, full of regret.

They both told me they would like to see more of the world. All their young lives, they had been confined to the minuscule surroundings of their small neighborhood. Freddie Lee said he had never been farther away from home than Albany (only about fifty miles away), where he had been sent as a juvenile delinquent, for playing hooky from school. Eddie told me he had never been farther than Augusta, where he served jail time. "I passed through Macon," he said. "We went through there when they was taking us to prison, but we didn't stay but an hour."

Their lives seemed to me an unbelievable tangle of misery.

They had both had numerous brushes with the law and told me they often found themselves ready to run at the sight of a police car.

"Outa habit," Freddie Lee said. "Them white polices git me in that car, I don't know what they'll do. When they come in here and stop and call you to the car, I don't go. I run."

They told me their most recent involvement with Americus police had taken place a week before I talked to them.

"Well, you see, one grabbed me," said Freddie Lee. "Well, I might've been in the wrong, but you know, this was about last week. His mama [their mother] called the law on me. See, I went down there to their house arguing, argued at them. See, I wanted to wear his clothes. He got a suit, one suit, and I wanted to wear it."

"I got two suits!" Eddie corrected him quickly.

"I wanted to wear it," Freddie continued, as if he hadn't heard his brother's correction. "I don't have a suit. They cost too much money. It's a three-piece suit. I know it was too big for me, but I wanted to wear it anyway. I told him I was gon' give him three dollars to let me wear it. Then I started to see if I could git him to let me give him one dollar, since he my brother, but she [their mother] didn't want him to do it, and I started arguing, because I was mad then.

"I wanted to go to this party. I was gon' take my girl friend, you know. I wanted to look nice. I went outdoors and was cussing. She got mad and throwed a shovel at me. It scraped my head, and she called the law. And we was going on home, me and my friend Larry, and the law passed by me.

"I was going around the curve and another police car was coming up. He backed up and said come here. I said, 'I ain't studying you.' He jumped out the car and grabbed me. I tried to resist him from taking me to put me in the car. He got me and throwed me on top of the police car, then after a while he let me down and tried to handcuff me.

"I got loose and ran. I heard a little girl scream, 'Don't shoot him!' He might've been reaching for his gun. I don't know. I guess I would've knowed if he would've got it. I was gone."

"Most of them white ones don't like to see you walking at

night, especially in the white neighborhood," explained Eddie. "I left my girl friend's house one night and walked back through the white neighborhood, and the police stopped me. They told me I better git my ass on home."

"You can walk all night in the black neighborhood," Freddie Lee said, "and the police don't even care. But if you try to walk through the white neighborhood, they'll say you trying to burglarize."

I was mesmerized by the tales of their lives. I sat there thinking that although they were not yet out of their teens, they had both been pretty much on their own for some time. Eddie told me that his mother was on welfare; that she had two other children at home with her, whom she took care of. He pretty well took care of himself.

"Nane one of us ain't got the same daddy," Freddie said. "I been staying with my grandmama a long time. Before that, I was staying with my mama in Randolph Alley. Then she left us and went to New Jersey. Then me and him was staying together. When she came back from wherever she was, she had them other children with her."

We were silent for a moment. I didn't know what to ask next. Then Freddie spoke again.

"You know," he said wistfully, "I would some of these days like to live in Florida or New Jersey. Florida look so good on the television, so much sun and water, and everybody got they own pool."

"I'd like to go live with my daddy in Connecticut — Hartford," said Eddie.

"He don't want you," Freddie said. "If he did, he wouldn't have left. My daddy 'round here," he continued, "but he living with another woman and she got fourteen children by somebody else. He taking care of her kids and ain't taking care of me." He paused and looked out the window through an opening in the faded curtains.

"He got me a job down to the peanut mill one time," Freddie Lee said. "I really don't conversate with my daddy much now, 'cause he got a jealous wife. She think I be talking this for my mama when it ain't really that way.

"But anyway, he got me a job at the peanut mill and it was going fine. We worked four days, and they just laid us off. They never called us back."

He looked at me straight on.

"I really want to go back to school," he said pitifully, " 'cause I'd like to take electronics. That's what I really like. I'm all right 'til I want something and can't have it. Then it give me the idea of taking it. But I don't wanna git in no trouble. I come close to stealing sometimes," he said. "I can't keep on like this."

"Yeah," said Eddie, "you see these people on television and white people, they have what they want. We can't never have nothing. I had me a job after I got out of prison, working up to the office equipment place toting typewriters.

"But they didn't do me right. I didn't work up there but two weeks. I only made 'bout thirty dollars for half a week, 'cause they wouldn't pay me right. They was 'sposed to be paying me two sixty-five an hour," he said, "but they wasn't. 'Cause I had a juvenile record. I quit." Silence.

"What about the way the races get along here?" I asked.

"This town, I'm saying it's separate," Freddie said. "Black and white go to school over there, but I don't think they [whites] want you to go to school with the white.

"On that side of town yonder," he said, "is the white folks' line. I can stay over here all night and won't nobody say nothing, but let me cross that line to the white folks' side and they ketch you.

"They gon' say you trying to break in. You try to explain to 'em and they don't wanna hear it. They'll take you down to the station, try to scare you to get you to tell them something on somebody else. They'll hold you for three days like that, seventy-two hours. I been down there three times like that."

Eddie had been looking through the opened door for several moments. He nodded his head an instant, then looked up at his brother. The faces of the bigtime singers stared at us from the walls.

"Y'all ever seen any of those people live, in concert?" I asked. They both shook their heads. They told me they had never been to a concert or live performance of any kind.

"I only know what's in the music they play," Eddie said. "When I listen to it, I can hear them talking to me."

"What do they tell you?" I asked.

"They be saying, 'Eddie Lee, git on up and git outta that town, see the world, git you some cash, move on.'"

"That's right," Freddie said, "git on outta here. If I could leave here, I'd git me a job making some *good* money. I wouldn't look back at all. I wouldn't come back. I know I'd miss my grandmama and some of my friends, but I wouldn't come back. Be a man of the world."

We all laughed, but there was pure fire in Freddie Lee's eyes. At that moment, their faces seemed so lit up to me that they nearly glowed in the dimness, like the album-cover faces on the walls.

"I'd like to just take off," Freddie continued. "See all them places they sing about." He was pointing to some of the singers on the album covers. "All them fancy places where they live, them fine cars and fancy clothes."

"Yeah!" Eddie said, in a voice almost a shout. "Yeah, yeah. You git so tired being poor."

12

In the Heart of
the Heart of the Country

BECAUSE I WAS so close, I couldn't resist seeing Plains. Half seriously, I had told Rankin and Minter that I was going to apply for a job at the Carter family peanut warehouse and at Billy's Service Station, to see what kind of response I'd get.

Plains did not make a good first impression on me. As I rode into town, I could feel my face harden into a frown. Signs of profiteering were everywhere. It was disgusting. The town was being choked to death by scamps trying to turn anything remotely connected with Jimmy Carter — the soil, air, water, trees, and dust of the town — into dollars.

I felt sorry for the ordinary townspeople, those who had seen their sleepy little hometown turned into a trashy-looking tourist-attracting bazaar full of cedar shingles, farm knicknacks, old plows, bent wagon wheels, and other assorted down-home memorabilia, to give it that proper just-plain-folks country look.

I passed Billy's filthy service station, which doubles as the home base for his tour-guide business. For a couple bucks, you can ride around downtown Plains and environs in the Peanut Special — a truck that is dressed up to look like a train. It is a very short trip. There isn't much to see in Plains.

The number of tourists making the pilgrimage here has dropped off tremendously since the glory days following the

1976 election, when thousands of people a day overran the town,
snapping pictures and scooping up souvenirs to show the folks
back home.

It was embarrassing now. There was only a trickle of tourists.
Attendants at Billy's gas station leaned against the Peanut Special
picking their teeth, watching the few tourists on the street saun-
ter from shop to shop checking out the trinkets. The attendants
could easily have been circus workers checking the animal cages
on the trailers, fanning flies, and wondering if life didn't have
more to offer than what they were experiencing.

The whole town had the look of a down-at-the-heels circus. It
was like watching Barnum and Bailey milk the last nickels out
of a country community. I kept waiting for them to fold up all
the seedy tents, load up the animals, and move on to the next
town.

Black kids hung out on the corners downtown, watching the
tourists. The boys waited for school to be over so the local
pool room, Billy's Playhouse, could open and they could take
to the pool tables and pinball machines. They were restless.
There was nothing else for them to do.

Just a block from downtown was the black neighborhood, a
string of sad houses stamped with the unmistakable mark of the
poor. One thing was clear to me. Black folks weren't making any
money off Jimmy Carter and Plains.

I had lunch — a bland barbecue dish — at the Korner Kitchen.
The waitress asked if I also wanted a slice of peanut pie, or some
peanut ice cream. I thought I would throw up. I left.

At the Carter warehouse, I was told that there were no job
openings at the time. I thanked the man in the office and left,
crossed the street, and made my way to Billy's gas station.

The young guy behind the counter looked up with a smile as I
entered.

"Looking for work," I said.

He shook his head. "Thangs awfully slow 'round here," he
said. "We ain't hardly got nothing for the people already here
to do. Sorry."

After a few more hours of hanging around, watching the

tourists, the young black kids, the ordinary townspeople who just wanted to be left alone, and the poor black folks who seemed to just stay in their houses, I couldn't take Plains any longer. At that moment, I couldn't think of a worse place to be. I left for Dawson, a town I'd heard and read a lot of bad things about.

• • •

Highway 45 took me into Dawson. Upon crossing a set of railroad tracks, I immediately picked up the pungent smell of peanut butter that came from the Cinderella Foods plant, a wing of Stevens Industries, Inc., which loomed like a giant troll guarding the entrance to the town.

The haunting smell followed me as I moved farther into town, checking out the layout of the streets and looking over the buildings and houses.

I knew the reputation this town had, and I thought I detected a more sinister odor in the air — the faint stench of racial hatred, mistrust, and ignorance.

This town had been brought into the national spotlight in 1977 when five young black men there were accused of murdering a white store owner and were brought to trial amidst an atmosphere of such hate that it brought back bitter memories of the wild lynch mobs that had meted out swift "justice" in the South a few decades before.

The case came to be known as that of the Dawson Five, and as the national media focused attention on the trial, it became clear that the five defendants were merely vehicles by which the town itself was being put on trial. The deep-seated racial prejudices of its citizens were bared for the world to see.

During the trial, all manner of vicious accusations flew across the courtroom, each side charging the other with impropriety in handling the case. There were charges that at least one of the defendants had been forced by the police to confess to the crime. Eventually, probably due in large part to the massive amount of publicity the case attracted, the defendants were set free.

Dawson had been forced to deal with its racial shortcomings

and the pent-up feelings released by the trial. It was trying to live down a bad reputation. A small town, Dawson had only about 7000 citizens. It was a cold town, and the coldness underscored my status as an outsider. I didn't see how I could get into the flow of everyday life there. The people didn't seem too hospitable.

On foot, I wandered around the central business district — the stores and shops, the courthouse and the city offices. Nobody spoke. It was almost like being in a big metropolis where nobody pays you much attention. I had to keep telling myself that this was Smalltown, U.S.A., where people are supposed to be easygoing and friendly.

It was late afternoon and I was hungry again, so I located a downtown café. It was called Mama's Kitchen. I went in, sat down, and looked around as the young waitress sidled over to me. Suddenly I realized I was the only person in the room who wasn't white. I was reminded of all the other times I had been in this predicament in the South. It was a strange feeling, something I'd never gotten used to despite the number of times it had happened. I felt naked, but I didn't want anyone to know I was afraid. I discreetly made sure I knew where all the exits were and who was seated next to them.

I ordered the Irish stew, since I noticed that a lot of other people were having it. I thought about the times in my old neighborhood when I was growing up when I had seen white people in clubs, stores, or blind pigs generally frequented only by blacks. Now I understood what they must have felt at those times.

I was afraid sitting there, but I couldn't admit it. Maybe this was Salisbury all over again, I thought. But maybe this time I wouldn't fare so well.

Suddenly I recalled all the lurid tales of violence I had heard and read about Dawson. Its bloody history appeared in pictures on the backs of my eyelids. I wondered if the same hate that had caused such mayhem against my people years ago was present now in this room, where all eyes darted away as soon as they met mine.

What were these white people thinking? That I was out of place here? Were they trying to detect the least bit of fear in me? I wondered if my situation was analogous to what people always said about dogs: that if you let them know you were afraid, they would attack.

The waitress seemed extra nice. Could it be that they were as uneasy about my presence as I was? Maybe to them I appeared to be some mean mother who had the balls to enter their sanctum and sit there not cracking a smile, as if it were all perfectly natural.

I finished my meal. I told myself to just be cool. I took my hat off and laid it on the table. The singsong conversations at the tables around me floated into the air and filled the room.

The door opened quickly and a nervous black man entered. His entrance was so tentative as to be an apology. He stared at me as if he were saying in his mind, "Boy, what the fuck you doin' sittin' up in here 'mongst all these white folks? You crazy?" He waited anxiously while the meal he had ordered was being prepared. It was clear that he didn't want to remain in the room one minute longer than he had to. When the order was ready, he paid and left, looking back over his shoulder at me as the door closed behind him. I sat picking my teeth, figuring that that would make me look tougher.

After a few more minutes of sitting there looking the place over, I got up, put my hat on, and walked toward the cash register.

"How was your meal?" the man who ran the place asked.

"Fine," I said. I paid him, went back to the table, left a tip, and walked out into the street. When I passed the glass window of the café, I peered inside and saw all those eyes still watching me. I saluted.

•   •   •

The man cursed loudly and drove his fist into the table top. The woman, whose face was puffy and dark, sat there expressionless, puffing a cigarette. The few other people inside the small black-operated café ignored the couple. I had been passing on the street when I heard the roar of the man's deep voice. The two men leaning against the plate-glass window outside were jiving each other and didn't seem to be paying any attention to what was happening inside. I stood in the doorway for a moment. Surely there was about to be a fight.

The man was short but heavily built, with thick shoulders and arms. His worn felt hat was cocked to the side of his head. His large eyes were filled with red blood vessels.

"Don't tell me that shit!" he said angrily. "I seent you with him!" He shoved a meaty finger in the woman's face. "I'll stomp your goddamn ass! Don't play that shit with me, woman!"

The woman sighed and looked away from the table, humming, as if her mind were traveling in another land.

"What the hell you looking at?" The man had turned on me. "This one of your *friends?*" he demanded of the woman.

I shook my head and backed out of the door. I thought he was going to get up from the table and come charging, but he kept his seat. The woman looked at me and smiled. I jammed my hand in my jacket pocket as I backed away.

"What you smiling for?" the man shouted at me.

"Minding my own business," I said. "I don't know nothin' 'bout you, you don't know nothin' 'bout me." The woman laughed. The man shouted something else that I couldn't quite make out, now that I was standing on the sidewalk, but it sounded like "punk motherfucker."

The two men outside were smiling and looking at me.

"What'd I do?" I asked. They shook their heads and shrugged their shoulders.

It was getting dark, and workmen were packing up their tools. They were finished for the day with restoration work they had been doing on the corner building that housed the small café and other black businesses.

"This is a tough town," I said. "Ain't nobody friendly?"

The two men smiled.

"Who owns this place?" I asked.

"Why you wanna know?" one of them, the younger one, asked.

"Just trying to be sociable," I said. "I'm new here."

"We know," he said. The other one smiled. This was worse than Charlotte. I knew I wasn't going to get anywhere with these guys.

"What's to do around here?" I asked pleasantly.

"Why you ask so many questions? That's all you do," the younger man said.

"How else can you learn?" I replied. They were not smiling. They seemed to be irritated with me. I stood there for a moment, looking at them look at me, before I slowly backed away to the curb and walked up the street toward my car. My ears were poised, listening for anybody who might be behind me, but nobody followed.

As I drove back to Americus, I thought about giving up on Dawson. In the two days I'd been snooping around there, I had gotten nothing but cold stares from nearly everyone I'd talked to.

• • •

The next morning when I woke up I knew I had to go back to Dawson for one more try. When I got there, I drove around town, taking the side streets and dirt roads, looking at the pitiful hovels some people lived in.

On one of the side streets, I wound up in the parking lot of a low-rent public-housing project, where a short stocky man in a skull cap was talking to a man in a pickup. The pickup drove off as I pulled into the lot.

I got out of the car and walked toward the stocky man. "How you doin'?" I asked.

"Passable," he said. We shook hands.

"Chester's my name," I said.

"Chester's my name, too," he said with a smile. "Alan Chester."

"Mine's Chester Fuller," I said. "I'm new around here, and I been having a helluva time getting anybody to tell me anything."

"People kinda tight with anybody they don't know 'round here," he said. "Where you from?"

"Atlanta," I said.

"You just visiting, passing through, looking for work, or what?"

"Looking for work," I said. "Actually, I'm a writer."

"Oh?"

"I'm writing about the South, how it has or hasn't changed for black people."

"Yeah?"

"I don't suppose you'd talk to me about your life here and what you think about the South over the last ten years or so?"

"I don't see why not," he said. I was surprised he agreed to talk so readily. I got my tape recorder from the car. Alan Chester told me he worked for the Dawson Housing Authority. His job was to make sure that things worked properly, including the plumbing, electrical devices, doors, windows — everything.

He said that only poor blacks, mainly single women with children, lived in the development we were standing in front of. Across town just a little ways was Dawson's other low-rent housing complex. According to Chester, only poor whites, mainly single women with children, lived there. There was no mixing of the races. "We tried to git some of the black people here to move in over there," Chester said, "but they wouldn't have no part of it. And it'd be just a plain waste of breath to try to git some whites to move in here. We just let 'em alone."

There were other things wrong with this town. Things that controlled peoples' lives, kept them in their places. Alan Chester knew about these circumstances that jerked people around like puppets. When he had stepped just a little beyond the role that had been expected of him, his own strings had been tugged, and it had nearly destroyed him.

The trouble had started a few years back. Chester was working for Stevens Industries, a large, diversified manufacturing concern. "I had been with Stevens for eleven years," he said. "The mess started after I bought a house on the [federal government's] 235 plan."

I watched this man closely as he talked. Telling the story seemed to hurt a little. He was a father of five, whose children ranged in age from three to eighteen. Earlier, he had told me how much it pained him that he couldn't afford to send his eighteen-year-old daughter to college, though she desperately wanted to go.

"See, I was 'bout to lose everything I had. That's why I left out from down there [Stevens]. Boy, that place down there, soon as they find out you bought an automobile or something, they fix you up where you can't make no hours.

"I see'd this was happening to me," he said. "I bought this house. House didn't cost but seventeen thousand dollars. I pay eighty-nine dollars and six cents a month. It ain't nothing fancy, but it's nice to us, 'cause we ain't been used to staying in nothing but what you might call a hut.

"I believe I was making a dollar eighty-five an hour at the time, driving a truck for Stevens," he said. "The house got four bedrooms and it's brick. We thought it was real nice, you know. We bought us some new furniture," he said with a smile. "Wasn't nothing fancy. We just didn't wanna put all that old junk in a new house.

"Well, everything was all right, I guess, until somebody down at the plant decided I was getting too big for my britches. First, I didn't know what it was. One week I put in six days and still they wouldn't let me make forty hours. Then I heard from somebody down there that one of the foremen didn't like it 'cause I bought a house in a new subdivision," he said.

"Man, it used to happen all the time. Somebody black git a new car, a new house, something nice, and all of a sudden they can't git no hours. A lot of people lost they houses behind that, lost they cars." He was quiet for a moment. I could see his mind working. He looked at me an instant before starting up again.

"First, I didn't think it was gon' happen to me, you know, 'cause I had been there eleven years," he said. "Done a good job for 'em, too. Never even brought 'em no speed tickets in all those years on the road."

There was pain in his face now as he continued. I found myself staring right into his eyes.

"I nearly lost everything," he said. "Everything. They wasn't letting me make no money and all those bills I had. I just couldn't make it. They would've starved me out.

"Don't git me wrong now," he said. "I don't think any of the big executives at Stevens knowed anything about this. I don't think they had nothing to do with it. It was these little old rat-rungs they got out there on the yard, these foremen — they didn't have no black foremen then. They didn't want you to git too close to what they had."

He told me he left Stevens to save himself from financial ruin. He went to work for the housing authority. But that was not the only full-time job he took at the time. He also went to work for a company that manufactures automobile bumpers. On the two jobs combined, he works eighty hours or more each week.

"It's the only way I can make it, feed my wife and kids," he said. "It's hard, but I always been willing to work. Just treat me fair, that's all I ask.

"Just about everybody 'round here trying to buy something nice got two jobs. You just don't git enough money per hour for a man to survive."

He told me he leaves his job with the housing authority at 5:00 P.M. each weekday. He then goes home and takes care of a few chores and naps for about an hour. Then he heads for his job at the manufacturing plant, where he works until around seven the next morning. After stopping at home for a little while, he heads back to the housing-authority job. This he has done for the past seven years.

"I don't really git sleepy until about Wednesday," he said. "I guess that comes from my days as a long-distance truck driver. I can go just about the whole week with little sleep, but on the weekends, man, I sleep the whole weekend. I don't have much time to enjoy my family, but I think they understand what I'm trying to do."

Even with two full-time jobs, life is still hard for Chester and his family. "With two jobs together, I still ain't making no money," he said. "I make a little over twelve thousand dollars a year, maybe as high as thirteen thousand. On my job at the plant, I bring home ninety dollars a week, after they take out. That ain't no money, but a whole lot of folks down here have to live this way. You have to, if you want anything decent for your family.

"So many people in this town working two full-time jobs must contribute to the high unemployment," I said. "That must be part of the reason why some people can't find one job."

He nodded his head in agreement. "That's bad," he said, "but what I'm supposed to do? I'm just trying to do good for my family, and ain't nobody got to give me nothing."

He told me that his birthplace was a few miles away, near Richland, Georgia, and that during the seventeen years he had lived in Dawson, he had seen some progress made in the relations between blacks and whites.

"You know," he said, "if you whup a cracker fair and square now, he just whupped. Used to be — and not long ago — white folks could do anything to you they want, and you couldn't fight 'em back. Now, you can whup they head."

His sentiments were similar to those of quite a few blacks I'd met elsewhere in the South. Many of these were older blacks who seemed to revel in the fact that at least they now had enough protection under the law to feel free to strike back at whites who tried to harm them.

"Another thing that's changed for the good," said Chester, "is that black women now got jobs in these mills and plants. They can git out of white folks' kitchens."

Not long after he said that, the noon whistle blew, and scores of black women spilled out of a nearby shirt-manufacturing company on their way to lunch.

"The thing now is to git some blacks running things in these plants," Chester said. "You ain't gon' ketch many young white fellows messing 'round in these mills and plants, though, 'cause ain't no money there. Most of them 'round here that don't hold some kind of office be carpenters, plumbers, something you can make some money at. 'Course, if they could come out there where I work and move right in as a foreman, they could make ten thousand dollars a year. But you can't come right in like that. They pretty much up to date out there. You got to come from the stump out there. They don't allow no discrimination at all, if they know about it.

"I just wish they paid enough money so I wouldn't have to work all the time. I don't wanna seem like I'm crying about it, 'cause I ain't. A man just do whatever it takes, you know? . . ."

I decided to go back to Americus to look in on my friends on Beale Street.

13

The Brothers Down Below

I WAS HAPPY. It was Friday, and I was going home for the weekend.

As I drove out of Americus that mild May evening, my whole body ached with anticipation, and I found myself smiling broadly and tapping my fingers against the steering wheel as a silly, cheerful melody ran through my head. I knew I would soon see my family.

• • •

The street lights were on when I turned onto my street in suburban DeKalb County and drove slowly past the houses of my neighbors. Many of them had mowed their lawns earlier in the day, and the smell of the freshly cut grass filled the warm night air. The street was still. No children played outside, and I was aware of the dull sound my tires made against the black-top.

The house was still standing, rising two stories into the darkening sky. My eyes scanned the brown bricks, the pale green paint and dark green shutters, and the row of green hedge under the living room windows.

The porch light was on. I pulled into the driveway slowly. When I got out of the car, there was a broad smile on my face. It had been a month since I'd seen them last. My wife and three daughters met me at the door. I reached out and grabbed them all, feeling their skin, hair, and bones. God, it was good to touch them, to hold them close.

I kissed them until my mouth was dry. At that moment, they were the four prettiest females in the world, and they loved me. Nothing else mattered now. Not the pains in my legs from the long drive home. Not the meal I had eaten with a poor family in Americus before I left for home — a meal of grits and eggs, which was all the family had. All that mattered was that I was home again, safe. We were together — my family and I — and it felt good.

The next day, to celebrate my homecoming, we fired up the gas grill in the back yard, put ribs and chicken on to cook, and stuffed a few beers into the freezer to get them ice cold. It was a scene from paradise — the meat sizzling on the grill, sending its alluring aroma skyward; the children running around the yard or playing on the gym set; and Pearl and I cooling it, sipping beer and waiting for the meat to get done. A storybook life, I thought.

When the meat was ready, I bathed it in barbecue sauce while Pearl rounded up the kids. This would be our first real meal of the day, and I couldn't wait to tear into it.

We sat down to eat. That's when it happened.

The meat stuck in my throat like a wad of bandages. I thought I was going to choke. I jumped up heaving for breath. Surely some strange sickness had seized me by the throat.

The storybook perfection was gone, shattered in an instant. Chills swept over me. Next came a tightness in the abdomen, as if I had already eaten too much. Then my body began to ache, the pain moving up my torso, through my limbs, and up my neck to my head. It became so intense I thought my head would burst like a ripe melon and splatter all over the patio.

Then the pain was gone as quickly as it had come, and I plopped down, tired and scared. A depression like heavy black mud settled on me, for I knew what was wrong.

I wanted to call Minter right away and tell him I'd had enough, that the project would have to end right then and there.

I did not want to face the poor anymore. I didn't want to go back to those shacks, with their rusting tin roofs and sagging floorboards, their broken-down furniture and cracked walls bearing pictures of the Last Supper, Jesus Christ, Martin Luther King, Jr., and John Kennedy.

I didn't want to stand in the dirt yards watching the flies buzz in and out of the torn screen doors, or look at the ravaged old sofas, leaking cotton and straw, on the porches and in the yards. I didn't want to see the babies in pissy diapers being followed by flies around the yards, playing happily, not yet understanding that they were doomed.

I was tired of playing the game of being poor. It had made me sick. It had made me feel guilty. Guilty because, for me, it was only a game. At any time while out there masquerading as a poor out-of-work soul, I could simply take off those secondhand clothes and head for my home in the suburbs, leaving all that misery behind.

As I sat there on my patio, I realized that that was exactly what I had done, and that was the root of my sickness. I understood just how far behind I had left all the poor people I'd met in the months I'd been on the road.

Here I was, cooling it with beer and barbecue, while the family I'd eaten grits with the day before in Americus was probably eating grits again, if they even had that. And what did Freddie Lee Mullins and his grandmother have on their dinner table? How could I have gotten so far away in only a few hours? How could I have forgotten all the pain so quickly? I was already turning my back on them again. And how could I? They were my people. They were me without my college degree, without my job and my middle-class lifestyle. They were me without the chance I'd had to climb the great American ladder of success.

In that frozen moment, I decided I would go back and face them again. I had to, for I realized that I bore them some responsibility.

Many of those to whom I had told the truth about my travels had thanked me for coming, for caring. They thought I had great power as a newspaper reporter, and that I might be able to help them with their problems. For them, I was a little ray of hope.

The bond was clear. They were my family too. No matter how poor they were. No matter how embarrassing they were with their niggerish ways and bad grammar. No matter how hopeless they felt. No matter how sad they made me feel. I could no longer go about my day-to-day life without thinking of them. They were a heavy burden to bear, but I would carry them as best I could.

I thought of Nadine Rouse in North Carolina, and what she had said about middle-class blacks, folks like me, the last time I saw her: "When blacks make it off the bottom, they don't even think about their brothers that's still down below. They just walk away and leave us like they don't want nobody to know this where they come from."

I wanted to let it all hang out — all the guilt I felt. I thought that if I got it out in the open, I could deal with it once and for all. I admitted to myself that I felt guilty because I had been too young to play an important part in the civil-rights movement of the fifties and early sixties.

I felt guilt because many others had gotten their heads bashed in, so that I could see my byline in the *Atlanta Journal.*

I felt guilt because of all the times I had been tired and hadn't wanted to hear from all those pro-black organizations who were trying to get articles in the paper about their upcoming protest marches and rallies.

I felt guilt because I had sometimes been short with them or failed to return their calls.

I felt guilt whenever I ran into down-and-out, unemployed old friends or classmates, who asked what I was doing. I hated to tell them I was a successful journalist, middle-class and all. It just didn't seem right.

With all that in the open, I felt a little better. I thought that at least I had a firmer grasp of who I was and where I was headed.

I thought more about the tremendous alienation that exists between middle-class blacks like myself and the forgotten poor. The gulf that separates us widens daily. Soon, it will be too wide to bridge. Poor blacks are beginning to hate us. One day, we will face each other across that gulf as strangers, perhaps even as enemies, and we won't even speak the same language.

We, the middle class, will be prisoners of our possessions, having to guard them with our lives. They, the poor, will desperately try to separate us from those possessions, so that they, too, can live. There will be no middle ground.

Perhaps it is already too late to stop this. The course is now being set. As the poor get poorer, falling further and further below the rest of us, racial distinctions will lessen in importance. We will be strictly a nation of those who have and those who don't have.

We must decide right now if that is what we want. Perhaps the decision has already been made, I thought as I sat on my patio, because fewer and fewer residents of the land of plenty are willing to venture into the land where the other people live — a land I will never be free of.

14

The Big Heart of Dixie

THE MAN followed me with his eyes. We were alone in the store. Outside, a handful of people moved cautiously through the downtown streets. Only one of them was black.

The man was biting down on his jaw, setting the muscles at the sides of his red face rippling. Breath came through his tensed nostrils in hard bursts. I continued to browse, looking over the stationery, the toiletries, and the rack where the transistor batteries hung like ornaments on a Christmas tree.

His eyes would not let me go, not even for a second. They encircled me like arms, and yet they were a camera, roving, moving in for close shots, then dollying back to keep me surrounded.

This man was disturbed.

"You gon' buy anything?" he finally asked.

"Just a minute," I said politely.

"You done looked over the whole place." He stood rigidly behind the counter, his left hand drumming the counter top, his right firmly gripping the cash register.

The eyes sneered at me. The struggle behind them was apparent. This man was trying desperately to maintain control over the powerful forces of hatred that swelled inside him. And he was losing the battle. I had irritated him beyond his ability to hold back the venom and anger, just by being there — by being black and casually strolling into the store as if it were perfectly normal, as if a war were not going on in the streets, the minds, and the hearts of this town. I had broken the code and ventured into his modest shop, which was being ruined by a boycott he couldn't understand, organized by nasty bands of nappy-haired pickets carrying signs and singing as they marched up and down the sidewalk outside the store every few days. He must have figured that I, a black, had come to survey the damage done by the picketing troops, had come to savor the success of the boycott, had come to watch him go down in defeat.

"Perhaps, if you'd tell me what you lookin' for, I could git it for you." Exasperation filled his voice and spread about the cluttered room, where trinkets hung from the ceiling, shelves of plastic-covered, brightly colored goodies hugged the walls, and glass cases containing jars, medicines, stuffed animals, candy bars, key chains, and other items rested on the tile floor like boxcars linked together in a train yard.

I could feel the heavy sighs that issued from his burly middle-aged body. He hated me even though he didn't necessarily want to. He hated me because he had to: because I was black and I was there in front of him while a boycott blacks had staged against the town merchants was scaring shoppers away and hurting him and his fellow store owners something fierce.

"I think I'll take these batteries here," I said, trying to sound the least bit cooperative. "How much are they?"

"They marked," he said sternly, "right there on the side."

"What about one of those candy bars, the Baby Ruth?" I said, pointing through the glass case.

"What about 'em?" he asked sarcastically.

"I'll take one."

"Three thirty-five, plus tax," he said, fingering the cash register. "You wanna sack?"

"Yes, of course," I said. He put the items in a paper bag, still watching me with indignation in his eyes, still grinding his jaw teeth.

"I'm not from around here," I said. "Just passing through."

"I can see that."

"Tell me, what's going on in this town? Everybody acting so strange . . ."

"If I was you, I'd just keep right on going. What's going on in this town is certain people need to be taught a lesson."

"Oh?"

"If I was you, I wouldn't hang around to see it happen. And it's gon' happen, sooner or later."

"I heard something about a shooting. What's that all about?"

"That's po-leece bizness. I don't wanna talk about it. You want anything else?" He was looking at the sack he had handed me only moments before.

"No. I think this ought to do it."

"You best be gittin' on then," he said firmly. "It'll be gittin' dark soon. If I was you, I wouldn't wanna be out on the streets at night right now. Crime's just got outta hand. Anything liable to happen."

I moved toward the door, looked back, stopped. "You have a good day," I said smiling, then moved through the door and out onto the nearly deserted sidewalk. The bell on the door clanged behind me, and I heard him mumble something that sounded like "bastard" before the door swished completely closed.

As I made my way along the sidewalk toward the side street where my car was parked, an elderly white couple approached — a pleasant-faced woman with strawlike white hair, and a thin, rubbery man with a cane. As they came closer, I inched aside enough so that they could pass easily. The old man nodded and the woman said, "Thank you, young man," and managed a frightened smile. I was stunned. It was the first time a white person had spoken to me on the street during the three days I had been in town.

I turned and watched the old couple hobble down the street and finally disappear around a corner. "Thank you, young man" rang in my mind. It was a simple phrase, but it was magnified in my thoughts because it was the first kind thing anybody had said to me, the first courtesy. I had almost forgotten about words like *courtesy* since I'd entered Gadsden, Alabama, but now I felt a little lifted up.

In a town on the brink of choosing up sides, with each side trying to gut the other, a little old man and a white-haired woman had smiled at me and offered a kind word. I found myself smiling as I hurried to my car.

• • •

That night I moved cautiously through Gadsden's dark streets, convinced that if anything tragic was going to befall me on my assignment, it would happen here, where fear and hatred, boycotts and pickets, already had the city on the verge of a violent explosion; where daytime sidewalks were filled with the intolerant glares of angry white merchants; and where, by night, numerous city police officers reputedly abandoned their blue uniforms of public duty for the white robes and pointed hoods of the Ku Klux Klan.

My fear of Gadsden bordered on paranoia, and local blacks had repeatedly warned me to be extra careful not to get "mistaken" for an outside agitator, in town to stir up more racial trouble. I had been told to be particularly wary at night. "These white folks in Gadsden don't play," one stern-faced black youth had warned.

I was glad that the meeting I wanted to attend on that particular evening was at a church in the black community, where I felt more at ease when moving about at night. The church was located on Henry Street, in a neighborhood I had come to know fairly well from roaming the streets on the black side of town for the past three days.

Because of the extensive publicity the racial troubles in Gadsden had garnered, I knew before I arrived that the situation was extremely tense. A sinister feeling had passed over me the moment I first crossed the railroad tracks and drove into the downtown area. Downtown seemed nearly deserted. Only a few cars were parked here and there on the main streets, and a few blacks and whites moved about like robots, keeping out of one another's way.

Police cruised the streets so frequently that they resembled an occupying military force making sure it could maintain control over the town it had just overrun.

Across the tracks and the highway, in the heart of the black community, anger and fear were widespread. There were those who ranted and raved at the drop of a hat about the things wrong with the town, and there were those who backed inside and closed their doors the minute you asked them about the racial troubles.

At the heart of all this was a twenty-seven-year-old black man with a wife and four young children, who had been gunned down in January by four Gadsden police officers. They had shot him fifteen times with weapons ranging from .357 magnum pistols to a shotgun, even though he had first been stopped for a traffic violation and was unarmed.

It was the shocking killing of Collis Madden that had rekindled the old fires of racial hatred and misunderstanding in Gadsden and brought the black and white citizens there to the point of attacking one another.

That incident, and the city's staunch refusal to fire the officers involved, had thrust many of the black residents of Gadsden into the streets, marching, picketing, boycotting, demanding the heads of the four lawmen. Since January, they had managed to get thousands into the streets for marches. People had come from all over the country — civil-rights activists, politicians. At one march alone, more than 3000 filled the streets of this industry-rich northern Alabama town where 25 percent of the more than 60,000 residents are black, where the bulk of those out of work are black, and where black residents wield far less political influence than their sheer numbers would indicate.

I had often been met with silence when I stopped older blacks on the streets of the black community and asked them about the shooting of Madden and the ongoing protest that resulted. Some merely looked up with pained faces and hollow eyes and said: "A shame the way they shot that boy. A cryin' shame."

One elderly lady wearing a black-trimmed red apron over a rumpled dress looked at me through teary eyes and backed me against the wall of her housing project with a bony finger, declaring in whimpers and sobs, "They jes killin' these boys like dogs. God in heaven know it's a shame. These young folks better wake up to what's happ'nin' to 'em. Lord 'a mercy." She backed off shaking her wrinkled head. "Don't mind me," she said. "Don't nobody else do."

Many younger blacks acted as if they were afraid to be seen talking to me. Some even asked me if I was in town to stir up more confusion and mess. They felt that if I was, they would suffer reprisals on their jobs. They told me that many of their friends had already been laid off by some of the companies around town, after being spotted participating in marches or pickets.

"Jobs 'round here too hard to come by if you black, to lose 'em like that," one young woman, with four children and no husband to help out, had told me. "You have to be cool, 'cause you never know who watching, and it might git back up there to Goodyear [the tire and rubber manufacturer], and your job could be gone."

Those who didn't avoid me like a leper were generally the ones who had been taking to the streets to fight the oppression of the "Klan-run police department" and the apparently insensitive city governing body, and it was through these vigilant souls that I had picked up word of the mass meeting to be held at the Union Baptist Church on Henry Street. It was to be a strategy session for the "continuing struggle."

Ahead of me, moving like ghosts through the dim evening streets, were weary blacks making their way to this meeting. They greeted each other weakly on the concrete steps of the old church, their voices announcing their fatigue.

For a long while, I stood outside watching them enter. It was like standing at the mouth of the tunnel in a stadium, watching bone-tired football players in dirty armor file through to the locker room, to rest and regroup for the second half. These people were meeting here to regroup, for their present struggle had begun in January, and it was now mid-May. There had been countless marches, pickets, and strategy sessions before this one.

They were mainly young and early-middle-aged people, though a few old heads were among them. Many of them were younger than I, and for me the Montgomery bus boycott and many of the other protests of the fifties and early sixties were just remembered images from the old Huntley-Brinkley Report. Television stood between me and those struggles in the streets of the South, between me and the vicious billy clubs of brutal state troopers and the slashing teeth of police dogs. Most of the young ones, like me, had watched the civil-rights and black movements from the comfort of their own living rooms.

The others — the ones marked by those early battles, carrying clear signs that they'd been through this sort of thing before — made me feel guilty, because I had not been there, had not shed my blood in a Birmingham jail or on the Edmund Pettis Bridge.

So far, I had been able to gloss over this feeling of discomfort and guilt by convincing myself that protest marches were a thing of the past, virtually meaningless in the present day, when the struggle was being fought on what I thought was a more sophisticated level. But here in Gadsden, there were people in the streets marching, singing, demonstrating. My rationalizations were being put to a test. Would they gain anything? Would their actions bring about the changes they desired? I had already seen one angry downtown merchant whose business had been badly hurt by their boycott. Maybe it was working.

Adding to my discomfort was the long-held fear I had of Alabama in general. I had grown up in Georgia in mortal fear of Alabama. During my childhood, friends and neighbors and the radio and television sets in our home told horror stories daily. There were bombings of black churches, vicious beatings of blacks by the Klan or by rowdy whites, attacks by police dogs, and descriptions of white firemen leveling crowds of protesting black men, women, and children with blasts from powerful water hoses. The sinister figure of George Corley Wallace stood in the doorway of the University of Alabama, blocking entrance to black students. I had the impression that no black person in Alabama could safely leave his house unless escorted by a contingent of national guardsmen.

And then there was the supposedly humorous story that made the rounds in the black community where I grew up, causing me days and nights of worry before I knew better. According to this story, signs were posted at intervals along the Alabama border that warned: "Read this, niggers, and run. And if you can't read, run anyway."

When I was a young elementary-school student, I heard the story of that sign so many times that I was terrified of Alabama, and I determined to make sure my feet never crossed that border. In my young mind, Alabama — the state that called itself the Heart of Dixie — came to symbolize the evil of the world.

I can remember sitting home with my parents many evenings in the late fifties and early sixties, watching film on the evening news that showed civil-rights marchers being clubbed and kicked all over the streets of Alabama by police officers and state troopers. I always wondered why those poor black folks hadn't paid attention to that sign and gotten the hell out of Alabama.

And though I knew better by the time I crossed the Alabama line, heading toward Gadsden at the beginning of the week, I had looked around for that sign, just to make sure it wasn't there.

• • •

The Union Baptist Church was warm inside, and the familiarity of the appointments made me feel immediately welcome. There is something about almost any church that is comforting at times when you're a little shaken by being in a new place. You always know how a church is going to look when you open the door and peer inside.

I sat down near the back amidst a group of people I had already seen or talked to during my stay in town. They looked up and smiled as I sat down. There were only about fifty or sixty people present. The leaders — two ministers and the president of the town's chapter of the Southern Christian Leadership Conference (SCLC) — had called the meeting and now stood below the pulpit, waiting to see if any late stragglers were forthcoming. After several minutes, the youngest of the three — Joseph Cole, the SCLC head — told a youth in the back of the church to close the door.

One of the ministers led us in prayer, asking for God's guidance during this "awfully hard hour of struggle." After the prayer, the man led the gathering in the singing of spirituals. It was like Sunday service. We started softly, slowly, like a boat swaying gently on the water. Gradually the feeling inside us grew feverish until we all clapped and stomped our feet in time to the surge inside our bodies. I looked around the small church and saw heads thrown back, mouths open, eyes closed, the singing rising to fill the room. It was powerful and it never failed. There is always something strengthening in spirituals, something liberating. The uplifting beat seemed to pull the walls of the tiny building closer around us, as if protecting us. Even the ceiling seemed to kneel to comfort us. I felt safe in that house of singing.

The singing calmed to a slow, lingering hum, with many heads still tilted back and eyes tightly closed. Bodies swayed softly now. The clapping and foot stomping had died away.

"In slavery time," the minister declared, "we got together down at the river and did exactly what we doing now. Oh yes. We ain't forgotten to this day, and can't ever forget, where we came from and who we are," he said. "From that time to this, it's been one battle after another." He looked out over the meager crowd shaking his head, his hands grasping the air.

"But we still here. Hear what I say? We still here, Gadsden, Alabama, and we gon' be here. White folks can think we just gon' lay down and die all they want to, but we got news for 'em. We gon' stand up and be counted 'til we get what's right. They can't go on killing us and beatin' us. Sending the Klan into our neighborhoods with the Gadsden Police Department, treating us any way they want to." The humming stopped.

"That's right," somebody from the audience shouted.

"Amen," said another.

"Now they've been surprised we been able to keep this thing up since January," he said. "We've had thousands of folks out in the streets. We've boycotted the stores downtown and in the mall. It's hurtin' 'em. Make no mistake about it, it's hurtin' 'em.

"But they've been expecting us to fall by the wayside," he said. "And some of us have. Each march, we dwindle just a bit. The white folks been praying for rain, 'cause they don't think we'll get out there and march or picket in the rain, but they just don't know. I say, we gon' keep movin', even if we get down to just me and Joseph Cole out there in the street, 'cause I know Joe Cole's gon' be there."

"I'll be wit' you," a man shouted.

"Me too," a woman said, "be right there every time. I don't care what nobody say. They can't take my job, 'cause ain't got nane to take. They wouldn't give me nane in the first place."

"Teach, sister," a young man said. "That's another thing we got to stay on 'em about, these jobs. All these plants and things 'round here, and they ain't givin' up no jobs."

"And those of us working at Goodyear and some of these other places," an older man said, "got to be careful, 'cause if they was to find out we at this meetin', I don't have no doubt our jobs wouldn't be there in the morning."

"That's right," a woman shouted.

"These things we up against, the things we fighting," the minister said. "And you can't forget this. Some of them who started out with us ain't here tonight. Some of them gon' be at the march tomorrow, I know that. They just couldn't be here tonight. But many have dropped off and we ain't gon' get nothing changed in this town by dropping off.

"Remember how hard it was for Jesus, but he stayed with it," he said. "We are meeting right now in the Lord's house. I pray that He is with us, 'cause with His help we gon' make it. And that ain't nothing but the truth."

He looked back to let Cole know he was ready for him to talk. "I'm gon' turn you over to our president, Joseph Cole, you all know him. He's brought us this far."

Cole was a tall, thin, dark-skinned man with close-cropped hair that made him appear boyish, though his voice was the voice of a man. His body was athletic and looked charged with energy, as if it would be no strain at all for him to crouch and leap skyward until his head touched the ceiling. He had the body of a basketball player, and the wide, innocent eyes of a schoolboy, but there was something about him that made you know this man was a leader.

The gathering quieted down and listened when he moved forward and began to speak.

"I know you're tired," he said. "I'm tired, too. We all are, but we haven't done anything yet. The time to rest is not now. We got this thing started, and we're going to finish it, if it kills us.

"I'm not going to talk long. I just want to say we appreciate your support and hanging in there. It's been tough. I know a lot of you got discouraged when we marched down to City Hall the other day to get into the commission meeting, and found out they had held the meeting earlier so they could get by us. But don't worry," he said calmly, with a slight smile on his lean face. "We got something for 'em. We definitely got something for 'em.

"Now tomorrow, we'll meet here about eight-thirty, right in front of the church here. We'll start the march at ten. I want you — everybody here tonight — to go home and call somebody up and tell 'em to come on out to the march. We need 'em, and they need to be in that march. There aren't many things any of us could be doing tomorrow that's more important than that march. These people are shooting us down. And I don't have to tell you Madden wasn't the first. But what we're here for tonight is to make sure Madden is the last."

"Amen."

"Preach it, doctor!"

"Tell the truth."

"Now," Cole said, "people got to understand the importance of this. A little marching now may mean you won't have to run in the future.

"Now we're going to line up at the church. The police department wants to provide us an escort, so we won't tie up too much traffic. They want to know the route we plan to take. We haven't told 'em, and we probably won't. That's their problem.

"Please, though, we don't want any violence. We've got to remain nonviolent, because if things get out of hand, that's exactly what they want to happen. We'll be playing right into their hands. The mayor has been going around calling me a troublemaker, a radical. He says we don't represent the law-abiding citizens of Gadsden. Don't worry about it. We know what we're doing and who we represent. But it's important to keep control. We can't have violence. And if anything happens, let them start it so everybody can see them for what they really are.

"When they come in our neighborhoods at night — the police and the Klan — to harass us, I say protect yourselves. I'm gon' protect myself. But these marches got to be nonviolent.

"Another thing I want to say at this point." He looked over the crowd carefully, from one end of the room to the other and back again. "There are spies among us. I don't know who or why, but every time we have one of these planning sessions, the white folks know what we going to do before we do it. All I got to say is I hope I never find who it is."

At this point, I noticed that a number of people had turned to look in my direction. It was the first time I had realized how heavy the camera was that rested in my lap.

"I want everybody who's with us on this to put up your hands," Cole said. "Show it by raising your hands." Hands flew up immediately. I didn't raise mine. All eyes were on me now.

Cole finally spoke, after staring at me for several seconds. "I'm curious about you," he said. "I don't believe I know you. You're not from here. Who are you with?"

Suddenly the pew I was sitting on seemed extremely hard, and my body began to ache from its cold hardness. It was as if all the flesh of my body had melted away, leaving my bones, brittle and cold, against the tough wood. I knew I had to tell them the truth, but even that worried me. I wondered if I would believe such a story as mine, if I were in their shoes.

"Actually, I'm a writer from Atlanta," I said, after several moments of hard thought. "I'm with the *Atlanta Journal*."

"Yeah," Cole said. An undertone of conversation swept across the room. Soon the whole church was buzzing.

"They sent you down here to see how bad these white folks are in Gadsden?" Cole asked.

"I'm traveling all over the South, seeing how black people are living now as compared to ten, fifteen years ago. I read about the troubles here and decided to come."

"Why didn't you just let us know who you were and what you were doing?" he asked. "I could've told you a lot."

"I've been trying to just blend in wherever I go, and observe. I've found you pick up more that way, and get a better feel for a place."

"You going to do a write-up in the *Journal* about Gadsden?" he asked.

"I'm pretty sure I will," I said.

"That's all right," he said smiling, "that's all right. You better be careful in Gadsden, though. Strange things happen to black folks here at night. Just be on guard. You going to be here tomorrow?"

"I'll be here."

"Good. Good."

The meeting went on, but when interest in me died down a bit I took the opportunity to ease out of my seat and make it to the door. Outside the church, I heard the singing start up again. I made my way through the scores of cars parked along the street and got into my car and left. As I topped the hill, I could see them through the back window of my car, as weary as when they had come, filing out of the tiny church, down the concrete steps into the dim streets. I didn't write in my journal that night but went right to bed. Just watching them and being among them had made me tired.

* * *

Someone was calling my name in a strange, shrill voice that penetrated my sleeping mind. The sound seemed to bounce off the inside walls of my head like a handball, forcing me into consciousness. The room was filled with light. It took several seconds for me to realize I was in a motel room again. I scanned the mediocre surroundings — the empty hollywood bed next to me, the portly television set with its expressionless face, the drab wallpaper, the nondescript carpeting, and the chair that could have come from the office of one of those down-and-out TV private eyes.

The room immediately threatened to pull me into that weightless mood of mediocrity and blandness brought on by awakening day after day in motel rooms filled with tasteless, character-less American wall hangings and furniture.

But the voice, that shrill voice, was there, just outside the window. I looked at my watch. It was seven. The voice spoke again, but unclearly. It was not my name being called. It was gibberish. I drew the curtains open, fanning away the dust. On the railing of the landing was a small grayish-brown bird with its tiny chest puffed out. The bird was making the noise. When I cracked the door to get a better look at it, it flew away, leaving me wondering whether it had somehow been sent to wake me by someone or something. I dismissed the thought as silly and headed for the shower.

It was a beautiful spring day, with a few people milling about downtown. The sun, already moving high in the sky, filled the valleys between the modestly tall buildings with warm, face-tingling light. I drove up to city hall, a new municipal building of smooth gray stone and glass which sat hugging the banks of the river that rushed past downtown in little sun-drenched ripples. With the sun reflecting off the new buildings and divid-ing into a rainbow, the whole area seemed to dance in the bright colors. It was a perfect day for a protest march, absolutely no rain in sight. Around city hall, however, police cars were everywhere, and burly, red-faced officers moved about the area with deadly serious expressions on their faces. Many had, no doubt, been called in on their days off, because of the impend-ing march, and it was obvious that they didn't like it one bit. There would be trouble, I thought. Those guys didn't appear to be in the mood for any nonsense. I made sure I had the camera and enough film to last.

•   •   •

On Henry Street, at least 200 charged-up black folks were lining up for the march. The roar of their combined conversations made them sound even larger in number than they were. After several minutes of getting lined up properly and receiving last-minute instructions, the marchers were off, and I fell in beside them, camera at the ready. We hadn't gone fifty feet yet, and already

I missed the security of my press card. It wouldn't be there to save me when the head-whipping started. Even though I walked alongside the column of marchers and wore the camera around my neck, I knew the police would treat me as one of the demonstrators. I wasn't dressed like a newsman. My head would get beaten, too.

• • •

In a spur-of-the-moment move intended to irritate the police escort leading the march, the demonstrators turned off the main artery of the black community, onto Sixth Street, cutting through one of Gadsden's largest and shabbiest low-rent public-housing complexes. The police were temporarily confounded, but, with much halting of traffic and hasty maneuvering, they managed to get in front of the advancing column once again.

Wide-eyed children and slouched-over elderly men and women, with the light of hope gone from their eyes, stared at the singing, clapping demonstrators as they moved through the poverty-ridden reservation. Off to the side, a knot of black youths had gathered on the cracked sidewalk as the marchers went by. Ignoring the police escorts, the youths were shooting dice. They talked loudly, arguing about who had what point to make next.

"Nine your point, nigger!" one shouted adamantly. "Don't try to pull that shit on me, boy."

The police ignored them, apparently feeling that the 200 marchers who refused to stay on an agreed-upon route through the city were enough for them to handle at the moment. After seeing that the police weren't going to interfere with the gambling, more youngsters moved over to join in the game.

"I got two on my man," one deep voice proclaimed.

"You bar this, then, chump," someone answered.

Cole, marching at the head of the line, was shouting for the black onlookers to join the march. Very few did. I could see the anger rising in his dark face as he shook his head in disgust.

"You'd better come on and walk with us today," he commanded, "or you sure 'nough gon' be running from the white folks tomorrow." His legions shouted their amens.

"Walk with us today," he repeated at the top of his voice, "or you'll be running from the white folks tomorrow. Walk with us today, or you'll be running from the white folks tomorrow. Walk with us today. A lot of y'all gon' be needing our help tomorrow. But you won't try to help yourselves today."

It seemed to take us forever to reach the heart of downtown, and by the time we turned onto the main avenue, a crowd of whites littered both sides of the street, forming a corridor for us to walk through. Police were in evidence everywhere. At one of the corners at the foot of the hill that leads up to the municipal complex, I saw two police-department sharpshooters atop a bank building, their high-powered rifles aimed at the glut of marchers in the street below. To make sure they saw me, I slowly aimed my camera, stopped, and took several photographs of them as best I could with the sun shining down into my face. When they saw me, they hid the rifles behind their backs. One of them waved.

Scores of blue-uniformed police officers in riot gear, carrying the longest billy sticks I'd ever seen, guarded city hall as if it were a medieval castle.

The marchers advanced in solid, determined steps until they were pressed chest-to-chest with the stern-faced cops who stood shoulder-to-shoulder, like a human wall, blocking the front doors of city hall. The marchers continued to advance until the opposing groups were pressed together into a tight sandwich of struggling humanity, arms and legs driving to resist the force in front of them, with the cops — nearly blue in the face from the pressure — dying to use those sticks, and the vigorous protestors singing loudly that they would not be turned around.

Behind the tangle of humans rooting at the door like several teams of rugby players going after a fumble, a half-circle of billy-stick-wielding cops surrounded the action, deep scowls showing through the plastic faceguards on their gleaming helmets.

Each time I stepped back to position myself outside the circle of enforcers, the officers moved back in unison, making sure to keep me within their ring of attack. Amidst the scuffling for position at the glass doors, deep grunts and groans issued from the contestants. Finally, Cole emerged from the huddle of bodies and demanded to speak to the mayor.

"This is our city hall," he asserted. "Every time we come up here, the door's closed. We paid for this building, and the mayor is here to serve us, too. Now all we ask is for him to meet with us."

"He ain't gon' talk to you long as you acting like this," said a small white-haired man in uniform, whom I later discovered was the chief of police.

"We can't get to see him any other way," one of the marchers retorted.

"He acts like he's scared of us," Cole said. "We just want to talk, that's all."

"We ain't scared of you," shouted a young red-faced cop who stood with a crowd of other officers on the lawn at the corner of the building. He was swinging his billy club back and forth in front of his burly body.

"As long as you insist on this kind of approach," the white-haired man said, "you ain't got nothing to talk to the mayor about. Besides, he ain't here."

"We're not welcome in our own city hall?" Cole asked.

"Not like this, you're not. I suggest y'all go on home."

It was hot by now, with the sun high above the buildings.

"All right," Cole said coolly, "everybody sit down right here in front of the door. If we can't go in there today, ain't nobody else going in there either. We'll sit here 'til closing time," he said to the chief.

"Well, buddy, we'll be right here with you."

After several hours, the tension had not lifted. The marchers continued to occupy the landing in front of the building, and the itchy cops paced around them like caged animals. Hatred filled the air like napalm. The least little ripple could have caused a disastrous explosion. The demonstrators had finished eating sandwiches they had ordered from one of the cafés on the black side of town, and Cole was making sure they picked up all the paper and other litter they had discarded on the ground. "We're going to leave this place as clean as we found it," he said.

The chief and a few of his men were now surveying the situation from a patrol car parked in the lot of the building. Everybody was tired now. Nerves were more on edge than ever. We were close to violence, I knew. My body shook in involuntary spasms, indicating just how close we were to warfare. I prayed nobody would get hurt.

Cole was working hard, talking to his people, trying to make jokes with them, keep them loose. He too, could sense the storm that lurked overhead, and I knew that was the last thing he wanted, for he realized that it would destroy everything he had worked for. Violence on the part of the marchers would taint the whole effort and would make the police seem justified in whatever brutal means they employed to quell it. He knew the cops would like nothing more than to be let loose on those who had caused them so much mental anguish.

"We've served our purpose today," he said in a self-assured voice. "We've made our point. Let's stay cool. Let them make the mistake, not us."

Off to the side, a group of officers were chuckling on the lawn next to a stand of trees. "Hey you," one of them yelled to a pretty young black woman. "I bet you can't pull a train." His companions doubled over with laughter, but the woman's husband, who had observed the incident, dashed for the officer who had made the remark. Several marchers rushed over to restrain him.

The cop, bent into a fighter's crouch, shoved the billy stick forward, then slapped it hard against the palm of his hand. "Come on!" he shouted. "Let the nigger go, let him go!"

The chief rushed from his parked car. The marchers hauled their companion away kicking and screaming.

"Let the sumbitch go!" the husky cop shouted after them. "Turn 'im loose!" The other officers continued to laugh, slapping their palms against their knees.

Transfixed by the experience, I could not move. My mind saw what was happening, and I thought, Oh God, this is it! I couldn't even raise the camera to my face. The scene somehow transported me back to an earlier incident, a day of bloody, club-swinging mayhem.

Suddenly, I was in the middle of Auburn Avenue in Atlanta, scribbling furiously in my notepad as scores of blue-suited, riot-equipped police officers beat and kicked hundreds of screaming black men, women, and children who were trying to stage a protest march without a parade permit.

I will never forget the viciousness of the attack. And it was 1974, not the Jim Crow fifties, not the riotous sixties. Nineteen hundred and seventy-four, one hundred and ten years after the Emancipation Proclamation. And it was not Birmingham or some place in Mississippi. It was Atlanta, Georgia, the Belle of the South, the city too busy to hate, the city with the best race relations in the country, the first major city in the South to have a black mayor.

Atlanta was a city with a black population approaching 60 percent, whose white residents were fleeing as rapidly as the surrounding expressways could carry them to the safety of the growing white suburbs. It was a city caught in the lie that was its image to the outside world.

The demonstration had been planned by Reverend Hosea Williams, then president of the Atlanta SCLC. During the movement days, Williams had been one of Martin Luther King's top lieutenants. He was the rabble-rouser. He would precede King into a town, stir things up, and get the black residents ready, so King could come in and show them the way out of their troubles. Williams was always referred to as a bull in a china shop. He was a street fighter, a scrapper, and he was effective.

Williams had called the march to protest the rising brutality practiced against black citizens by the Atlanta Police Department, under the leadership of its tough chief, John Inman. During the previous year, some twenty young blacks had been shot down and killed by members of the department's stakeout, decoy, and regular patrol squads. The latest victim was a sixteen-year-old kid, who had been shot by an officer while the boy was supposedly tussling with the officer's partner over the patrolman's gun.

Incensed by the string of killings — all ruled justifiable homicide by the department's internal overseers — Williams led a series of protests at city hall and at the police station, demanding that Inman be ousted as chief and that excessive violence on the part of Inman's men be halted.

But this march against death, which Williams had conceived during the protests outside city hall and the police station, was a brilliant scheme. It had all the potential for drama that the early sit-ins had had. He intended to bring the whole situation — the killings by the police, the racial climate in Atlanta, the struggle between the black mayor and white police chief for control over an essentially black city — starkly into the public eye.

It was a stroke of genius. The body of the sixteen-year-old youth slain by the officer's gun would be hauled through the streets of Atlanta atop the mule-drawn wagon that had carried the stilled body of Martin Luther King, Jr., to its resting place six years before.

The mother of the youth at first agreed to the plan, but backed down at the last minute because of pressure from city officials and from then-governor Jimmy Carter, who was already preparing for his 1976 run for the presidency.

Angered by the turn of events that threatened the success of the march, Williams vowed that the protest would go on, even if he had to ride atop the wagon himself.

"I've been asked not to go on with this march," Williams told the crowd gathered across from King's gravesite — the scheduled starting point for the demonstration. "City officials, the mayor, preachers all over this town have asked me not to do it," he shouted. "They appealed to the boy's mama, and she decided at the last minute not to let us use the body. But we're going to have a body — mine. And I'm not listening to these chicken-eating, money-loving, Cadillac-driving, bullshitting preachers. We're gon' have a march!"

Williams and his lieutenants pulled the creaking wagon by the yoke, and hundreds lined up behind it as the march began. People littered the sidewalks of Auburn Avenue, staring keenly to see what the police were going to do, because the marchers had refused to apply to the police department for a parade permit, and Inman had vowed to stop the march as an illegal parade.

"We don't need no permit to march," Williams had declared. "It's our right, and nobody gon' take that away."

The marchers sang and clapped as they passed the King entombment and the Ebenezer Baptist Church, where the young King had succeeded his father as minister. The rain that had threatened for several days held back as the marchers moved up Auburn through a cheering sidewalk throng toward downtown.

Something curious was happening. At each side street leading off Auburn, I noticed police officers, in cars or on motorcycles, blocking the streets to traffic trying to reach Auburn. Were they cooperating with the marchers?

The singing shouts of the demonstrators filled the air, and reporters and camera crews were busy running in front of and alongside them as they charged onward.

As the procession neared Courtland Street, there was a sudden ominous silence. The roar of the singing and shouts of the protesters had ended abruptly. There was a slight, almost imperceptible, hesitation in the march, the wheels of the wagon slowing to a crawl before picking up speed again. Walking backward, facing the marchers, I could not immediately see what they had seen ahead. When I turned to see what had caused them to pause, I was almost blinded by the shocking blue glare of brilliant sunlight reflected off the dark blue uniforms of the sullen cops who stood shoulder to shoulder across Auburn Avenue, from sidewalk to sidewalk, like a massive human fence, each man wearing a riot helmet and wielding a billy stick. I looked across the line they formed with their blue-suited bodies, and the image of all those black boots glistening in the sun struck me like a hammer. The men were so close together that it was impossible to see the street behind them. Only the tall buildings of downtown Atlanta rose above them, assuring me that there was still a world behind their backs. The cops stood silently, their eyes bearing down on the marchers.

Williams led his legions on. When the column of marchers reached the blue wall, a police major stepped forward and warned the marchers that they were conducting an "illegal" demonstration and that if they didn't end the march, the police would be forced to act. Williams and his lieutenants listened intently to the major. When the officer was finished, those pulling the wagon began to move ahead, closer to the human wall. Someone pushed the wagon from behind, and it surged into the wall.

With that, the police rushed into the marchers, grabbing and swinging. The wagon, a relic, was smashed back against the curve, buckling on its back wheels. People went down and children screamed as they scurried to get clear of the collapsing wagon.

Marchers cried out in agony as billy sticks crashed against their skulls, shoulders, and faces. It was a nightmare of horrid sounds — screams, shouts (OH MY GOD! DON'T HIT ME NO MORE PLEASE! OH LORD, DON'T KILL ME! DON'T STOMP MY BABY!), the wicked sounds of wood meeting flesh, clothes tearing, and boots crunching and skidding against the pavement of the street.

People went to their knees, twisting, swinging, trying to get away. Cops straddled marchers prone on the concrete, pinning them down and beating them about the head with their sticks. The demonstrators tried to run, pushing themselves to their feet in an effort to escape the onslaught of the bloodthirsty fighting force, but their escape routes were blocked by Atlanta police cars or uniformed troops on motorcycles.

It was a well-planned massacre. Yet it was surreal and civilized, if savagery can ever appear civilized. Even in the midst of all the flying billy sticks, the kicks, the knees to the groin and the back, even as I heard lips burst from the impact of the licks, and bones creak from the blows, I was never struck by the sticks swinging all around me, for I was working in my suit and tie, with my press card and notebook to protect me.

Within moments, the mounted patrol had entered the fray. Cops on horseback waded into the crowd swinging their sticks, their horses knocking down and trampling those who couldn't get out of the way. Cops came near me and almost swung at me, but when they saw that I was writing in my notepad, they diverted their blows onto the heads of less fortunate souls. My hand ached from trying to write it all down, all the madness.

The struggle seemed to go on forever, until finally the horses began to back away. Most of the marchers had been rounded up and thrown into paddy wagons. The cries had died to whimpers and occasional pleas for help from those captured.

As I raced downtown to follow up on the charges against those arrested, what stuck in my mind was the image of that beaten and broken wagon slumping like a wounded paraplegic in the debris-littered street. For me, at that moment, it was a sad symbol of the civil-rights movement in the South in the seventies. That wagon couldn't get up off its knees. It was a has-been, a relic, a ghost of things past, just like the NAACP, SCLC, CORE, and a score of other old civil-rights groups that were still desperately trying to hang on to memories of the glory days, the days when they were wanted and supported, the days when they walked with their heads high, carrying the hopes and dreams of a people on their shoulders. Now they were all broken-down wagons with no proud black stallions to pull them.

●   ●   ●

The noise made by the small cluster of cops gathered on the grass taunting the demonstrators brought me back to the city hall in Gadsden, Alabama, where Joseph Cole was rounding up his marchers so they could go home. It was past 5:00 P.M. now, and all the city employees had left work. The marchers had done their duty for that day, Cole told them.

"They knew we were here," he said. "You better believe they knew it. And they know we'll be back until we get what we want."

The cops in the cluster made faces and threw slurs, but Cole got his people away from the complex without incident. They were tired from the day-long siege. There would be another meeting at the church that night, and the demonstrations would continue.

●   ●   ●

In America, hilltop living is usually reserved for the rich, who have a penchant for hanging their expensive houses precariously on the faces of our cities' tallest mounds. Take, for instance, the lavish homes that dot the northern California mountainsides.

But the hill that affords a panoramic view of Gadsden — the

river winding its way gently past downtown, the tree-shaded streets and the railroad tracks separating the haves from the havenots — rises like a huge, clay beast, out of the city's impoverished black community up to a table of dusty land sparsely covered by grass and weeds, where two decidedly modest houses stand alone in the sun.

These unpretentious dwellings, with no baths or running water inside, are the homes of Mattie Dupree, thirty-seven, her thirty-three-year-old sister, Johnnie Mae Taylor, and their thirteen children. They live atop this hill, but they are far from rich. They would be totally out of place in the uppercrust hills of San Francisco, for they have known only the bottom of life in America.

It is a curious image — their living so high above the city, so high above the very society that relegates them to this country's socioeconomic basement.

"Gadsden is rotten," Mrs. Dupree said, leaning her heavyset, big-boned body against my car. "They sho' don't b'leeve in helping no black folks here. The way them polices shot Madden, it's a crime. The polices here treat black people like dogs. They can't ask you a simple question, and then when you go to answer it, they tell you to shut up. Just like you ain't grown yourself. That's the way they do. Them polices is rotten down there in Gadsden."

I had stumbled onto this woman by chance. Out of curiosity, I had turned off Tuscaloosa Avenue, the backbone of the black community, onto one of the side streets, just riding and thinking, taking in the meager houses and the children playing games in the street. Several turns led me to the hill, and finally to the two houses, where I eventually wound up talking to Mattie Dupree.

"They say the polices stopped him [Madden] for a traffic violation," she said. "I don't care what they stopped him for, they ain't have no business killing him. He was so young, in his twenties. A wife and three or four chillun." She shook her head in disbelief, questioning the fact of the killing though she knew it was a reality.

"Another thing," she said, "the other day when nine or ten polices walked off their jobs 'cause of the federal grand jury looking into the killing, they say them polices sliced up they police-car tires and a whole lotta stuff of the city, but that never did come out in the paper. Ain't that something, the police slicing up the city's tires?"

"The grand jury has already declined to indict the four officers involved in the killing," I said.

"Well, we all knew they wasn't gon' do nothing," she said angrily.

"The paper today said the walkout of the nine officers resulted from an incident last week, when the local Fraternal Order of Police voted for a work stoppage," I offered. "They were supposedly protesting a one-day delay by the city in returning the four officers who shot Madden back to work after the grand jury decision. I had thought they were never suspended."

"They shoulda been fired," she said. "That's the whole damn point."

"The paper also said the Gadsden chapter of the United Klans of America has asked the city commission to dismiss all charges against the nine who walked off the job, and 'get on with the business of running the city.' "

"The business of killing black folks," she said softly and looked away. "What you going 'round talking to people for? What you gon' do, write it up?"

"Yeah."

"Where?"

"In a few newspapers," I said. "Maybe I'll even write a book."

"A book?"

"Yeah," I said. I reached into the car and got the camera off the front seat. "Let me take your picture so I'll remember what you look like."

"You know what I look like," she said bashfully, "you don't need my picture."

"If I write about you," I said, "people will want to know what you look like."

"You can remember how I look. I look too bad for a picture . . . Well, man, you know how I look, like a nigger with her hair plaited up." She smiled and looked away.

"I ain't kidding about these folks in Gadsden, they rotten," she said. "These white teachers at the school put your chillun out of school for the least little thing. I wish we still had our own school so we wouldn't have to send our chillun up there. One teacher put my boy out of school, say he talked back to her. My son said a white boy spit on him in class, and the teacher wouldn't do nothing about it. They didn't put the white boy out," she said angrily. "They hurry and up put my son out. I had to stay off work and go up there. Teacher told me my boy mumbled back to her under his breath. You can't put no child out of school 'cause he mumbled. Good gracious! Wouldn't be nobody left in school."

"Do the police ever patrol this area?" I asked.

"You kidding? You can't git nane to come up here. I don't be worried with nobody breaking in up here, though," she said, "'cause I ain't got nothing for nobody to take. Every penny I make goes for gro'cy [grocery]."

"We don't git no welfare, no food stamps. I used to be on food stamps when they first come out. Now I just buy what I can at the store," she said. "If I don't have the money, I don't git it. We do without.

"We don't have to pay no rent. Me and my sister have owned these two houses for about fourteen years now. Yeah, they'll sell you these old broke down houses, but they won't loan you no money to fix 'em up.

"I spend seventy to eighty dollars a week on gro'cy. We use butane gas to heat these things. Cost me over one hundred dollars a month for gas. I have to pay it by the week, you know, so much every time I git a payday. I make one hundred ninety-seven dollars, sometime it be two hundred dollars, every two weeks." [She is a maid at a local hospital.]

"Feeding these chillun and keeping this place warm takes all my money," she said. "If I had to pay rent, too, I wouldn't be able to make it. I got seven children of my own, from eleven to eighteen years old. Then I got two of my dead sister's kids."

Some of the children had gathered around the car where Mrs. Dupree and I stood talking. A demure young black-haired girl with glistening black skin leaned against the fender of the car. Her thin lips were chalky white, and her fingers frail white sticks. She was eating from a box of Argo starch. Though she was narrow to the point of being skinny, her round little belly protruded above the top of her pants. In my mind the image became exaggerated, her stomach expanding like a balloon until she was one of those emaciated Biafran children whose bones were visible beneath sagging skin and whose bellies were swollen as if about to burst. Those children had stared at me from CARE posters on city buses, and from magazine photographs, during the civil war in that country a few years ago.

Mrs. Dupree was talking again now, pulling me away from the girl and her starch. "We don't even have no septic tank," she said with a sigh. "We've been trying to git one to put between the two houses. Ain't no way we could afford two. If we could git one, and even if we couldn't have a bathroom in each house, we could have one bathroom. But the city commission said we couldn't do it that way," she said sadly. "They say you got to have one septic tank for one house. I know they got rules down there and they 'sposed to protect people, but the rules hurting us. We just ain't got no bathroom.

"These old houses all we got, and won't nobody here loan us a dime on 'em. And ain't nobody gon' give you no septic tank," she said firmly. "You can b'leeve that."

"What about the Madden killing?" I asked.

"Shoot, they got black folks in this town over a barrel," she said. "Black people scared to even talk about it. Scared they gon' lose they jobs, and jobs hard to come by for us. Where I work, they ain't hired nane black boy as an orderly, but they've hired plenty of white boys. They treat me all right, but some of them heifers, they try to talk to you just like a baby, 'cause you black. I been there six years.

"Some of these other businesses like Goodyear got blacks working, but the blacks take so much from 'em — they won't go to the meetings or the marches," she said. "They scared to death to be seen, 'cause they know them jobs'll be gone.

"And only a few black folks own businesses. All of them on

Tuscaloosa Avenue [the heart of the black community]. Ain't nothing downtown. Downtown belong to the white folks. Used to be a black clothing store downtown, but it closed down. Oh yeah, I think Pete Young's Café still on Sixth Street, but that's all."

I thought about a conversation I'd had with a young minister the previous evening, outside the Henry Street Baptist Church. He told me about a black business downtown that had caught fire a few months earlier. The black owner called the fire department as soon as he discovered the small fire. But it took the fire fighters so long to respond, according to this man, that the owner had gone into the business and removed most of his belongings before the building burned to the ground and the firemen finally arrived to look over the ashes. "If it's on fire and owned by somebody black, if you can't put it out yourself, it's gon' burn down," the man had said.

"Gadsden is a rotten place to stay in," came the familiar refrain from Mrs. Dupree.

"Have you ever thought of leaving? Starting over somewhere else?"

"I used to think like that all the time," she said wistfully. "I ain't never had enough money to git outta here, with these nine kids. I don't like Gadsden, but I ain't able to go nowhere else. I started once to go to Detroit. I did have a sister and a brother. My brother still there. My sister died, and I just never did make it."

Neither of us said anything for several seconds after that. I turned and looked out over the rim of the hill at the busy city sprawled below us. Even the children were quiet now. Again my mind questioned the effectiveness of the civil-rights movement, all the publicity and ballyhoo it had received over the years. There was no denying that it had forced progress, opened jobs, neighborhoods, and schools to those who had previously stood outside looking in. But only a few had benefited to the fullest — a very few. Not the masses. They were still living like Mrs. Dupree, like Nadine Rouse and Ola Davis, like those tired souls in the housing project on Sixth Street in Gadsden, like the people on Beale Street in Americus, Georgia, like Eddie Lee and Freddie Lee Mullins, like Alan Chester.

When you think about it, mainly the people who were out front, the leaders — Julian Bond, John Lewis, Jesse Jackson, Vernon Jordan, Andy Young, and other elite civil-rights fighters — are the ones who moved into elective office, government jobs, and other positions of influence in this country. They were the gifted ones, the ones with advantages from the beginning who probably would have assimilated easily into the majority society anyway.

I didn't want to talk to her any longer. I said good-by and was starting my car when she leaned her plait-covered head into the car and said: "Don't forgit the meeting at the church tonight."

"I won't. S'long."

The kids waved as I pulled away. The thin girl with the white-fingered hands smiled.

* * *

The leaders of the Gadsden protest figured they had finally come up with a way to surprise city officials and force the mayor to confront them. They decided at the meeting at the church that instead of following their usual practice of lining up and march-ing down to city hall, singing and chanting and demanding to see the mayor, they would split up, get into several cars, and drive downtown, arriving at short intervals.

People would get out of their cars, proceed inside city hall in inconspicuous groups, and head for the bathrooms on the second floor where the mayor's office is located. Once they were gathered in force on the second floor, they would suddenly appear in the mayor's office, and he would be forced to deal with them face to face for the first time. They were convinced that this would work. It was now Friday, and I had planned to leave Gadsden early in the day, but I decided to stay and see how it all panned out.

That morning, they met at the church and left in small groups at regular intervals. Many of the marchers got inside city hall this time, past the police guards, the cops assuming they were just average citizens there to pay utility bills. But that was as far as they got. The second floor was closed off. They were turned away again.

• • •

After I left Gadsden, I continued to follow the progress of the demonstrations through the media. A week after my departure, Hosea Williams, who was national president of SCLC at the time, led a group of about fifty protesters into city hall, to the second floor. There they camped outside the mayor's office. According to Williams, whom I talked to later in Atlanta, Gadsden police rushed in and locked the doors of the mayor's office, with the mayor and police chief inside refusing to come out.

"They kept us out in the hall," Williams said smiling, "but we got what we wanted. We sat out there on the floor and sang. It shook 'em up. We made our point. They wouldn't even come out and talk to us. But Gadsden's generally a racist town. It's always been that way. One of the most inhuman beatings I can remember we took was in Gadsden during the time of the Birmingham movement."

Williams said that Gadsden police "nearly beat those kids' brains out down there. They were on their knees, and they were just a-beating 'em, beating 'em all over the head and face, neck, beating 'em like they were dogs. It's a typical racist situation, a southern town . . . The attitude of the general public is usually portrayed by the officials, and those officials were beating those kids.

"They don't have a helluva black population down there, only about twenty-five percent, and even with the large industry they have there, black folks still have a helluva time getting jobs.

"There was no reason in the world for the police to kill that boy [Madden], except they just vented all their racism and hatred on him," Williams said. "Shot him fifteen times, one was a shotgun and one a magnum pistol. I heard rumors that he was going with a white girl."

I shook my head. I had heard the same rumors when I was there.

"They shot that boy about that white girl," Williams said. "The same old racism . . . You see, I don't know what people mean when they say 'New South.' Because when you talk about the bottom line, that means blacks will have equal access to total American life. Black babies will have just as good a chance as white babies, because black mothers will be getting good prenatal care. A black man or woman will be able to get a job in keeping with their ability."

Williams, who is also a Georgia state representative, believed that little progress was being made through state governments. "For instance, in the Georgia legislature we have the second-largest number of black elected officials of any state in the union, and we are still powerless. And unless you play ball with the white racists — and even if you play ball with 'em — you can't get anything beneficial to black folks through that legislature. You can come up with something that looks good on paper that you have to develop a story out of, you know, that you have to carve a victory out of it. All those black legislators up there. So what? What difference does it make for the black constituent? None!

"And I'll be frank with you. If you want to get something through the Georgia legislature, you come up with something anti-Atlanta, antiblack, or antipoor, and it flies through.

"So when you talk about the 'New South,' I don't know what you mean. Right here in the black mecca — Atlanta — we have lost ground economically over the past fifteen years. The black economic base has been shattered," he said. "We've got a black mayor of the city, half the city council is black, the majority of the board of education is black. We've got a black school superintendent, a black as head of the chamber of commerce, and we are sixty percent of the population," he said, "yet we control less than three percent of the wealth . . .

"If you are going to talk about that few of us who were able to escape poverty, and the few of us who have been allowed to fill window-dressing positions, that's nothing new. They had house niggers during slavery. All these blacks who have been elected to public office don't excite me. You can't single out some unique individuals who've excelled. When you talk about the difference between the sixties and the seventies, you have to decide if things are better for the black race as a whole.

"The majority of black folks are just as bad off as they ever were," he continued. "People talk about all this so-called black political power in Atlanta, but what good is having a Jesse Hill [president of Atlanta Life Insurance Company and an influential Carter supporter and adviser] as president of the chamber of commerce, while black businesses in Atlanta are going bankrupt left and right?

"I cannot judge black progress by the progress of Hosea Williams or the progress of Jesse Jackson. There is no 'New South,' here, in Gadsden, or anywhere else. It's the same Old South. They've thrown off one false face and put on another." He was clearly angry now. "What New South? What New South?"

15

Home

THEY DECIDED to end my journey early. In the beginning, we had talked about my being on the road in the South for five or six months, but now they were calling the project to a close after three months and four states.

"I think you need to come in and sit down and write what you've got," Minter said in a hollow voice. "See how it looks. If you need any more, you can go back out. What you think?"

For a long time I did not respond. I knew their minds were made up, and the costs of the project were piling up. I had known this moment would come. I had never believed it would last six months. And from the beginning, I had strongly suspected that those early plans for me to spend a week each in New York, Washington, Detroit, and Los Angeles at the close of the southern project, to compare conditions in those places to conditions I'd found in the South, would never materialize. I had been in the newspaper game long enough to know that all those projects that begin with lofty goals and fat budgets inevitably shrink in value, from the newspaper's point of view, as the bills come pouring in.

"What about New York, Washington, Detroit, and Los Angeles?" I asked.

"We may still do that," Minter said perfunctorily, "but right now I think you need to write what you've got."

It was funny how during all those lonely nights I'd spent in strange roadside motels, listening to the rain pound the roof and, often, watching it seep through cracks in the ceiling or sweat down the battered walls, I'd thought of how wonderful it would be to just call off the whole thing right then and there, call my wife on the phone, and tell her I was on my way home — that I was through suffering just to see how people lived on the other side.

I often convinced myself that I had done my duty, had been uncomfortable enough, had seen the shanty towns and bleak low-rent housing projects, the reservations where the poor were bound together in despair. Nobody could blame me for walking out, I thought.

Yet now that I was being told that the project was over, I did not feel the sense of relief I had anticipated. Inside, I was still holding on to the misery, the memories of the people's faces, their dank rooms and wood-burning heaters, their outhouses and raggedy porches, their looks of long submission that immediately told you that these people had been engaged in a lifelong battle with the world, and that the world had won.

"What you think?" Minter asked again.

"Whatever you say," I said. "It's your world," I added, remembering a phrase the brothers on the corner often used.

"What?"

"We'll see what it looks like when it comes out of the typewriter," I said. Minter shook his head. I left the office, for at that moment I couldn't bear to talk to him another second. I didn't quite know why, but he suddenly seemed to me to represent power, incredible power. He could begin the project, then end it whenever he wanted to. The very room we had been in, his office, in the midst of that huge newsroom, was a center of power. The people I had met on the road would be out of place in his glass-enclosed office high above the sidewalks teeming with inner-city life. They would feel awkward moving about in that world where people made decisions about the vast community that spread out below them.

The newspaper was like all those businesses I had visited while looking for work, where I never once found a black face behind a desk of real authority, never saw a black in a decision-making position. I had left Atlanta and discovered conditions essentially the same as those surrounding me where I worked every day. But here they existed in such a sophisticated form that you forgot they were there.

It is the same everywhere. Your color still matters in the South, in this country. In the newsroom you sometimes forget that. But out there in the world where people are struggling just to get up off their faces every day, it is never forgotten, not for one minute. The reminders are everywhere: their own howling stomachs, the trip into the backyard to the bathroom, no jobs, no money, no hope.

Summer was on the way, and I was home again trying to settle back into the routine I'd left, but it wouldn't work. Things were not the same. Faces I'd seen on the road haunted me as I drove to and from work. The wrinkled hands of wizened old black ladies, their bottom lips full of snuff, moved before my eyes. Scrawny dogs with drooping eyes padded across my mind. And as I drove through Atlanta streets, the poor leaped at me from their housing projects and slum neighborhoods, waving their bony hands.

When I first began the project, we had agreed that I would not masquerade as a poor out-of-work black in Atlanta, because I would surely be recognized and the project ruined. Now I wished I had tried it, though I knew what I would have found: many of the same things I found elsewhere.

Atlanta, hailed as the black mecca of America, with its large black bourgeoisie, its impressive number of black millionaires, its sizable throng of black skilled and professional workers, has, like other American cities, another, uglier, side. It has more than its share of poor, unemployed, and underemployed blacks. It has its massive public-housing projects, nightmares of architectural horror that provide breeding grounds for rats, roaches, and crime.

Like other major cities, it has been abandoned by large segments of the middle class and is becoming a city of the very rich and the very poor. It is wrestling with these problems, because it is fortunate enough to have a measure of sensitive leadership. Still, it is not, as it has long billed itself, "the city too busy to hate." Its reputation for excellent race relations has always been a bit overblown.

As John Cox, former head of the Butler Street YMCA and now an airline executive, told me in 1973, when I was researching an article on race relations in the city: "There has never been elimination of segregation. There have been book decisions, but birds of a feather still flock together. Consciousness of kind overrides the law."

What I wrote in that article seven years ago is true today. I approached the article from the standpoint that in order to find out whether or not there is genuine mixing of the races, one must determine whether blacks and whites continue to associate with one another after the work day ends.

This is, in part, what I wrote:

> To get there you walk up three flights of creaky stairs. The building sits on Spring Street, and the stairway is dark and narrow, the walls charred — evidence of a not-so-long-ago fire.
>
> You pay a buck to get in, stand to be searched for weapons before being led by a vivacious black hostess to the bar or a table near the stage where slinky black dancers twist and undulate to the throbbing, head-pounding, foot-stomping beat of a soul band.
>
> The music is loud, but that is the way the people like it. They clap, tap their fingers against the table tops, shake their feet, and croon with the singers — the men with their ashy arms around their women, both sipping their drinks.
>
> A lot of cab drivers come here for entertainment. With their chariots-for-hire parked outside, they sit scattered about the small nightclub drinking beer and shouting encouragement to the wriggling, shaking dancers.
>
> A young black man and his white date lean against a wall near the back of the club, and no one seems interested in their presence. They are caught in the movement of the same throbbing beat, and move and clap with the music, but are always looking around to see who is noticing them.
>
> A few blocks away, on West Peachtree, modishly dressed,

middle-class white men and women crowd into their favorite nightspot.

The fashionably dressed host treats the customers with jokes as they enter and walk across the carpeted floor to the long bar, or wait to be led to small tables that bear these signs: "This table is for four people. To remain seated here, one drink per person must be ordered every hour."

The club has no trouble enforcing the rule, for the patrons drink heartily, and the slender waitresses in skimpy skirts are kept running among the tables.

The band is informally dressed, good and loud. Enthusiastic couples crowd onto the dance floor during every number, whether it is a ballad, a rendition of pop or hard rock.

A black face here is cause for staring.

Atlanta is a segregated town. Not segregated by law, but by the consent of the citizenry.

It is a hustling, bustling town by day, with black and white cops flooding the downtown streets with their walkie-talkies and night sticks.

A city of sidewalks filled with black and white faces going to and from work, schools, courts, cafeterias, and stores. A city of tall, integrated office buildings, where leggy black and white secretaries ride the same elevators.

A city of long-hairs and short-hairs holding doors for each other as they enter the same banks and coffee shops.

Atlanta is, like all other big cities, a city of multisocieties and multilifestyles — a city where the different cultures, different races tolerate each other by day, because that is the only way the work will get done.

With a few exceptions where there are some genuine friendships between blacks and whites, the two races go their separate ways when the work day ends, to their separate havens of food, fun, and pleasure . . .

And as I drove through the city — my city, where I was born in what is now the charity hospital, and raised in the bitter streets — I knew things had changed only minimally since '73 when I'd written those words. And the same went for the South in general. Yes, there had been some change. More blacks held public office. More blacks sat in key government jobs. The black middle class was growing, but so was the lower class.

For the masses, things had changed only in the sense that now they had perhaps even less hope, because they were being abandoned by their fellow blacks who had climbed out of the gutter and onto the white man's sidewalk — those who had once stood beside them and fought the same hunger, the same despair; those who now had no time for that kind of fighting.

•   •   •

I had come to dread actually having to write about my experiences, to relive them at the typewriter, because I would have to fashion my story into a form that would enable other people to understand and feel what I'd felt.

When I had first come back to the newsroom, the reporters had been stunned to see me. They were shocked to learn that I had not quit at all, but rather had been on a "secret assignment." They seemed impressed by the scope of the project and the amount of money spent to pull it off. As word of my assignment spread throughout the building, expectations of what would come from my typewriter, as a result of this effort, skyrocketed, until I could no longer work at my space in the newsroom without people stopping by periodically to talk about my experience.

I decided to do my writing at home. But the fear that I would not be able to produce something that would satisfy the sky-high expectations hounded me even there. For the first couple of weeks nothing came from the typewriter. It wouldn't obey me. It was a retarded child sitting before me cold and distant. There were too many facts, too many faces, too many dreams. The images kept me awake at night. Words danced in my head, but by the time I could rush downstairs to the typewriter, they would be gone, like ghosts slipping into the darkness. And my biggest fear was that nobody would want to read about what I had experienced. Only a very depressing story would come from that typewriter.

The writing went torturously slowly, but within a month and a half I had produced a ten-part newspaper series, which I suggested to Rankin and Minter should be called "Down Here on the Ground: Poor Blacks in the 'New South.' "

The series was published under the title "A Black Man's

Diary," amidst a plethora of publicity and a public reaction that nearly flattened me.

The paper's publicity department told me that the producers of NBC's *Today* show wanted me as a guest, and the *New York Times* News Service bought syndication rights for the series and distributed it to more than 500 newspapers in this country and abroad. Cards, letters, and phone calls from people all over the country and from several foreign countries poured in by the thousands. I was suddenly being sought after by local radio and TV stations for appearances. Colleges and civic groups wanted me to give speeches. I was interviewed by several newspapers around the country.

How could I have been so wrong about the response I had expected? People everywhere told me how much they were moved by what I had reported, and wanted to know more. The paper had to hire a temporary secretary just to handle all the mail, and the amount of mail and calls that came to my home kept my wife and me busy for weeks after the series ran. And something else happened that surprised me.

In response to the plight of the Rouse family, whom I had written about in the second installment of the series, people began sending money to the *Charlotte Observer* — which had run the series — to help the Rouses.

The paper sent a columnist to check out my story and reported that he had found the things I'd written about and more. In response to the tremendous reader reaction, the *Observer* set up a fund for the family, to channel the money they were receiving through the mail. Within a couple of months, the donations exceeded $14,000, enabling the Rouse family to purchase a new house on nearly two acres of land.

Two North Carolina colleges offered scholarships to Mrs. Rouse's daughter, and Mrs. Rouse had several job offers. Because of the kindness of concerned people all over the country, their lives were changed completely, almost overnight.

When I first heard from the columnist at the *Observer* that all this was happening, and saw the stories in that paper, I was gratified that I had been, in a small way, the catalyst for such an outpouring of human warmth and compassion.

The *Journal* wanted me to go back to North Carolina, visit the Rouses, and write about their "new life." I couldn't go, and I could not explain why, but I felt it would not be proper. Another reporter was sent, and I felt embarrassed when I read her story, in which Mrs. Rouse thanked God that I had happened upon them. There was a picture of the new house, with its bright new kitchen and indoor bathroom.

I later talked to Mrs. Rouse by phone and told her how happy I was for her and that I would like to help in any way I could, because I knew the struggle was not over for her and her family. Just hearing her voice moved me so deeply that tears inched down my cheek as I held the phone to my ear. I wiped them away before my wife saw me.

"Who was that on the phone?" she asked when I hung up.

"Mrs. Rouse in North Carolina."

"What did she say?"

"She told me about her new house. She said she was very happy."

"That all?"

"That's enough."

She had gotten more than the acre of land she'd been dreaming of all her life, I thought. And she wouldn't have to drape a sheet across two sticks, as she had said she would do.

My initial joy because of the Rouse family's good fortune did not last long. Even though I was happy for the Rouses, I could not forget Eddie Lee and Freddie Lee Mullins; I could not forget Ola Davis and Alan Chester. Nobody had helped them, yet, and probably nobody would. I could not forget all those miserable souls I had seen and hadn't written about. And there were those I hadn't even seen, who were living on the ragged edge and would soon be lost forever in society's dung heap.

Even among the poor, there are the fortunate and the damned. The Rouses were fortunate. So many others were damned.

• • •

The newspaper's management was ecstatic over all the publicity and my sudden celebrity status. I could imagine the pats on the back that must have been taking place in the corporate offices on the ninth floor. I knew the wheels of their minds were turning: What could they do next with their wonder boy? What social evil could they send him after now, to prove that this was no fluke, that the *Journal* was indeed a real newspaper in the noblest tradition? I waited on pins and needles, for I was still reeling from my experiences on the road.

Within a short time, an opportunity for the paper to show me off again presented itself. During the time I'd been gone, a shadowy but growing movement was taking shape, gaining ground in isolated pockets around the country — on the California coast, in the Midwest, and in small southern towns.

The Ku Klux Klan, that lame and believed-dead old warhorse of racism and fear, popped up in Oxnard, California, in several Midwestern cities, in Alabama, and finally in Mississippi, where it was now making a strong bid for a comeback, or so it appeared from wire-service reports.

The Klan's rejuvenated popularity in the South was not lost on Minter, who had been kept abreast of the cross burnings and demonstrations the racist group was staging throughout Mississippi. In Jackson, a rash of cross burnings plagued the city, including one at the entrance to an all-black housing subdivision, two at a black-run television station, and one outside a liberal newspaper that carried editorials condemning Klan activities.

North of Jackson, in Tupelo — the hometown of the late Elvis Presley — the alleged beating of a black jail inmate by two white detectives had sent angry black residents into the normally quiet streets of that northeastern Mississippi trading center, marching, boycotting, and picketing. And who was there to meet them? The Klan, using its new-found public-relations tactics, which included press conferences in rented hotel rooms, where members took off their pointed hoods for the cameras and proclaimed that they were white and proud, proud to wear the KKK robe, proud to stand up and stop the niggers from taking over the country.

I was soon dispatched to Mississippi, much to my fear and displeasure.

16

Encore, Mississippi...

Mississippi. I tried to conjure up a central image of it — the land of cotton, the namesake of that mighty river that feeds the midsection of this country.

Images flew through the darkness behind my eyelids like flashes of light — bellybusting blues of B. B. King; the deep, joyous eyes of Fannie Lou Hamer as she spoke about the Delta and the hope she had for our people there; the straight-edged prose of Richard Wright, screaming from the page; and the powerful lyrical writing of Tennessee Williams and Eudora Welty.

Medgar Evers appeared to me, standing in the driveway of his home, then being laid to waste by a rifle blast. Next I saw Philadelphia, where the bodies of three civil-rights workers were found in 1964, buried under an earthen dam.

In my mind, their blood was still sinking deep into the coal-black earth, into the roots of trees, vegetables, and grass, into the stomachs of cows, into the bodies of the people.

I had expected more of a nightmare, something like the ghoul-ish paintings Rod Serling always posed in front of while intro-ducing stories on *Night Gallery*. I was prepared to see the shacks that lined the elevated backroads, their roofs rising only as high as the roadway, each shanty sitting on the dusty ground below the road like an egg in a carton. But I had not expected the ter-rible beauty of the night-black soil, so rich it looked as if it could feed the world. I hadn't envisioned the green vegetables growing out of the black earth; the bolls of cotton standing out like white eyes in the dark fields; the gentle hills framed by the horizon; the winding, black-topped roads; the sun sinking like a huge orange tablet in the autumn sky; and the sweet sound of crickets in the bushes along the highway. Highway 49 snaked through the Delta and I saw the beautiful aspects of Mississippi as well as the damned.

The 1978 *World Almanac* calls Mississippi the Magnolia State, ranking it thirty-second among the fifty states in land area, and twenty-ninth in population, with two-and-a-half-million people.

Hernando de Soto explored the area in 1540 and discovered the Mississippi River in 1541. La Salle traced the river from Illinois to its mouth, and claimed the entire valley for France in 1682. The area was ceded to Britain in 1763, and American settlers began to appear soon after.

During the American Revolution, Spain seized part of the region and refused to leave even after the United States acquired title to it at the end of the war. The Spanish finally relinquished it in 1798.

Sixty-three years later, in 1861, Mississippi, which had entered the Union in 1817, seceded. Subsequently, Union forces captured Corinth and Vicksburg and destroyed Jackson, the present state capital.

According to the *Almanac,* "soybeans have taken over as Mississippi's largest crop. The state ranks third in cotton production. Other farm products include pecans, sweet potatoes, rice, sugarcane, poultry, and eggs."

The fields rushed past the window as I drove toward Greenville, where I would spend the night before continuing to Tupelo. They were laden with cotton — millions of white puffs suspended on the skinny fingers of cotton plants. It was more cotton than I'd ever seen in my life. The almanac had said that cotton was no longer king among farm products, yet here in the Delta the fields of little white bolls seemed to fan out forever. All that cotton, and not a single soul was bent over picking it. I supposed there was now some machine to do the job, sparing the poor blacks whose lot it had been, in years past, to suffer the heat of the sun, and the endless bending, to harvest the precious crop.

The streets of Tupelo were filled with cars, all bearing license plates proclaiming Mississippi the "hospitality state." I did not get a warm reception in the birthplace of Elvis, however. This prosperous trading center in northeast Mississippi, a racially divided town of some 30,000 people, was the scene of a sixties-styled war where your skin was your uniform.

Judging from the reaction I got at the dozen or so hotels and motels where I went in search of lodging, I might have been a leper or, worse, a carpetbagging Yankee of a hundred years ago, in top hat and spats, shouting, "Piss on the Confederacy!" At each establishment, I was confronted by a slightly nervous clerk who quickly told me there was no room at the inn. Blame was placed on two huge conventions, which had every room in the town sold out for a week, I was told. This I thought curious, since none of the parking lots outside the motels were filled. Had all these room-grabbing conventioneers walked to Tupelo? I asked myself.

I found a phone booth and called each of the motels I had already visited, to see if I could make reservations. I called the Holiday Inn, the Ramada Inn, the Townhouse Motel, and the Traveler's Motel, all on Highway 45.

Over the phone, clerks at Holiday Inn, Townhouse, and Traveler's told me they had plenty of rooms, and that all I had to do was "come on over." The Ramada Inn desk clerk said that there were no rooms available for that day, but that they would certainly be able to accommodate me beginning the following day, "for as long as you'd like."

With slogans from national advertising campaigns running through my head, I chose the "people-pleasing place," Holiday Inn, where "the best surprise is no surprise."

The two women behind the counter seemed stunned as I made my entrance for the second time. When I informed them that they had a reservation for me, and gave them my name, there was total silence in the lobby for several seconds. Neither of the clerks moved. They just stared at me with discomfort, almost horror. I waited for several awkward seconds, not wanting to do or say anything that might lessen the embarrassment they obviously felt.

With a sudden start that frightened me, both lunged toward the counter to give me a registration card.

By this time, a fortyish white guy, dressed in the polyester uniform of a traveling salesman, had entered. He seemed nonplussed by the scene he had just walked into. His huge brown leather bag dangled like a lead weight at the end of his short arm. The woman who reached the registration cards first handed me one. The other lady finally turned to help the gentleman in the polyester suit.

"Can I help you?" she asked in a frail voice, almost as if she was afraid he was going to make some preposterous request.

"A room, please," the man said in a strong southern twang. I suddenly had the sensation of being outside of myself, outside of the room, watching the whole funny scene through the plate-glass door. I was determined to keep up a serious front.

The lady waiting on the polyester-clad gentleman looked over at me. "Do you have a reservation, sir?" she asked the man.

The man shook his head.

"Well . . . " Again she peered at me. Her eyes seemed to be pleading. I couldn't help but smile, though I fought to keep it small, not overly generous. "I think I can find something for you," she finally told him.

Glancing outside, I noticed the same white man with brown hair and thick brown mustache I had seen outside all the other motels I had tried in Tupelo. He was leaning against a wall watching me. I had noticed him at all those other places, but had told myself that he was just somebody else trying to get a room. Still, I hadn't seen him get out of his car at any of the other motels. He had just sat behind the wheel watching, and his eyes had turned away whenever I looked in his direction.

Now he was out of his car, and instead of turning away when I looked at him, he stared back. It stopped me in my tracks. Finally he walked toward the parking lot at the rear of the motel.

I checked the room number on the key the woman had given

me. She'd told me that the room was at the back, on the second floor of the two-story motel. I drove around back, parked, and was about to start unpacking the car, when I again saw the man staring at me. He stood in the shadows of the soft-drink machine across the parking lot from me.

I got back into the car and sat there watching him watch me. After several minutes, he took the cigarette from his mouth, tossed it to the concrete, and walked briskly toward a gray late-model Ford station wagon parked diagonally across from where I sat in my rented Toyota.

When he opened the door to get into the wagon, I started my car and pulled into the stall behind him, blocking his way. I don't know what possessed me to do that, but it was a sudden impulse that I obeyed without thinking about the possible consequences.

When he looked back to see what was happening, and I saw the shock on his face, and what I thought might even be a tinge of fear, I felt as if I had been plunged into the middle of one of those espionage movies where almost anything can happen. I fantasized about being a hit man who had discovered he was being followed and had trapped his shadow and was about to finish him off.

I quickly picked up my notepad and wrote down the wagon's license-plate number. When I backed out of the stall, the man shot out past me, roared through the parking lot to Highway 45, and sped into the downtown traffic.

When I had finally settled into my room, I called Rankin and told him about the incident, giving him the license number I had written down. He called back within an hour, saying that he'd gotten somebody in our Washington Bureau to check the plate through the FBI, and that some of the guys in the city room back in Atlanta were investigating it through the local police.

It turned out that the car was registered to a corporation in Clinton, Mississippi — a city less than a hundred miles from Jackson. The FBI and the law-enforcement people in Clinton knew little or nothing about this enterprise.

I told Rankin to forget it, that I didn't think I was in any

real danger. He called back about two hours later with the
names of several local people I could call on if I found myself
in a situation where I desperately needed a friend. I told him
not to worry, but I made sure to write down the names, just
in case.

I finally fell asleep that night, sometime near the end of the
Johnny Carson show. I had lain in bed wondering who the man
with the mustache was and why he was interested in me. Was it
possible that he had seen me on the *Today* show and wanted
to check me out?

I wanted to know why the hotels in town had given me such
a hard time. Did they think I was an outside agitator, there to
help the blacks who were boycotting and picketing? Did they
treat every out-of-town black the same way they'd treated me?
And if they wanted to know who I was or what I was doing
there, why didn't they just ask? And what about this corporation
the car was registered to? Was it connected with the Klan?

As I drifted toward sleep, I told myself that the whole thing
was just a coincidence, that the man with the mustache had
not been interested in me at all, and that I was just a bit paranoid.
I tried to persuade myself to think positively about the whole
experience and to believe that the next day would go smoothly.
Deep down, though, in the region of the mind where scary
things grow, a tiny voice kept warning me that my troubles in
Mississippi were not over.

The days that followed proved the voice to be right.

•   •   •

It had been a protracted battle there, this racial struggle that
started months ago when black demonstrators demanded that
two white police officers be fired, after a federal court had
ordered them to pay $2500 in damages to a black prisoner they
had been accused of beating in the city's jail.

Tupelo's whites were stunned by the demonstrations. They
had been blind to the growing frustration on the part of blacks,
over high unemployment, poor housing conditions, and a score
of other problems.

"I just don't understand it at all," one middle-aged white

woman told me. "We've always had good relations with our blacks here in Tupelo. We didn't have all that nasty business they had other places in the sixties. We've been nice to them . . ." she said tentatively. It was more a question than a statement. "We just never had that kind of trouble."

"You've got it now," I said. "You've got the sixties ten years after everybody else."

"I guess," she said, shaking her head. "Lord, I guess . . ."

The initial demonstration triggered a series of boycotts and pickets of white-owned businesses, and almost weekly marches by blacks demanding better jobs, better pay, and more services from the city administration.

The Ku Klux Klan, having decided that the conditions were right, with the country moving headlong into uncertain economic times, seized the opportunity to try to make a comeback. Accounts appeared sporadically in newspapers across the country concerning some white group or individual who saw affirmative-action programs and aid to minorities as abridgements to the rights and freedom of whites.

Whites throughout the United States have a growing, insidious fear that "reverse discrimination" is rampant in the land, and that they are losing ground economically and legally, almost daily, to upwardly mobile blacks and to the hordes of Mexican and Asian refugees coming into the country to compete with them for a rapidly dwindling pool of jobs.

In the past three years, Mississippi and Alabama have seen a steadily increasing amount of Klan activity. Klan crosses were burned in front of a black-run television station, and at the entrance of a middle-class black residential area, in Jackson, Mississippi, late last year. In October, 1977, a dozen crosses were set ablaze across southern Mississippi in one single night, and Fayette's black mayor Charles Evers spotted a Mississippi Highway Patrol employee and his wife trying to burn a cross near Fayette.

The Klan, created in 1866 by a few former Confederate soldiers in Pulaski, Tennessee, as simply a social club, was showing signs of new life, even though as late as 1972 federal officials had estimated that the combined membership of the nation's steadily dwindling eighteen Klan organizations was no more than 4500 — down from some three to five million members in the 1930s.

Taking advantage of what he saw as an opportunity to rebuild his failing Invisible Empire, Bill Wilkinson, a thirty-six-year-old former electrical contractor from Denham Springs, Louisiana, hotfooted it over to Tupelo in 1978 to organize counterdemonstrations against the blacks who were boycotting and picketing there. Wilkinson's Klan started out by "monitoring" the marches and protests staged by blacks in Tupelo, but soon it was holding membership rallies, countermarches, and cross burnings.

Before he formed the Invisible Empire, Wilkinson was associated with the leader of another Klan group, David Duke, a twenty-nine-year-old college graduate who headed the Knights of the Ku Klux Klan and who has publicly labeled his former associate — Wilkinson — as "a very little man with a Napoleonic complex . . . a man who has never read anything in his life . . ." The enmity between the two has grown so severe that Wilkinson forbids himself to even mention Duke's name.

Having established his headquarters in Metairie, Louisiana, Duke has been engaged in a national campaign of public appearances, before civic, community, and school groups, designed to change the image of the Klan. Seeking to dispel the prevalently held image of the Klan as a group of illiterate, shotgun-toting rednecks, Duke has moved away from the shadowy secrecy that was a Klan trademark in years past, into the bright lights of television cameras and convention centers.

"We're not just a bunch of fools running around in bed sheets," he has said, adding that he espouses nonviolence as preferable to the methods used by Klan groups in the past. He advocates the use of "ballots rather than bullets." To this end, he has sought out younger, more articulate whites for his organization and has succeeded in recruiting a number of high school students across the country, many of them angered by forced busing in their school districts.

Though Duke is more sophisticated than Wilkinson and most other Klansmen, his basic message is still unabashed racism and staunch anti-Semitism. He has said that he is convinced that Jews are the behind-the-scenes manipulators of nearly all the books marketed in this country, the movies produced by Hollywood, and the scripts written for television. He has also said that if he were in control of America, he would turn his back on Israel and become more friendly with the Arab world, whose oil the U.S. depends upon.

Duke advocates closing America to all nonwhite immigrants seeking to make this country their home, particularly illegal aliens crossing the Mexican border. "We are literally being invaded by Mexico," he has reportedly said. "And, if they continue to come in by the millions, they will sweep away our culture and our rights."

It was fortunate for Wilkinson that the United League of Mississippi — a black civil-rights organization that claims some 62,000 members in northern Mississippi — took to the streets of Tupelo, joining with local blacks to protest the beating of a black prisoner in the city jail. It was the perfect opportunity for him to bring his tired old cult of hocus-pocus and nigger hate to Mississippi and to the eyes of the press and the nation.

Though Wilkinson admitted that his following was "small but bold," he insisted that he could see tremendous potential for growth, from the ranks of hard-working white people tired of seeing "the niggers running off with everything.

"If I had to pin it [the rebirth of interest in the Klan] down to one thing," he has been quoted as saying, "I would have to say affirmative action. It's just that white men are tired of seeing their employers forced to hire niggers and promoting niggers over white people. And, of course, there's busing, this lax judicial system, the Panama Canal, and taking the troops out of Korea."

During the months he had been in Tupelo, Wilkinson, a Napoleon in white sheet and pointed hood, had kept his army engaged in night maneuvers — burning crosses and, reportedly, shooting at blacks from speeding cars. There had been several incidents in which gunfire was exchanged between blacks —

who had been arming themselves since the Klan turned up — and Klansmen out patrolling Tupelo and communities in surrounding towns. Several times, marches and countermarches by the Klan had produced near-violent confrontations, and police had made numerous arrests.

From talking to blacks in the streets, I discovered that it was not uncommon for Klansmen to ride through town with submachine guns lying on the seats of their cars and pickups. And many of them posed for television cameras and news photographers, brandishing weapons from their apparently powerful arsenal.

The constant reports of shootings at night, of "innocent" blacks being fired on by whites, inspired rumors of even more shootings and killings of blacks by whites, and this in turn prompted blacks to further arm themselves and travel in groups at night.

It had gotten serious. The little face-off between the rejuvenating Klan and the black protesters led by the United League had reached the point where neither side could back down. The future existence of each group depended on soundly trouncing the other, sending the beaten members scurrying in shame.

Everywhere I went around town, the tension was noticeable. Laughter was guarded. Even blacks when among other blacks moved about animatedly, with the jerky motions of those whose nerves are on edge. It was impossible for me to relax around them. And around whites, I found myself feeling very self-conscious, or just scared that something would happen suddenly and I would have to defend myself or run.

Downtown, a steady parade of picketers tried their best to ward off shoppers, and disgusted merchants spat retorts to them through store windows. I could see the angry lips moving, but the sound was muffled by the glass.

Police cruised the streets constantly, waiting to see what each new night would bring. Would the Klan hold a rally? Would there be a black–white clash? How long would this go on?

I sat in on sessions in which blacks were plotting a boycott of the county fair that had just arrived in town, and wondered what countermove the Klan would employ.

Blacks on the street talked freely about the Klan; about the machine guns in open view on the seats of cars; about how they believed that the Klan not only was above the law, but was the law.

I soon learned that there was more than a little truth to that allegation, because one night Wilkinson's boys rented space in a local motel and held a rally, during which a handful of recent converts removed their robes. Two of them turned out to be law-enforcement officers not ashamed to let the world know that they had taken up the hood and the cause.

Blacks in Tupelo made it clear, however, that the days when they feared the men in white sheets were long gone. "We are nonviolent," one of them told me, "but we are not cowards. It's not like eight or ten years ago. If a man in a white sheet wraps himself around a black man today, I say, 'Woe be unto him.' That black man is going to fight."

The absence of fear on the part of Tupelo's blacks, who comprise less than thirty percent of the city's population, was buttressed by the outward strength of their firebrand leader, Alfred "Skip" Robinson. A forty-two-year-old father of seven and building contractor from nearby Holly Springs, Robinson was the founder and head of the United League. He operated out of an old converted house near downtown Tupelo, where he held meetings with League workers, arranged speaking engagements to raise funds for the organization, and sifted through reports of shootings and other acts of violence by whites against blacks in several northern Mississippi counties.

Robinson's office was sparsely decorated. A few blacks lingered about the front steps or porch at all times of the day. I don't know whether they were there for security reasons or not, but I could see how their presence would be a deterrent to anybody considering doing harm to Robinson, at least in Tupelo, because many of those cluttered around the front of the house were burly and gave the impression that no nonsense was tolerated.

Since I'd been in town, I'd been told of several shootings of blacks by unknown assailants on the dark streets of Okolona (a nearby town) during the previous three weeks. It had also been reported that, just a few days before I arrived in Tupelo, a white man in a pickup had driven up next to a black man at a traffic light in Okolona, shot him twice — in the arm and in the leg — and driven away. According to the report, police there knew who did it, but refused to do anything. The League was trying to check this out.

"That's the kind of thing we're up against," Robinson said vehemently, as he showed me to a straight-backed chair in the tiny room that was his office. A desk, his chair, the chair I sat in, and a telephone were the only furniture.

I had not expected him to look the way he did, and stared at him a long time while shaking his calloused hand. Dressed in denim pants and jacket, he was one of the fiery denim-clad orators and community organizers I had thought were now an extinct breed. With him sitting right in front of me, it was as if the clock had not ticked one second beyond 1966.

His appearance was lionlike. He had a gray mane of thick hair, and sideburns framed his dark face and intense eyes.

"This thing goes back farther than outsiders realize," he said. "It didn't start a year ago when that white grocer in Shannon killed that black man who he said insulted his wife. It didn't start with the beating of that brother in jail here. This thing has been seething. Black folks have always been mistreated in Mississippi. We don't get our share of the good jobs. It's still like we don't have no rights. They try to treat us any way they want to, but that's got to stop. We ain't gonna stand for it no longer," he said sternly. "No longer."

"We got out in the streets after the beating at the jail," he continued. "We've been demanding the firing of the officers involved, and that the mayor, who got a heavy black vote, and the police chief, resign.

"But we've taken it farther than that," he said. "There are deeper issues involved — equal job opportunity and black economic development. White business interests been cleaning up off us in this region from the beginning, but where are your black businesses? Ain't none. They've been holding us down long enough."

Robinson said that his contracting business had suffered since he formed the United League, and that his house in Holly Springs was once burned down by "bastards" he suspected were Klansmen or Klan sympathizers.

"It's cost me a lot," he said matter-of-factly. "I been in the civil-rights movement since nineteen fifty-eight, because it's something that needs doing. It's got to be done. Right now, we are taking up where the movement of the sixties left off. The movement never quite got to Tupelo then, but we've brought it here now," he said.

"This time it's not about integrating the neighborhoods, integrating the schools," he continued, "because, in many ways, integration was the worst thing that ever happened to black people. For one thing, we lost so much of our identity, things that were our own. There used to be more black school principals in Mississippi, before integration, than anywhere in the country. Now, around here, you can count 'em on one hand. Integration has made us suffer even more."

The more I listened to him, the more I became convinced that he was an anachronism. His rhetoric was right out of the sixties, and his voice had the tone of the fiery street-corner speeches that had urged a generation of young people into America's angry streets.

He told me that he was genuinely concerned about what he saw as an attempt by racists to eliminate blacks in this country, and that he was very distrustful of any kind of family planning. "Black genocide," he said knowingly. That was a term I had not heard in a long time.

I wondered how long such tactics from the past could hold the imagination of this generation, how long he would be able to persuade those now following him to stand fast.

"Don't underestimate the power of what we are saying," he warned. "The United League already has over sixty-two thousand members in thirty-three counties here in Mississippi, and it's growing every day.

"You see, a lot of folks got off the movement train in the late sixties, to take a rest, and never got back on," he said. "Some of them got good jobs, headed up foundations or organizations that got a lot of government grants. Some of them got elected to office or took government jobs, but I never got off that train, 'cause it was clear to me the job had not been done, and it still ain't been done.

"You can just walk around this city and see how white folks are living, then see how black folks are living, and you know the job ain't been done. It ain't been done nowhere in this country. Don't let nobody fool you.

"What we are in right now is the midst of the American human-rights struggle. These protests in this state will continue. The movement is here to stay. This is just the beginning."

Robinson told me he had formed the League because the older civil-rights organizations like the NAACP seemed no longer effective.

"I tried to get the NAACP involved in what we're doing in Tupelo," Robinson said, "but they told me the NAACP couldn't come out and involve themselves in a boycott. They've done some good things in the past, and I've worked with 'em, supported 'em, but they're not doing the job now. I've heard some of them don't want me to continue with this, but if I have to fight the NAACP as well as the Klan to get what's right done, then I'll fight the NAACP. Right is right, and we're moving forward here. If they can't help us, they can just get out the way."

∙ ∙ ∙

The picketing dragged on downtown and at the fairgrounds, but each day there seemed to be a few more blacks in the stores.

The Klan held a few press conferences, in which they reaffirmed their position as guardians of the white race and vowed more cross burnings and rallies until the niggers were driven back to Africa.

The Klan rallies held at night just outside town attracted less than two hundred whites, most of whom attended only out of curiosity. I kept a safe distance from the goings-on, and watched Wilkinson gather his men in a circle around a huge flaming cross while he preached the same old racial hatred the

Klan has espoused for decades. He promised the white onlookers that the key to solving the problems of this country lay in their joining forces with his mighty Invisible Knights and doing "the job this weak gov'ment won't do."

It was pretty old stuff, and the image of these whites — grown men with decent jobs and loving families — carrying out the ring-around-the-rosy ritual, wearing white sheets and hoods while circling a flaming cross, seemed absurd. It was like a bad high school play, an ill-conceived comedy struggling to take itself seriously.

I knew then that ultimately the Klan could not survive. It was indeed dead. The Klan, as we had known it and feared it, had not come back, could not come back, because time had destroyed it. The sheet had been lifted by the FBI's infiltration in the sixties. It had been crushed by adverse public opinion brought on by its own deviltry and excesses. The mystery was gone. We had all finally seen it for what it really was, and we were no longer afraid. The Klan was exorcised from the public imagination, and now only the myth remained.

The splinter groups that were forming all over the country, bearing the bones of the old beast, would not be able to revive the original monster. With their new leanings toward openness with the media, and their ironic use of old civil-rights tactics such as marches and press conferences to draw attention, they were exposing themselves to daylight. With the mystery gone, we could never fear the Klan again, only despise it. Our fear was what had given the monster its strength, its life. Once we knew that those sheets merely hid crazed men, human like the rest of us, the magic disappeared.

Tupelo made me sad, sad that it was necessary for blacks to protest. But there was a need. They were mistreated, they did not have equal access to jobs, and there were still — as I later found out — separate and unequal waiting rooms for blacks and whites in at least one doctor's office in the area. It saddened me to see that man had not made any progress in his quest to learn how to solve even the most minor differences among social groups without resorting to drastic measures. It was as if we were living in an ongoing farce, in which nothing was given to anyone unless there were demands and/or threats of violence.

Tupelo made me sad because I was watching it repeat the same old mistakes; because in the end the past meant nothing to us. We were living only for ourselves, for now, for the future.

Tupelo also made me sad because I realized that the fate of the town and its people was in the self-serving hands of the United League and the Ku Klux Klan.

• • •

The League had planned a big march in Okolona for the following weekend. I couldn't stay for it, so I decided to leave for Jackson after one more day. I didn't know that the Holiday Inn had another little surprise for me — something to ensure that I would remember Tupelo always. The trouble the little voice had warned about on the day I arrived was about to come to pass.

It was the middle of the night. I was sound asleep in my room when I suddenly became aware of loud noises invading my sleep. I stirred, then came fully awake, realizing that somebody had unlocked the door to my room and was trying to force his way in through the chain latch. I jumped up in bed.

Maybe it's my shadow with the mustache, or the Klan out nigger hunting, I thought.

"Who is it?!" I shouted in the manliest voice I could muster.

"They rented this room to me," came the answer, in a gruff voice deeper than any I could ever mimic. "I been on the road all night. I'm tired and I'm going to bed!"

A huge, hairy forearm was jammed in the crack between the slightly opened door and the door frame.

"There's some mistake," I offered.

"Yeah," the voice said, "yours. You better git outta my room. I ain't in no mood for playin'."

I walked to the door. I had no weapon. The man outside the door was huge, a truck-driver type, with a massive pink face and oily hair. His reddish shirt sleeves were rolled up past the elbow, and his arms were the size of my lower legs.

I moved back to the bed, put my hand under the pillow and

brought it around in front of me, hoping it would suggest that a gun was concealed underneath. I pointed the pillow toward the door, making sure the man could see it. I wasn't about to open the door.

"If you don't get away from this room so I can sleep, there's going to be trouble," I said.

"But it's my room," he insisted.

"You better check with the desk," I said. "I ain't got time for this foolishness. And if I were you, I'd get my hand outta that door." I stared menacingly.

He studied the situation for a moment, then backed away from the door. I listened as his heavy footsteps moved down the corridor to the steps, then down the steps to the ground.

In a few minutes, he was back with the manager, who demanded that I open the door. I showed him the receipt I'd gotten from the desk when I checked in three days before and paid my bill in advance. He apologized, saying that he had not known I was in the room and that there was a new man at the desk that night.

"Sorry for the inconvenience," he said. He was a short, portly, balding man who nodded his head a lot. "Something like that would've scared me to death," he said, an odd smile on his face. "Again, I apologize."

They left, the trucker glaring at me as he backed away. I could tell he didn't want to turn his back on me. I closed the door, called the front desk, and asked the clerk if he had a wake-up call scheduled for me for six that morning. He said yes. I asked him how long he had worked at the Holiday Inn. He said nine years. I thanked him and hung up the phone. I couldn't go back to sleep, so at four-thirty in the morning I showered, shaved, got dressed, packed, and read until sunup. Then I spent my last day in Tupelo, watching the League and the Klan try to outmanuever each other.

•   •   •

Nearly two hundred miles south of Tupelo, to Jackson, is where I went looking for Bill Minor.

Operating out of a small rented office building on a quiet side street near downtown Jackson, Minor, a fifty-six-year-old crusading journalist, has managed to keep his tiny newspaper, the *Capital Reporter,* alive, despite the hardships he has had to face because of his editorial stands against local politicians, the power company, the downtown business power structure, and the Ku Klux Klan.

His scathing columns in the *Reporter* have resulted in the loss of much-needed advertising revenue for his paper, which reaches about 6000 subscribers weekly, and have brought him plenty of trouble from the Klan.

On separate occasions — following editorials about the reemergence of the Klan in Mississippi, and about some of the organization's activities — Minor's office had been vandalized, equipment had been sabotaged, and a huge flaming cross had been laid against the front of the building, destroying the electrical lines feeding the office.

Since December of 1977, Minor had been chronicling the "comeback" of the Klan in the *Reporter,* and it was apparent from a glance at the newspaper's office that his crusading had been at great cost. The large plate-glass window out front had been shattered. Covered now by a huge sheet of plywood, it reminded me of the bandaged storefronts in Atlanta's Summerhill section following the riot of 1966.

The shattered glass was the first physical sign of the Klan's displeasure with him, Minor told me. That incident was followed by others. A typesetting machine had been vandalized, and the most recent attack had been the flaming cross, which was spotted by an off-duty Jackson fireman who managed to knock it to the ground before it ignited the entire building.

The withdrawal of ads from his paper, the denunciation of him by politicians he has taken to task in editorials, and the "warnings" from the Klan have not stopped Minor, who was the Jackson correspondent for the *New Orleans Times Picayune* for better than twenty-eight years before resigning to run his own paper.

"I've been here thirty years, I've got my house paid for, the newspaper is mine. As long as I can still get up in the morning, come to the office and the building is still here, I'll keep on writing what I feel is right," said the soft-spoken, fast-talking Minor.

The cramped office of the newspaper could have been declared a disaster area. There were copies of newspapers, old photographs, tearsheets, scraps of paper, boxes, and clutter everywhere. Chairs were hidden under old newspapers.

Minor has had to find help wherever he can, since he's had little if any money to pay his employees. Help usually comes in the form of a college student or recent graduate who needs the experience more than the money.

Traffic in the tight office was constant. People stopped in off the street to tip Minor off about underhanded dealings and backroom arrangements at city hall or at the capitol. The tips came in faster than he could ever hope to check them out, but ads and subscriptions came in much more slowly. It seemed that a lot of ordinary people admired Minor and read him, but they didn't necessarily subscribe to his paper.

To help support the paper, Minor writes columns in seventeen other Mississippi newspapers and often takes stringing jobs with national magazines, since there are not many people alive who know and understand the Mississippi political scene as well as he does — a knowledge he has taken a lifetime to acquire. But despite all his efforts to hold his paper together, every day and each new problem bring with them the real possibility that the next day will be the *Reporter*'s last.

"My kids haven't shown all that much interest in it," he said sadly, "and the young people who come through here use it to gain experience so they can move on. And I don't blame them. I can't expect any of them to share the same dream I have. Their dream is to work for the *New York Times* or the *Washington Post*. They want to make a decent living and still change the world.

"When I was young, I had this dream of owning my own paper," he said. "Now that I'm old, the dream is old, too. This paper has meant a lot to me. I've been able to do what I wanted to do — speak out about things I think are wrong. How many times does a man get to do that without fear he'll be fired or pushed aside?" he asked philosophically. "I decided a long time ago I'd rather have this than be rich or famous. It's been enough."

Minor, who with his rugged good looks and long graying hair looks like a Hollywood stunt man, has boldly laid much of the blame for the Klan's surge of violent activity in Mississippi on the doorstep of the governor's mansion.

Minor told me he believed that then-governor Cliff Finch had given an air of official respectability to the Klan by appointing numerous "old-line segregationists" to key jobs in state government, while at the same time approving — "for the first time in history" — a charter of incorporation for the Invisible Empire, Knights of the Ku Klux Klan.

"You see," Minor said, "Finch picked up a heavy Klan vote in his march to the governor's office back in 1975. Now, according to many observers in state government, he's repaying that debt in political patronage."

Minor showed me several copies of the *Reporter* that carried editorials outlining the connection he was trying to make between Finch's appointees to government jobs and the rise in Klan activity around the state. "Earlier this year," Minor had written in one 1977 edition of the paper, "L. C. Murray of Natchez, the second-ranking official in the United Klans back in the 1960s, was given a plush job in the State Aid Road Division by Finch."

Subsequent editions of the *Reporter* singled out other "longtime segregationists, oldline Klansmen and members of the old White Citizens Council," who, according to Minor, had been appointed to state jobs by the Finch administration. Among these was one appointment to a key position that was, Minor felt, highly ironic. Minor wrote that "Finch pushed the hiring of Charles Blackwell, formerly a Klan attorney in Laurel who was involved with many of the Klan figures in the Neshoba [County] . . . cases [violence against civil-rights workers], as chief counsel for the State Department of Public Welfare." (This agency administers programs vitally important to poor blacks.)

"Correspondence which was secured by the *Reporter*," he

continued, "showed that Attorney General A. F. Summer sought to discourage the hiring of Blackwell, but the governor's office insisted that Blackwell be hired."

"One of Finch's earlier appointees," Minor wrote in another edition, "was Elmore Greaves, a well-known pamphleteer and spokesman for white supremacy during the heyday of segregation. Greaves, who was named by Finch to the Mississippi Agricultural and Industrial Board, had been called before the House Un-American Activities Committee in its 1966 investigation into the Ku Klux Klan. Greaves had refused to answer questions as to whether he was a member of the Klan and had taken part in several rallies."

Minor wrote in the same edition that "When the State ABC board recently hired a new director, Finch saw to it that James 'Buster' Treloar, former sheriff of Yalobusha County, got the job. Treloar was known back in the 1950s as one of the worst race-baiters among the state law-enforcement fraternity.

"Just when the state was trying to live down the bad image that the Emmet Till case had given it in 1955, a black man was beaten to death in Treloar's jail, and several white witnesses saw the sheriff club the man with his blackjack.

"Treloar was indicted, but quickly acquitted by an all-white jury. A *Time* magazine story of the trial reported that Treloar, with a big grin, said afterwards, as he picked up his blackjack, he had to get back to round up 'Niggers.'"

I spent an entire day with Minor, even accompanying him to the funeral of his former high school English teacher, who was to be buried just across the Mississippi border in a small Louisiana town. A funny thing about it was that I was the only black present at the funeral services, and the reception afterward at the home of a white family. I was simply introduced as a friend of Minor's, and somehow I was not at all self-conscious about being the only black in a throng of whites.

All during the drive down there, Minor and I had talked about race relations, the Klan, violence, and fear, and yet during the funeral and the events that followed, all those problems seemed distant, like things of the past. I only thought of the woman who'd died, and all the nice things people said about her. It was as if I had somehow been released from race, freed for the moment from having to think about it.

． ． ．

I felt I had to ask Finch about some of the comments Minor had made concerning the governor's appointees to state office.

A spokesman for Governor Finch told me that if any of the governor's appointees were segregationists, it was "not to his knowledge."

"If so," said Bill Bartlett, "it is something that was in the past, not today. Governor Finch has put together a black and white coalition. His entire administration has been for all the people. He is not an advocate of any group, but he recognized the right of assembly of any group as long as they do it in a manner that is in the letter of the law."

Bartlett told me that the state would step into the Tupelo situation "only at the request of the local government. So far, there has been no such request." He insisted that the racial troubles in Tupelo could not be compared to the demonstrations of the 1960s. I told him that to me they seemed almost identical to those protests.

"Mississippi has made great strides in race relations," he countered. "These two groups [the United League and the Ku Klux Klan] are minimal in size. What they are having there is a difference in philosophy. It is not the nineteen sixties all over again. The sixties are gone. This situation cannot be equated with that time. It is all this publicity that adds momentum to these groups and keeps them going," he declared.

True, to a small extent, I thought. Both groups were actively seeking publicity, and needed it in order to grow. But it was not true that if the media went away, the problems that gave rise to the protests would go away. I was convinced that even without publicity there would still be protests in Tupelo, and maybe even more violence. I told Bartlett this. He did not agree.

"It's all this publicity that keeps 'em going," he insisted.

I thanked him, and we ended our phone conversation. I continued to think about Mississippi, about Minor, and especially about Tupelo. All over northern Mississippi, United League members and other blacks were at that very moment planning further demonstrations. At the same time, Klansmen were plotting what they would do next to bring the niggers to their knees.

There is this little difference of philosophy in Tupelo, Bartlett had said. Just the difference that causes bloodshed, I thought; the kind that shatters people's lives. And what is war, I thought, but a difference in philosophy?

III

Aftermath

This is a very small planet, and we are entering a period of uncertainty that is bound to
make us very selfish, and smaller . . .
— Paul Theroux

17

The Road from Here,
Part I

THE STORM of publicity that swept over me after my articles
were published brought me hardly any happiness or peace of
mind. The television appearances, the interviews by foreign
journalists, and the requests for speeches failed to fill me with
the sense of personal satisfaction I had assumed they would.
These were things I had secretly longed for all my life. I had
wanted to feel that people actually listened to what I had to say
— hung on my every word, even — and applauded me.

I had always longed to be a celebrated writer, a man of ideas
whom people recognized on the street and smiled at or waved
to. "Mr. Fuller," they would say in my dreams, "saw you on
the Carson show. Enjoyed you very much." Or, "caught you on
the Cavett show. Very nice."

And people did stop me on the streets of Atlanta. Beaming,
they would tell me they'd seen me on a certain television show
or heard me interviewed over the radio, or that they'd read my
series or read about some award I'd just won. They'd wish me
luck and tell me to keep up the good work. This went on for
weeks. Being a small-time celebrity only embarrassed me and
deepened my sadness, for each time celebrity treatment was
accorded me, I was reminded of the people whose unfortunate

lives had made all this good treatment and instant recognition possible for me. I was haunted by sad eyes, by people with simple ways who asked for little and received even less.

Along with my sudden celebrity status came the realization that people were clearly more affected by, and interested in, what I'd done than what I had found. They got very excited and wanted to know all about why I'd taken on the assignment, what clothes I had worn, where I had stayed, how I had traveled, how I had changed the way I talked — all of the mechanical and cosmetic details. They wanted to know if I was ever afraid. The conditions I had described — the lives the people led, the suffering they endured — were not nearly so magical and interesting to them. It was part of a phenomenon I had noticed about people in the news business. It had always struck me as odd that certain journalists, certain television interviewers and anchor people, because of the way they wrote or talked, became such recognizable personalities in the public's mind that they somehow became even more important than the news they reported.

I was tormented by a feeling of impotence, as if I were somehow spinning my wheels, standing around accepting plaudits while children went ragged in Americus and ate grits three times a day.

At the office, Rankin and Minter felt we had a great series on our hands. They basked in all the publicity and encouraged me to keep the stories coming, to go back on the road. Before long, the expectation that I would win a Pulitzer for the *Journal* was so strong in the newsroom that it became impossible for me to relax there any longer.

"Nobody ever won it without going after it," Minter told me. "I think you've got a helluva chance. And besides, what you're doing is important on its own. Look at it, that woman in North Carolina getting a brand new house because of what you wrote. That's more important than fifty sessions of Congress. I think you can win the thing," he said conspiratorially. "But you've got to want it," he added solemnly.

Now I knew what was expected of me, at least from the newspaper. But what could I do for those sad people living on the edge of the abyss out there in the New Dixie? Simply writing about their plight did not seem enough.

Nonetheless, I took to the road again, this time as a reporter asking questions, trying to find anybody who could offer solutions to the problems of the poor and dispossessed in the South.

With the help of people who had read the series, I came across three programs designed to help those I had written about. They are examples of the good that I feel can be done on a larger scale in this country, if we as a people are more willing to improve things for the less fortunate.

Two of the three programs are government-connected, while the other is run by a religious organization. All three are located in states I had visited earlier, but I did not learn of their existence until after I'd already written the initial newspaper series.

The first program I investigated took me back to Americus, Georgia, where I found a set of houses for the poor that differed from the worn-out shotgun shacks I'd encountered on Beale Street. These were by no means fancy houses, but they were new, roomy, and well insulated against the harsh blasts of winter. They were cheap, but for many of the poor and needy they were indeed a blessing. For me, the surprising story behind these houses was that they were built without any government assistance; no taxpayers' money was involved. The houses were sold to the poor at cost, and no interest was charged. The outfit behind this project is called Habitat for Humanity, and one of the principal figures behind Habitat is a man named Millard Fuller (no relation to the author).

• • •

The young woman smiled at Millard Fuller — a lanky forty-three-year-old lawyer from Montgomery, Alabama — as we entered the house. There were strands of gray in his dark hair, and his metal-frame glasses seemed too big for his face. He moved with the awkward grace of Washington Irving's Ichabod Crane. It was clear to me that this man was well liked here. The young woman was Mrs. Sarah Moore, twenty-six. She, her twenty-eight-year-old husband, Henry, and their three children had been living in this house built by Habitat for Humanity since March, 1978. It was a modest home with three bedrooms and a den, and, according to Mrs. Moore, it was immensely better than the low-rent apartment the family had lived in previously.

"We lived in these apartments not far from here," she said, "and had a two-bedroom place for eighty-one dollars a month. Now, we got our own home with three bedrooms, a den, and it's our own place and we pay only ninety dollars a month.

"At the apartment, they [the management] were all the time sending us letters saying we had to do this, had to do that, or couldn't do this or couldn't do that. It's hard to live that way. In our own home, we can fix things up just like we want. It's just so much better. We never thought we could own our own home this soon."

This housing program was a side of Americus nobody had told me about when I was here before. No one I met then had mentioned Habitat or the parent organization behind it — Koinonia Partners. The work being done here for the poor is so basic that it is actually stunning in its simplicity. Houses are being built for exactly what they cost — no profit margin, no interest added. Those poor people fortunate enough to be chosen can buy houses with about $700 down and monthly notes ranging from $45 to $90 for 30 years. It was incredibly simple, yet I found it hard to believe that it really worked, perhaps because I, like so many others, had been conditioned by the massive waste of big government to think that anything that is not complicated and doesn't have umpteen layers to administer it has no chance of succeeding. But here it was working, and there were scores of happy families who had been able to move out of crowded shacks and low-rent apartments into their own comfortable homes, at prices they could readily afford.

"You talk to government bureaucrats," said Fuller adamantly, "and they have all kinds of excuses and reasons why they can't do what we're doing. They tell us what we're doing can't be done, even though we're doing it. They won't do it, because if they solve the problems, they'll be out of their jobs. And you know they don't want that."

• • •

Koinonia Partners is a nonprofit, privately supported cooperative farm community a few miles from Americus. At the time I visited, it was composed of approximately thirty-four families who still believe in the ideals of the community's founder, the late Clarence Jordan, who first envisioned a Christian farming community that would exemplify "the kinship of humanity both black and white." In 1942, on land off Georgia Highway 49, Jordan, with his wife Florence, began to explore "ways and means of productive farming under a life style patterned on the Christian community called Koinonia in the Greek New Testament," according to the group's literature. In the beginning, the community was often hassled by people from the surrounding towns and by the Ku Klux Klan, because of its belief that blacks and whites could live together peacefully.

Down through the years, there were several acts of vandalism at the farm, boycotts against the commune's products, and repeated demands that Koinonia members get out of Georgia. Somehow the commune survived those lean and threatening times. Since 1968, the partners, using donations from people all over the world, have been building low-cost houses for poor people, mainly in Sumter County. To date, more than 100 houses have been built, all with cash as it comes in, and more were under construction when I visited, with others planned.

According to Ted Swisher, the twenty-nine-year-old coordinator of Koinonia Partners, "In the ten years we've been building these houses, we've never had to foreclose on a single house."

"People often get behind in their payments," added Fuller, "but we try to work it out with them, and it's worked so far."

Money for construction comes mainly through what is called the Fund for Humanity. Families currently living in the houses built with money from the fund are repaying, in house payments, more than $3000 a month. This money is used to build other houses. As evidence of the tremendous need for what Habitat and Koinonia are doing, the partners said that they had over 200 applications for the 28 units that were under construction in Sumter County.

"It's our feeling here," said Fuller, "that it is better to do what you can than to sit and bemoan the bigness of the problem. You will never get a majority of people in this country to get involved in anything. You have to work with the dedicated few, those of good will, and accomplish what you can. That's what we do."

• • •

Millard Fuller sat behind a desk in a house on West Church Street that had been converted into a law office which he shared with another attorney. Next door, the "international" headquarters of Habitat for Humanity was situated in another converted house. Fuller is executive director of the housing venture formed with the blessings of the Koinonia Partners over three years ago. His goal is to extend to other areas of the world the housing programs and practices started by Koinonia in Sumter County thirteen years ago.

Already, Habitat had built homes, and indeed whole communities, in Zaire, Africa, Fuller said. They were considering projects in Tanzania and Zambia, and programs were underway in San Antonio, Texas; Morgan, Tennessee; Johns Island, South Carolina; and Immokalee, Florida. I was shown slides of the work being done in Africa — modern villages containing clusters of sturdy-looking houses, recreation centers, and community buildings, all constructed with concrete blocks. Fuller showed me a statement of the Habitat operation's income and expenses for the first nine months of the year. According to the statement, more than $270,000 in gifts and donations had been received and nearly $260,000 expended.

Listening to Fuller talk, absorbing his boundless enthusiasm and seemingly unshakable belief that people can help change things for their less fortunate brothers, it was easy for me to understand why so many people all over the globe send money to help Habitat. This man could sell fleas to a pest-control company.

"I made a fortune in business back in Alabama," he said.

"I thought you were a lawyer," I said.

"I am," he answered, "but I didn't make no money as a lawyer. I had a direct-mail business with my partner, Morris Dees. [Dees is known nationally as an expert political-campaign fund raiser.] We were in school together, and when we got out, we decided we were going to make some money. And we did. You wouldn't believe all the money we made through the direct-mail business. Man, I had a fortune," he said. "Twelve years ago, I had plans on the drawing board for a $150,000 home on a twenty-acre lot in a plush new subdivision just outside Montgomery. A little farther down the road, my business partner and I owned two thousand acres of prime farm land," he said with a smile. "My wife and I never built that house, though."

Fuller said he had a religious experience in 1966 and turned his back on his business and fortune and decided to devote his life to Christ.

In 1968, he brought his family to Koinonia, where he served a stint as director, helping the partners build up a sagging mail-order pecan- and peanut-selling business. With his legal experience and considerable business acumen, he soon helped get the farm's enterprises into high gear.

After living in Africa for several years, Fuller returned to Koinonia and set up Habitat. About two years ago, he moved his family from the Koinonia community to a house in a close-in city neighborhood. The all-white neighborhood, which bordered a squalid, all-black neighborhood, didn't receive Fuller and his family very warmly. "We found piles of broken glass in our drive-way every morning for two weeks, when we first moved," he said. "They all knew I was associated with Koinonia.

"It's really a shame we can't get blacks into the houses in this neighborhood," he lamented. "They are really a bargain. Whites are moving out. You can buy them for twelve thousand dollars or a little more. They're still very good houses, but it would take a courageous black family to move in here, because this is still a tough area of the state. I wouldn't feel right encouraging any blacks to move in, because there could very well be trouble, you know, bombings and the like. And I'm not kidding.

"But if blacks ever did start to move in here, it would make our work a lot cheaper," he said. "We could help them buy these houses and renovate them, probably, cheaper than we can buy land and build new houses. But like I said, it could be very dangerous. Very dangerous. So right now, it's just a thought."

• • •

During the time I was crisscrossing the South to examine the programs I mentioned earlier, I also looked in on former and current black leaders and many whites who had been human-rights activists in the fifties and sixties. I interviewed others by phone and even went to Washington to talk with the head of the U.S. Community Services Administration (the current federal antipoverty agency), Graciela Olivarez. I also spoke with Sargent Shriver, who had spearheaded Lyndon Johnson's War on Poverty, and Stuart Eizenstat, President Carter's chief domestic policy adviser.

Their thoughts on the matter were not encouraging. In fact, many of those who had been considered leaders during the civil-rights days — those who had suffered at the hands of angry state troopers and billy-club-wielding jailers, so that all U.S. citizens might have equal access to the advantages of American life — were as disturbed by the present lack of progress as I was. They could not offer much hope, and they seemed just as worried as I am that very few people in this country appear at all concerned about the problems of the poor.

"I try to be very hopeful and optimistic about change," said John Lewis sadly. Lewis led his share of marches during the dark days of the movement, particularly the Selma march, and once headed the Student Nonviolent Coordinating Committee (SNCC) and the Atlanta-based Voter Education Project (VEP) — an organization that has been instrumental in registering millions of poor blacks and whites all over the South. The increase in the number of black elected officials in the South over the past few years can be explained in large part by the VEP's successful efforts to register the previously disenfranchised.

Lewis, at the time of our conversation, was a top administrator in the federal Action Agency, a position he was appointed to by

President Carter after making an unsuccessful bid for Georgia's Fifth District congressional seat vacated by Andy Young when he took the job as United Nations ambassador.

"I try to remain hopeful," Lewis repeated, "but I just don't see the initiative, the will to solve these problems. The actions of this Congress clearly showed it was looking out for the greedy and not for those in need. And when I speak of the needy, I'm talking about a whole segment of the American population, not just in the South. Even in places like Maine, where you don't have a great many black people, there is a large concentration of poor whites, and I'm not kidding when I say they are struggling just to survive."

Lewis's remarks reminded me of a statistic that Graciela Olivarez of the Community Services Administration had said was one of this country's well-kept secrets: that most of the poor people in America — 16.7 million of the 25 million people listed by the government as being below the poverty level — are white.

According to Olivarez's breakdown, 7 million of these 25 million are disabled or handicapped; 3 million are elderly and live on fixed incomes; nearly 7 million are children; and about 2 million work full time at the minimum wage and still can't escape the vicious clutches of poverty.

Lewis said that part of the reason for the current lack of progress in dealing with the problems of the poor was "this dangerous trend — caring only about yourself.

"I feel so helpless sometimes," he said. "So limited."

After a long silence, he continued. "It's going to take something to shock us all. We are sowing the seeds for trouble, for major conflict in the future, with this attitude that 'I got mine, can't worry about you.' These desperate people are not going away. I see hundreds of young men here in Washington on the street corners, with nothing to do, standing there, no jobs, nowhere to go. We haven't learned anything from recent history. We are in for a season of conflict. Maybe it's already too late . . . I don't want to be a prophet of doom . . ."

There was another long silence.

"A new kind of organization is needed," he finally said, the words exploding from his mouth. "Masses of people would have to be well organized and mobilized. A new force, a new type of organization that would organize people from the bottom up, not from the top down. It would be hard work, damn hard. It would require dedication like you've never seen."

"Are you too tired to do it?" I asked.

"No," he answered. "I'm not too tired. You know, I question my being here [in a government job]. I question my whole role here. I've said on several occasions that I might be more effective outside than here.

"If anything, I think we are losing ground in the fight that so many of us gave a lot to. We are slipping. If ever there was a time when there is a need to get black people, poor people, registered to vote, it is now. Combine them with the Chicanos in the Southwest. You could have a powerful coalition to change things in this country.

"But too many people get caught up in protecting their positions," he said, toning down. "They become blind. I've told a lot of people since I came here that they need to get out of Washington. Get out of the office, walk the streets, visit the South, New York, anything. Because you lose touch here. You lose touch with the problems . . ."

Ruby Hurley, who had also put her shoulder to the wheel during the movement, was another person I looked to for answers. She had spent thirty-five years with the National Association for the Advancement of Colored People, twenty-seven of those years in the South. Until June 1978, she had served in Atlanta as regional director of that long-standing civil-rights organization, but the frustration of seeing many of the gains won during the fifties and sixties slip away and experiencing difficulty in "getting people to move on anything" helped her make up her mind to retire.

"The frustrations were taking their toll," she said. "Things are worse now for black folks than they've ever been, and they're going backwards. The New South is mainly an illusion created by newspaper people. And because a few black folks are making a name for themselves or building their own personal empires, we just sit back and accept what the papers say.

"One reason I don't have any regrets about retiring is that I look around at all the people who are benefiting from all the hours and pain other people put in during the movement. These people enjoying these positions and finery don't even know how they got them," she said sadly. "They know nothing about the civil-rights movement. They don't understand from where we had to come."

There was much heaviness in her voice, as if it were many voices wound into one, and those voices, like a sad chorus, were tinged with sorrow.

"A lot of them are running around here believing this notion that Atlanta was — somehow — always different from other places," she said. "Not as racist."

"They didn't have to ride the trains into the Jim Crow station. They don't know anything about the wall one of the former mayors built to keep Negroes out of Peyton Forest [a residential subdivision]. They don't know what Talmadge was like when he was governor. People have a tendency to see what they want to see and close their eyes to all else," she said vehemently. "You can't get this well-to-do younger bunch to do anything now. Most of the middle-class blacks of today didn't have any share in getting where we are today. They have no concept of what it was like. That goes for the young politicians, too. They have no concept.

"I don't know what it's going to take to straighten things out, and I'm scared to death. The NAACP is not even the same. All of those who knew what it was like are gone. We've got a whole new crew running things, and they don't know what it was like. They don't have the things pushing them that pushed us . . . I'll never forget what it was like. I still remember talking to Medgar [Evers] that Saturday morning back during the sixties. And that Monday he was gone. Shot down. I could've been with him. You don't forget things like that."

The more I thought about what Ruby Hurley, John Lewis, and others had said, the more the image formed in my mind of a tremendously muscular black beast, a giant with powerful shoulders and arms, and massive legs, but no head. Part of the problem

— and probably a small part — is that black people in this country are in the midst of the most serious leadership crisis to face us since slavery. At a time when there is an urgent need for someone exceptional to emerge from that nebulous throng of people who have at one time or another been called leaders, few seem willing to speak up on behalf of the poor and disadvantaged.

Vernon Jordan, head of the National Urban League, has been consistently critical of President Carter's initiatives (or lack thereof) on behalf of blacks and the poor. In a way, he has emerged as a consensus leader, along with Jesse Jackson of Operation PUSH (People United to Save Humanity).

But it is difficult to determine whether Jordan and Jackson are fully sanctioned by the people they claim to represent, or whether they are merely leaders invented by the typewriters of reporters and editorial writers throughout the country. There are arguments on both sides.

Jackson and other black "leaders," including the national president of the Southern Christian Leadership Conference, Joseph Lowery, have taken a strange turn in recent times. They have seemingly abandoned, for the moment at least, the domestic concerns of black folks here at home, in favor of dabbling in Henry Kissinger–style shuttle diplomacy in the Middle East. Jackson has been photographed hugging and kissing PLO leader Yassir Arafat, and insisting that the PLO be given a greater role in the solving of that troubled region's problems. Meanwhile, here at home, things continue to get worse for poor blacks and whites; unemployment climbs and desperation deepens.

"We can't get together on anything," Ruby Hurley said. "Blacks are so interested in making a name for themselves. Vernon Jordan is still raising hell, but a lot of other blacks are envious because he has emerged as the senior black leader.

"In a very real sense," she said, "black politicians have lied to the people. They promise them they are going to do all these things that only they can do for them, and they never intend to deliver. We've got to become more sophisticated politically. Decisions are made on the golf course while we're dancing or having our big dinners at the Peachtree Plaza. It is just too damned important. We can't keep wasting whatever political power we get.

"We've got seventeen blacks as mayors of cities in Mississippi," she said, "but who is teaching them how to be mayors? There has got to be an end to this selfishness and egotism. Those blacks, leaders, who can, must help others. It's the only way we're going to survive."

One former activist I talked to asked not to be identified, because he blamed a lot of the current woe faced by blacks on the "so-called black leaders" — people he had worked with in the past.

"It is my view," he told me, "that blacks are going to lose this thing as long as it is played out the way it is. We've got all these media-created leaders — and the people have gone along with them — who didn't do anything during the movement. You didn't see them anywhere. People like Vernon Jordan and Jesse Jackson did show up sometimes, but they're in there with Roy Innis, Coretta King, and Ben Hooks of the NAACP.

"They're what I call sophisticated superfly. They talk a good game, but they don't even know what it's all about. Or worse, they know, but pacify the people with smooth speeches and these hollow calls for more jobs programs. Those programs are just maintenance. We need something more basic than that — economic participation, our fair share. We are not going to get anything economically until we confront the people who make the economic decisions."

Lonnie King agreed. King, who was ousted as head of the Atlanta chapter of the NAACP in the early seventies because he disagreed with the national office over how the Atlanta school desegregation matter ought to be handled, is now in private business, with offices in Atlanta and Washington, D.C.

"We as a people need to stop worrying about the social aspects of integration and concentrate on economics," King said. "Show me the black economic clout in America. It's not there. And money is power. We need to stop blaming whites so much, because there are things we can do to help ourselves. For instance, planning. There is not a black group in America that has plans for where black people ought to be in religion, economics, politics, et cetera, in the next few years. Nobody is planning how we can leverage the factors of production — land, labor, and entrepreneurship — for the benefit of black people. That's what it's all about."

. . .

Again I was on a roller coaster. The interviews usually plunged me into deep despair, leaving me with a feeling of almost total futility. Then the programs I had chosen to investigate and write about would fill me with a fresh sense of hope — not exuberant hope, but a flame of belief that things didn't have to be as bad as they were, and that there were answers — somewhere. All I had to do was find them.

The second program I investigated was operating just north of Charlotte, North Carolina. By the time I left there, I was once again on the rails going up.

Marcia Kuhn, an energetic lady with a knack for inspiring people to want to help themselves, met me at the Charlotte airport and drove me to her office in the predominantly black Kingville community in Stanly County.

Kingville, she told me, was the target area for her project, which is called Human Resources Development Program (HRD). I knew we'd arrived as soon as the lush farmland lay behind us and we entered a small community of tiny houses and narrow roads — the enclave of the poor. Across the way, I could see the school that had been abandoned during integration and now provided offices for the program, which is operated through the North Carolina community-college system, with forty-seven of the state's fifty-seven community schools participating.

"The Human Resources Development Program," said Ms. Kuhn, "was started about four years ago. It was designed to identify hardcore unemployed and underemployed adults; to recruit them; teach them how to get a job, and how to keep a job once they land one."

HRD works. The cases of three former participants convinced me of that right away. One of them, a thirty-three-year-old mother of three, had been separated from her husband and was struggling to raise her children while receiving welfare and food stamps. The woman wanted to work, but had never had any success in getting a job. She entered the program, and graduated two years ago. After graduation, she landed a job as a production worker with a local firm that manufactures electrical parts, and she's been working ever since. During the Christmas season of 1979, she even held down a part-time job in addition to her regular work, to help make ends meet. More than anything else, she was proud of the fact that, since taking the job, she had been totally off welfare and had successfully supported herself and three children.

Another woman who completed the program had been in desperate need of work. At age thirty-one, she had been unemployed for more than three years when she got into the program. She has worked as a teller with a local bank for the past two years, thanks to the HRD training she received.

And then there was the twenty-two-year-old man who had been laid off from a factory job and needed work to support his wife and new baby. The fact that at the time he could read and write at only a third-grade level made it extremely difficult for him to find work. According to Ms. Kuhn, the young man was expected to soon complete work for his high school diploma. He had gotten a job as an assistant dog warden for the county.

These were people who had been tossed on life's trash heap and forgotten, because they had little education, or no job skills, or didn't know how to interview for a job, or didn't know how to hold a job. For various reasons, they had been relegated to the welfare rolls, to poverty and hopelessness. That is, until Marcia Kuhn found them.

The sturdily built, dark-haired woman showed me reports on the program that were filled with strange terms like *competitive efficiency funding earnback index,* and other abstract concepts used to analyze and evaluate the success of the project. I also met the people whose lives had been changed by the opportunity to work and make their own way in the world. Formerly, when they had been wards of the welfare system, each monthly check had often done more to make them feel frustration and a sense of worthlessness than it had to provide them with real assistance.

For me, the people I saw and the turns their lives had taken spoke volumes about the worth of this program.

In the two years Marcia Kuhn had headed the project in Stanly County, the taxable income of participants had increased by $162,361, she said. Many of the "students," as she called them, who ranged in age from eighteen to middle age, had never held steady jobs before joining the program.

During that same two-year period, according to Ms. Kuhn, the program saved more than $29,000 in county public-assistance payments, because some previous welfare recipients were able to get off assistance entirely.

According to Ms. Kuhn, it cost the state about $5 million to conduct the program in fiscal 1978 — including $2 million in federal CETA funds. Nonetheless, the state was able to reduce its welfare payments by $1.9 million because of the program, she said, and graduates increased their taxable incomes (state-wide) by $6.9 million.

"That is a significant thing," she said proudly. "Almost seven million dollars in taxable income added to the state's economy. And there is something even more significant. All those people who had felt left out — many on welfare — were able to get jobs and earn money, feel like they were contributing. Some of them for the first time in their lives."

When you get down to it, the program is simple. Common sense is applied to a classroom situation. Participants are given six-to-eight-week classroom courses in how to find jobs and how to hang on to them once they are obtained. Almost everything is covered. "I mean, it is basic," Ms. Kuhn said. "We're not here to help those who are college material. There are enough people around to help those. We pick up the people who have been left out and are untouched by most other programs. These people are usually living very desperate lives, living on the edge.

"And giving them a job is not the answer by itself," she said. "We get them in classroom situations. We teach them how to interview for a job. How to find jobs in the newspaper, how to call for an interview, the very fundamental things that most of us take for granted.

"These people can't take anything for granted. We try to teach them the value of being on time for work, how to handle criticism from supervisors, and how to turn themselves into better workers. We often let them play-act situations, with them being the employer and other students acting as job applicants. We help them understand how to fill out applications and job forms of all kinds. We have personnel managers from all over the county come in and talk to them. When some students get jobs during the course, we are able to use their on-the-job experiences as discussion material in class.

"I suppose most of our graduates earn right around the minimum wage, but there are others who come back to visit and they now have jobs where they earn more than I do," she said.

"What we try to do in the beginning is zero in on exactly what kind of job they're interested in, whether it's a clerk's position or in a mill. We want to know if they like third-shift work, or like wearing uniforms, or what. All those things are extremely important."

It is not always easy to convince people out of work or on welfare that they can benefit from the HRD program. "I've literally gone from door to door trying to get people in this program, because I knew we could help them," said Ms. Kuhn. "Sometimes it is hard to get people to want to help themselves. They often have so many problems and so many excuses. When they need understanding, I can understand them. When they're just plain lazy, I'm hard on them, because they've got to understand they have families and responsibilities, so they've got to work."

Another aspect of this program that really impressed me was the amount of effort made to find out how former students were making out in the workaday world. Ms. Kuhn and her staff try to track down every student who graduates from the program. They monitor the students' progress every few months, to see if they are still employed. "We have tracked them as far as North Dakota," she said, "and most of them are still on their initial jobs or have gone on to better positions.

"We also have a program set up in the local prison, where we help those who are about to be released or placed in work-release centers. We've had a lot of success with that, too," she said happily.

The more I thought about the HRD program, the more I wondered why North Carolina was the only state using it. According to Ms. Kuhn, government officials in Washington were studying it, and the government in Egypt was getting ready to install the system there, after examining the North Carolina project.

It certainly looked good from where I sat.

•   •   •

The final project that caught my interest took me back to Greenville, in the Mississippi Delta, where some of this country's poorest people struggle to live on some of the most fertile land in this part of the world.

In the heart of downtown Greenville, a port city of some 47,000 — at 819 Main Street, to be exact — in a cluster of offices filled with nicely dressed, important-looking business people and secretaries, I found a black financial empire slowly taking shape in the midst of devastating poverty.

The corporation is called Delta Enterprises, and its growing list of subsidiaries had gross sales of more than $5.8 million in fiscal 1977, placing the company in the number 58 spot on the 1978 *Black Enterprise* magazine listing of the nation's top 100 black-owned companies. Revenues for fiscal 1978, I was told, were expected to top $7.5 million.

Delta Enterprises is a holding company of the Delta Foundation, a minority-controlled Community Development Corporation (CDC) begun in 1970 by fourteen black community groups in Greenville. It is currently funded by a $4.2 million, two-year grant from the federal government's Community Services Administration. According to Graciela Olivarez, who headed the CSA, the Delta Foundation has quietly emerged as one of the most successful models for rural development anywhere.

At the helm of Delta is Charles Bannerman, a handsome thirty-seven-year-old northerner raised in Harlem, New York, and Columbus, Ohio. He is chief executive officer of Delta Foundation (the CDC) and Delta Enterprises, the holding company that handles the three profit-making companies that form the outfit's financial nucleus.

Bannerman, who strides through the corporation's offices with the self-assured air of one who truly enjoys power, told me he first came to Mississippi in 1966, after graduating from Ohio State University. Lured south by the civil-rights movement, he had intended to stay for only a year.

"Like most northerners," he said, "I spent my life rejecting my southern roots, and when I first came south, I had the typical New York arrogance. I soon learned, however, that the people were warm and friendly. If anyone was ignorant, it was I."

As president of Delta Enterprises, Bannerman now oversees a budding empire that employs more than 350 people, with a combined payroll for the three companies that approaches $2 million. This is certainly welcomed in the Mississippi Delta, where the sixteen river counties that make up the region have a median family income that ranks among the state's lowest.

Delta Enterprises currently operates Fine Vines, Inc., a manufacturing concern that turns out more than 1500 pairs of blue jeans weekly; Mid South Metal Stamping, Inc., which produces commercial and residential attic fans, and folding wooden staircases; and Electro Controls, Inc., which manufactures electronic pressure switches, relays, current sensors, and dri-reed switches for the aircraft and computer industries.

Fine Vines, whose biggest customer right now is the J. C. Penny Company, is located in Greenville, not far from the Delta Enterprise offices. Mid South Metal Stamping has plants in nearby Memphis, Tennessee, and in the small town of Sardis, Mississippi, while Electro Controls is located in Canton, just north of Jackson, the state capital.

"When we first opened Fine Vines here in December of 'sixty-nine," Bannerman said, "we had seventy job openings, and seven hundred people showed up looking for work. That's how bad it was. This is an area that had survived on farming. Cotton was king, but when farming became more and more mechanized, the people weren't needed anymore. There was no industry to absorb them."

Despite the progress Delta Enterprises has already made, and the wide ray of hope it has brought to many of the Delta's people, Bannerman is reluctant to call the company successful. "Rather than say we're successful," he told me, "I just like to say we're growing. And that's something I believe will take a long time to convince other people of. We are growing and coming along probably because we are in Mississippi. There are opportunities for blacks in Mississippi that are unavailable anywhere else," he said. "There's a tradition of black entrepreneurship in the South, and in Mississippi there is a sense of black self-determination stronger than in any other state. It's possible to get things accomplished in Mississippi, in terms of concrete aid to people, that could never be achieved in New York."

During the eight years the corporation has been in existence, there have been many subtle changes, often prompted by the realities of the business world, that have given Bannerman and his staff a new sense of business savvy and maturity.

"At one time, we had all-black management," Bannerman said. "I was like a lot of new businessmen. I figured that if we had money and a market, we could make it. I now know that money isn't the answer: it's management. Today, I'm interested in skills and talents rather than race."

Although all of Delta Enterprises' plants are now managed by whites, most of whom have several years of experience in their respective industries, young blacks hold several key management and executive positions within the organization.

One of those young black executives is Henry Myles. Myles is a Greenville native in his mid-twenties who went away to college and thought he'd never return there to live, because job opportunities for upwardly mobile blacks were nonexistent in the area — until Delta Enterprises, that is.

Myles is director of public affairs, a position that affords him the luxury of countrywide business travel and a middle-class lifestyle he never expected to enjoy in his hometown.

"I was fortunate that Delta Enterprises was in full operation when I got out of school," Myles said, "because otherwise there would have been very little for a person like me here. So many of my friends — all talented people — had to go elsewhere. After you spend four years in college, you sure don't want to go back to work in a mill or in the fields.

"Here at Delta, we're giving young people a chance," he said. "We can't hire everybody who needs work, but we've got a good start. This is something that has almost no limits, and it can serve as an example for people in other areas of the country. It makes me tremendously excited about the future," he added. "I definitely think we're in for solid growth."

Bannerman, who describes himself as a city boy who came to the country, added, "I'm trying to get people to think more positively about Mississippi and the South. A lot of people who left the South to find work in the forties and fifties, return here to die," he said. "I'm trying to convince people that it's now possible to return here and live."

18

The Road from Here, Part II

SINCE THE Great Depression of the thirties, the federal government has played an ever-increasing role in our daily lives, and over the years we have turned increasingly toward Washington to seek solutions to the problems that plague us as a society.

Though many people have warned of the dangers of asking government to do more and more for us, and of allowing government to take on more responsibility for our lives, the warnings have largely gone unheeded.

In this country, despite the fact that it erodes individual freedoms and overburdens the federal budget, government is our protector. For that reason, I decided to make Washington, D.C., and our national palace there — the White House — the last stops on my eye-opening and saddening journey.

During the Depression, when countless Americans were poor and when a great number of those who had never known poverty before were in dire straits, the federal government didn't turn its back, and we have expected it to step in at every crisis since then. Aside from God, it seems that the federal government has been the only hope for the poor.

It was in 1964 that Lyndon Johnson, in a flurry of pomp characteristic of the times, declared all-out war on poverty in America. There was all the attendant ballyhoo — newspaper headlines from coast to coast — and all the sincere enthusiasm that usually accompany such noble pronouncements.

But not long into the battle, another war came into the picture — this one in Southeast Asia, where America's honor was at stake. And the much-heralded war against poverty in this country got into trouble. Since then, this brainchild of Johnson's vision of the Great Society has been much-maligned, kicked around, picked apart, ridiculed, and left for dead. But it is still alive. It has never really been declared defunct.

Former president Richard Nixon, however, nearly dealt it a death blow when he ordered the dismantling of the old Office of Economic Opportunity (OEO), which, at the time, was command headquarters for the war-on-poverty effort. But even though most of the programs started under OEO were farmed out to other government agencies — the Job Corps, the Department of Labor, Head Start, the Office of Education, and so forth — they are still going strong. In fact, they are currently funded at much higher levels than they were during the Great Society days.

OEO's low-key successor, the Community Services Administration (CSA), has been quietly continuing the fight to provide hope and opportunity to the millions of poor and underprivileged across America. This job is more difficult now than ever before, because helping the poor is no longer in vogue.

"People don't see poverty as an issue that affects them," Graciela Olivarez said. "People see themselves working harder and harder and taking home less and less, so the natural reaction is to step on the guy right below you. It is like child abuse. You take on the most helpless to vent your frustration.

"There is a strong shift to the right now," she said. "We are following the patterns of history, the pendulum swinging back and forth between periods of liberalism and periods of real conservatism. The swing is to the right now, and that makes it tougher to bring about meaningful change for the poor. A lot of people don't want to hear about the plight of the poor. They've got their own sob stories."

The beating the government's antipoverty effort suffered at the hands of angry critics within and outside of government was so severe that today almost no one seems willing to stand up and raise a voice for the poor. One gets the feeling that the old leaders and poverty fighters are shell-shocked.

"Even the churches are playing it safe now," said Mrs. Olivarez. "Poor is still a four-letter word. Nobody speaks for the poor. Nobody wants to step forward, because we all know what happens to people who step forward. They get knocked down. Also, I think too many people associate poverty in their minds only with minorities — blacks, browns. But more than fifty percent of the people we help are white.

"Too many of these people who helped us put together the coalition we had during the sixties to fight for civil rights apparently think the battle is won. But it's not. I travel around this country a lot, and I see those people out there who need help desperately.

"I run into people with church groups, civic organizations, and other social groups, and when I ask them if they can help, a lot of them start quoting from the Bible. You know where it says something about, 'The poor you shall have with you always.' Okay, so it says that. But it doesn't say that there has to be twenty-five million of them every year."

•   •   •

Sargent Shriver, the man who headed up Lyndon Johnson's War on Poverty and who unsuccessfully sought the Democratic nomination for president in 1976, reared back in a chair inside an office of his powerful and well-respected Washington law firm located in the Watergate Complex. Shriver is a man of seemingly undying optimism.

"Something definitely can be done," he said, in a voice that reminded me of Hubert Humphrey, Lyndon Johnson, the Kennedy clan, the Peace Corps, and scores of liberal causes that came and went with the sixties. "If the American people so desire, something can be done about the troubles of the poor. We *are* the government, you know," he said with a smile. "It will take a catalyst to shake us up."

Remembering what John Lewis had told me earlier about the possibility of our having to face a season of conflict and racial unrest because of high unemployment and the conditions the poor must live under, I asked if he was referring to racial troubles when he spoke of a catalyst to shake us up.

"I don't say race riots," he replied, "because that's not a big enough calamity. It's got to affect everybody. A gigantic depression would do it, would change people's attitudes. A very serious calamity of any kind could do it. You see, there is a natural tendency of politicians to operate from one crisis to the next, and if we don't change, we will pay a heavy price.

"I found out one thing while running the War on Poverty, which is this: You don't get somebody out of poverty by giving them a job or by giving them a handout, by giving them welfare or by giving them a house, et cetera. That's why our slogan in the War on Poverty was 'a hand up, not a handout.'

"What we were trying to say is this: If you will do something, you who are poor, then we will do something. This is not an insensitive, barricaded, fortresslike society where nothing you do will ever get you progress. If you were willing to go to school, you could get into the Upward Bound program. If you were old and didn't have income, you could become a foster grandparent, et cetera.

"So what we were giving — we hoped — was bait to motivate people to help themselves get out of poverty. Now, I believe that poverty can only be overcome that way. We just need to do all the things that were developed in the case of the war against poverty. We can do them better now. We've learned so much since then. And there are many improvements that could be carried forth," he said.

"When you look back on the war against poverty, how much do you think was accomplished?" I asked.

"My response is going to be counter to what most people today will be telling you. The generally accepted revisionist, neoconservative viewpoint is that the War on Poverty only threw money at problems and didn't solve any of them. From my viewpoint, that is pure hogwash, baloney."

I smiled. I had not expected him to use the words *hogwash* and *baloney*. Somehow they didn't sound right coming from him. He seemed annoyed.

"Let me give you an example," he said, gesturing with his hands toward the window that looked out on Washington, the sun-draped buildings towering over wide streets. "A large number of the best-educated people who are lawyers in America," he said, "including professors as well as practitioners, will tell you that the legal-services program started by OEO, by which legal services were provided to the poor free of charge, may well have been one of the most significant developments in the political history of this country. That's not a quotation from me. That's a quotation from many key people. Presidents of the American Bar Association, justices of the U.S. Supreme Court, and general lawyers.

"Having said that, I don't mean to imply that the program by itself was able to take millions of people out of poverty. That would be absurd. But it surely helped many people get out of poverty, and it eliminated a form of poverty. Poverty is not only economic," he said, in an aside.

"It eliminated a form of poverty which is discrimination, or helplessness or powerlessness on the part of millions of people."

What about all those powerless, helpless people I'd seen? I was thinking as he continued to speak.

"That program was started with an initial appropriation of about fifteen to twenty million dollars. The United States government today is putting two hundred and fifty million dollars a year into that program.

"We had a program called Head Start. People in education, especially in early-childhood education, universally across this country will tell you — I am almost sure they'll tell you — that that program was the most significant new development in early-childhood education in this century in this nation. We started that program with about fifty million dollars. The program is now running up eight hundred and fifty million dollars," he said with a smile.

"People would say that just proves that government people are crazier than ever, because they're putting more and more money into these programs. But the reason they are putting more and more money into these programs is because these programs have been researched and studied by scientists and the government, and they have proven to be the most effective programs in our nation directed at those particular problems.

"I could go on and on with other programs we developed during the War on Poverty, but what I'm trying to say is simply that the specific programs — every one of them started by the war against poverty — exist today in much larger magnitude than they did when we started them, and every study of them concludes they have been extremely helpful for the poor and for the health of the American society as a whole, not just the poor but the lower middle class, the upper middle class, and the super rich . . ."

Shriver was highly critical of the Proposition 13 movement and other tax-reform efforts of that ilk, which he categorized as "the current guruism."

"The current idea," he said, "that if you could just stop government altogether, the rest of us — this is the quote — free private enterprise would bring about all these happy improvements with no government, except, maybe, policemen and firemen and school teachers. Well, I think that is childish, and there has never been any proof in history of any society where that was true. Anarchism has a very great appeal to rather immature minds. It is juvenile to think that a highly complicated industrial society like the United States can function effectively without government.

"The answers to the problems of the poor lie in doing all those things that were started during the war against poverty, and doing them better, bringing back the great liberal coalitions that were alive in the sixties, all those people who were exhausted by the Vietnam War and depressed by Watergate, those two tragic blows . . .

"But let me say I have no belief or illusion that any government or any structure of society — communism, anarchism, monarchy, democracy — is ever going to be successful in making a heaven on earth for everybody here. That is not going to happen."

"Not only won't there be heaven on earth for many people,"

I said, "but some people won't even have a decent life. I've seen them. Today, with all the programs we have to help, so many people don't get help. They are isolated. They've never heard of the War on Poverty."

"That's right," he said. "You're not going to have a decent life for everybody, because the word *decent* changes from era to era. Ninety percent of the people in the United States today live in a different place, a better place than ninety percent of the people did who started this country. Ninety percent of the people who started this country were out chopping down trees and living in wood huts with no running water, no electricity, no gas, no nothing. They were living by the sweat of their brows, with their two hands, and they had nothing in terms of creature comforts.

"But still we see some people today who are not in the mainstream, whose housing is substandard according to our standards and who are suffering from deprivations, which are inequitable today, even though that person may be better off than his forefathers were five hundred years ago. By today's standards he is poor. What does all that mean? It means to me that, at any time in history, there are always poor people, people who are not as well off as other people in that society at that time."

After I thanked Shriver for seeing me and left, I thought hard about the last thing he had said — that there would always be poor people — and there was no doubt in my mind that he was correct. But it seemed unfair to me that the burden of poverty always falls on certain groups. It has always been a fact in America that a larger proportion of blacks and other minorities are poor in our society than whites. To simply make peace with yourself and accept the fact that there would always be poor people seemed gravely unjust, a cop-out of the worst kind.

Many people are poor in this country because of discrimination; because the stairways out of deprivation are not equally accessible to all. If opportunities for a better life were open to all, it would be much easier to accept the fact that some of us would always be poor, because then it would be possible to blame the individual for his plight.

Now, however, we — society as a whole — are responsible for the poor in our midst. And I kept thinking about some of the people I had seen who had less than enough food to eat, ragged clothes, ragged houses, and nothing to look forward to but more of the same misery day after day, week after week. I knew I could never explain to them what they had done to deserve their station in life; what they had done — as Langston Hughes wrote in a poem — to be so black and blue.

• • •

My final stop was the White House. It had come to that. If any lasting answers were to be found, surely I had a better-than-even chance of finding them in the house where major decisions affecting us all are made each day. It was my second trip to Washington, but my first chance to actually set foot inside the White House.

Standing at the wrought-iron gate, looking through the black bars at the immaculately kept lawn, the winding walkways and curving drives, and the White House itself, looming like an elegant lady of the most proper breeding, I realized just how far I had come from Beale Street in Americus, Georgia, where the roofs are tin and rusting, and the toilets are outdoors and give off an incredible stench. I could also understand just how far James Earl Carter had come, because Americus lies in his home county of Sumter, and the houses on Beale Street are only fifteen miles from his home in Plains.

Jimmy Carter knows the people I had met on my journey. He has lived among them. He remembered them during his presidential campaign, appealed to them, made them promises of more jobs and a better America. They are still waiting for him — their neighbor — to make good on those promises. They and I have become convinced that he has not been remembering them quite as much since he moved into the house that stands inside the wrought-iron fence on Pennsylvania Avenue, like a monument to the American way of life.

But I was in Washington to talk to Carter's top domestic-policy adviser, Stuart Elliot Eizenstat, a thirty-five-year-old former

Atlanta lawyer who is now one of the most powerful men in government. It is often said that on domestic issues, Eizenstat generally knows the mind of the president better than anyone else, including the president.

I went to Washington to ask questions for and about the troubled souls I'd met in the big cities, small towns, and backwoods hamlets of the "New South." I went — with their sanction, I think — to find out whether any help was on the way; whether they could expect any changes in their condition in the near future; whether they could expect any changes ever. I took them with me in my notes and in my head, because I knew that was the only way most of them would ever get there. Their voices were in my recorder, and their pain and puzzled faces still exploded in my mind. In theory, the White House is their house, but in reality it doesn't work out that way. In truth, I don't think they'd be welcome there if they went.

I arrived on the day President Carter was to sign the recently passed Humphrey-Hawkins full-employment bill in a big ceremony to be attended by influential blacks from around the country.

I stood outside the gate for what seemed an interminable period, waiting to be admitted. There was some problem; I had not been properly cleared in advance by Eizenstat's staff.

When one of the guards, a burly white guy with a cold, rigid face, opened the gate momentarily, for a network newsman to leave the grounds, a middle-aged, matronly white woman, who had been standing in front of me begging the guards to let her talk to the president "just for five minutes," squeezed through. She bolted across the lawn like an NFL running back, her huge purse dangling from her shoulder.

The burly white guard was not gaining on her by the time she had made it halfway across the lawn, but a lithe black guard took off like a shot from the guard station and brought her crumbling to the ground with a flying tackle. As they were lifting the woman up from the lawn like a sack of laundry, I was admitted inside and led to the west wing, through a series of doors and halls.

Being inside the White House was an awe-inspiring experience
— the opulent decorations, massive ceilings, and brass-handled
doors. It can almost make you forget what it is like inside those
houses in Americus, with their sagging floors and lack of running
water — the other side of the tracks in America.

People were everywhere — all smart-looking sophisticated
types. These were the same kinds of people I had seen in plush,
big-city law firms. But this was the White House, where a lot of
the people's business is conducted, I had to keep reminding myself.

Stuart Eizenstat, an angular man whose looks made me think
more of Boston and New England than of Georgia, sat behind a
desk in his spacious and tastefully decorated office. He looked
almost too official to be true. I had the feeling that he was not
really there in the flesh; that I was looking at a Norman Rockwell
painting of a severe young man sitting behind a very large desk.
But he was real. When he spoke to me, there was Georgia in his
voice.

I had been advised earlier that Eizenstat could give me no
more than thirty minutes to talk about poor people's problems,
and their future in this country. I accepted the terms, after trying for several days just to reach him and, later, having my appointment shifted around at the last minute because of "pressing"
business at the White House.

Although this meeting conflicted with other, longer-standing,
appointments, I agreed to it, because Eizenstat's office had told
me that if I wanted to talk to him while I was in Washington, I
would have to do it then. Eizenstat was scheduled to meet with
the president following his thirty minutes with me, and, after
that, he and his wife were leaving immediately for a weekend
retreat.

I had no delusions that I was anyone of real importance to
Eizenstat. I was not a powerful senator or a visiting foreign
official, so I had only the slightest hope that my visit would make
some difference in the way he viewed the poor, and what he
would do to help them.

I began by asking him if he thought we'd already reached the point in this country where there is a permanent underclass, completely outside the mainstream of American life.

"Well," he said, "I think that's a good question. No one likes to think so . . . I think a lot depends on what you mean by underclass. Clearly, there will always be a group that will be lower on the totem pole than others, because there has got to be a top and a bottom to everything . . .

"But the question is whether there is a necessity that that be one particular group, and, second, how low that really is, because an underclass — and I think that's a fair description of at least a small segment of the population — means not simply people who happen to make less than people at the top, but rather people who make so much less, and whose conditions are so poor, that they really are out of the mainstream of life."

Not only was Eizenstat the quintessential bureaucrat; he seemed the consummate politician as well. I knew already that this interview was an exercise in futility. Nothing meaningful would come of it.

"I think that some progress is being made in reducing the underclass," he continued. "I think a lot of the jobs programs we're working on, particularly the way we're targeting them, are going to help in that regard."

He talked about the CETA program and similar federal programs already in force, and how they would be changed and improved. Still, I was not impressed. Then he showed me a chart dealing with unemployment figures and talked a great deal about "economies of scale." I was speaking to a position, not a man; to an adviser, a pacifier, a mouthpiece in a suit.

"You'll notice that black unemployment is roughly twice white unemployment," he said, pointing to one of the charts, "but you'll also notice that in terms of the growth in the number of jobs, if anything blacks are actually getting a greater percentage of the jobs in their comparable categories, so that while there is still a big differential, they're catching up. But that's not to say there's still not a problem as you describe. I think it's, in many respects, a fact of life that it's going to be years before this underclass is chipped away at. But I don't think it's impossible. It's very hard, but not impossible."

I told him about the widespread attitude on the part of very poor people that nothing will ever help. I pointed out that many of them had been down so long that they now believed down was where they were supposed to be.

"Is there anything government can do to help people out of this negative self-image?" I asked.

"I think a lot of the self-image problem — which I think is a real problem — comes because of generation after generation of welfare dependency . . . I'm a believer that a decent job goes a tremendously long way toward improving one's self-image and getting one out of the feeling of hopelessness.

"But the interesting thing is that, in some respects, in the rural areas it's more difficult to do than in the urban areas. In urban areas, you've got CETA sponsors working out of the mayor's office, you've got concentrated groups of people you can work from. In the rural areas, people are so dispersed it's very hard to reach them individually . . . But I think welfare reform is one of the real keys to the self-image problem you talked about."

"Do you foresee any special programs coming from this administration that would attack rural poverty?" I asked.

"We had really two sets of programs," he said. "One is a targeted tax credit which gives an employer three thousand dollars in the first year and fifteen hundred dollars in the second year, if the employer hires a young person between eighteen and twenty-four who is poverty-level or below. This goes after poor individuals by giving tax incentives and training subsidies to employers, whether they're in rural or urban areas.

"Secondly, and although it was in our urban policy, all of the tax incentives, all of the programs like the national development bank, which would provide subsidized loans and expanded grants to private industry, would go whether they located in a distressed urban or distressed rural area. It would be equally available . . ."

Urban, urban, everything is urban, I thought. Rural America is low priority.

"For example, under our proposal, a company looking for a spot could reduce its financing costs for a plant by sixty percent, if they went into a targeted area," Eizenstat continued. "And the targeted rural area would be just as available as the targeted urban area, so we're hopeful that by encouraging business backers to move in we do create job opportunities. But, you know, no one will deny that it is a painfully slow process."

"Is there any chance that anything on as grand a scale as Lyndon Johnson's Great Society will come out of this administration?" I said.

"Well, we think, in some respects, our urban policy is on that type of scale. [What?!] And our jobs programs are, but in terms of anything beyond that, I think our budgetary constraints are such and inflation is such that we could not do it."

"How much do you think racism has to do with the kinds of people who end up in poverty?" I asked.

"I don't think there's any question that discrimination is a factor," he replied. "Whether it's the predominant factor, I can't say, but it's certainly a factor, no doubt about it. Lack of training, lack of educational skills, lack of mobility are all factors. But there is no question in my mind that a factor — if not the predominant factor — is still an overlay of discrimination.

"Again, one of the reasons I'm not overly pessimistic about the future in terms of poverty is that I grew up in the South, and when I look back to only fifteen, seventeen years ago, the changes are traumatic in terms of the breakdown of race consciousness, the breakdown of discrimination. However, I'll be the last to say we're all the way there in this country, by the way, North or South. But we've made terrific progress, and that has helped bring many more blacks into the mainstream.

"If you look . . . there are some very interesting figures about the growth of the black middle class in the last ten years. Since the time of the Great Society started, there has been tremendous increase in the black middle class, people making between ten and thirty thousand dollars . . ."

I told Eizenstat that one of the things that had bothered me during my travels was the presence of many of the same conditions that had existed in the sixties before the riots. There was the same kind of seething rage, particularly in the rural areas, where there were none of the social-service agencies that pacify people in the bigger cities. I mentioned small children playing in abject poverty, oblivious to how bad off they really were, unaware that society looked down its nose at them. But in ten years, they would understand the horrors they were living in. Would we be prepared for their reactions?

"I think there is no question but that a country pays a heavy price for the poverty it has," Eizenstat replied. "People don't see that immediately, because to them poverty is a very distant sort of thing. They rarely come into contact with people who are in poverty. But society pays an enormous price in terms of the fact that the frustration you referred to manifests itself in antisocial conduct, which itself is not only — just from a purely academic standpoint — very costly economically, but in terms of society is very costly.

"You know, when you've got modern communications, even the poorest people either have or have access to a television. They see that life is not the way they're living it . . . and they want a piece of the action . . ."

"What do you think happened to all those people who were socially active in the sixties, who formed the coalition that the civil-rights bill and all those things grew out of?" I asked.

"Well, I think a number of things happened to them," Eizenstat said. "First of all, the goals that were set then were very easy goals to rally around — the right to vote, the right to eat in a restaurant, the right to sleep in a hotel, the right to go to any school you wanted. Those were so fundamental and so basic that they were easy issues. I don't mean easy in the sense of passing, but for those interested in the cause, it was simple, a clear-cut cause.

"Those issues are now behind us, and the issues of employment and job hiring and affirmative action versus quotas are infinitely more difficult. They cut across those groups, so that the first thing that has happened is that issues have become more difficult. We've gotten rid of the ones that were so morally correct that it was easy to rally groups around. The issues are much more complex. They're economic now. And economics, people see that as if you're giving something to somebody else; maybe you're taking it away from them . . .

"Secondly, a lot of people who were active, students and others, are now ten or twelve years older, with families to support, jobs, and they don't have time. The issues have changed, they're more complex. And the people have sort of grown up and are going about their own business now. And the new generation of young persons and students tends to be much more insular . . ."

My thirty minutes were nearly up, but I asked Eizenstat one more question. In terms of this administration's priorities, I said, where do the problems of the poor fit?

"When we came into the office," he said, "the president said repeatedly that our number-one job was to get unemployment down. We've gotten it down almost two full percentage points . . . We've created six million new jobs, we've stimulated the economy. The reason inflation is our number one domestic economic problem is (a) because of the obvious impact it has on poor people, people on fixed incomes, on consumers, on business investments. But (b) — and equally important, maybe more important, if inflation continues unabated — it's not just that in some intellectual way it's bad, but that it will have a direct impact on employment, and one of the things the president will be saying at the Humphrey-Hawkins signing ceremony is that if we can't lick inflation, can't keep it under control, then it's going to be very difficult to do anything further, because you won't get the growth to generate jobs."

Time was up. We shook hands. I was shown out of the White House. My hotel was at the other end of Pennsylvania Avenue, and, as I walked back to it, I found myself preferring to think not about my just-completed conversation with Eizenstat, but rather about Millard Fuller and his program in Americus; the project in North Carolina, which got people off welfare; and Delta Enterprises in Mississippi.

I veered off Pennsylvania Avenue and strayed downtown, through a few neighborhoods. I saw people, hundreds of people, some of them obviously poor. I saw poor people hanging out on the corners, their heads bent down. I wondered what Eizenstat would say to these people, how he would talk to them. Could he talk to them?

By the time I reached my comfortable hotel room, it was dark and I was tired. I wanted to sleep but couldn't. I kept wondering what Eddie Lee and Freddie Lee Mullins were doing back in Georgia, and whether there was any way I could get them into the White House to meet Good Ol' Stu. There was no way, just as there was no way they'd ever have decent jobs or live in decent houses. No way at all.

* * *

Now, months later, I sit at my typewriter and conclude that for the poor, the road from here is dim, filled with potholes and treacherous turns. In this country, there will never be mass relief for the underprivileged. But I cling to Millard Fuller's philosophy: instead of sitting around lamenting the hugeness of the problem, you do whatever you can. Small victories are possible, like the ones in Americus, Georgia, Albermarle, North Carolina, Greenville, Mississippi, and other programs scattered throughout the country.

And though a lifetime of weeks has passed since I masqueraded as a native in the land where poor people live, the sadness lingers in me. I still don't know what I can do to help those people I came to know, except keep on asking questions, keep on writing about them and their problems. Yet I know that for me, that will not be enough.

It is unquestionably true that things are going to get much worse for the underclass in this country. I have accepted that, but still it hurts. It is hard to swallow the fact that for many of those I saw languishing on America's backdoor steps, the road out of despair is getting longer and more difficult. Still, it is not yet totally dark, because a few determined souls manage to find their way safely, every once in a while. They are the lucky ones.

I wish I had more hope that we all could pull together and change things for those who are less fortunate, but my faith in us is not too strong. Yet because history is filled with events that demonstrate the indomitability of the human spirit, I am not totally pessimistic. And because there is always God, there is always hope.

CHET FULLER, winner of several journalistic awards for his *Atlanta Journal* stories, has also received the Gwendolyn Brooks Literary Award for poetry. He is an Atlantan by birth, a graduate of Gustavus Adolphus College in Minnesota, and presently a Special Assignments Writer for the *Atlanta Journal*.